A LESSON FOR EVERY DAY

6–7 YEARS

MATHS

6–7 YEARS

A & C Black • London

Published 2010 by A & C Black Publishers Limited
36 Soho Square, London W1D 3QY
www.acblack.com
ISBN 978-1-4081-2545-8
Copyright text © Hilary Koll, Steve Mills, Caroline Clissold 2010
Editors: Dodi Beardshaw, Jane Klima, Marie Lister, Clare Robertson, Lynne Williamson
Compiled by Mary Nathan and Fakenham Photosetting

The authors and publishers would like to thank Ray Barker, Fleur Lawrence and Rifat Siddiqui for their advice in
producing this series of books.

A CIP catalogue record for this book is available from the British Library.

Printed and bound in Great Britain by Martins the Printers, Berwick-on-Tweed.

A & C Black uses paper produced with elemental chlorine-free pulp, harvested from managed sustainable forests.

Contents

Introduction

A Lesson for Every Day: Mathematics is a series of seven photocopiable activity books for the Foundation Stage and Key Stages 1 and 2, designed to be used during the daily maths lesson. The books focus on the skills and concepts outlined in the National Strategy's *Primary Framework for literacy and mathematics*. The activities are intended to be used in the time allocated to pupil activities; they aim to reinforce the knowledge and develop the facts, skills and understanding explored during the main part of the lesson and to provide practice and consolidation of the objectives contained in the Framework document.

A Lesson for Every Day: Mathematics Ages 6–7 supports the teaching of mathematics to children aged 6 to 7 by providing a series of activities to develop:

- processes for using and applying mathematics in real situations
- skills in talking about the mathematics in real situations
- essential skills in counting and recognising numbers
- the learning of simple number facts
- an understanding of ideas of addition, subtraction, multiplication and division
- spatial vocabulary in order to increase awareness of properties of shape and measurement concepts
- learning in how to sort and record information in a variety of ways to answer questions and solve problems.

On the whole, the activities are designed for children to work on independently, although due to the young age of the children, the teacher may need to read the instructions with the children to ensure that they understand the activity before they begin working on it.

Extension

Many of the activity sheets end with a challenge (**Now try this!**), which reinforces and extend children's learning, and provides the teacher with an opportunity for assessment. These might include harder questions, with numbers from a higher range, than those in the main part of the activity sheet. Some extension activities are open-ended questions and provide opportunity for children to think mathematically for themselves. Occasionally the extension activity will require additional paper or that the children write on the reverse of the sheet itself. Many of the activities encourage children to generate their own questions or puzzles for a partner to solve.

Organisation

Very little equipment is needed, but it will be useful to have available: coloured pencils, counters, cubes, scissors, dice, glue, coins, squared paper, number lines, grids and tracks, 2D and 3D shapes, a variety of different classroom items.

Where possible, children's work should be supported by ICT equipment, such as data handling programmes on interactive whiteboards, or computer software for moving pictures or photographs to show similarities and differences between groups and also charting information. It is also vital that children's experiences are introduced in real-life contexts, such as those portrayed in home/role play areas and through practical activities and number or nursery rhymes that they know. The teachers' notes at the foot of each page and the more detailed notes on pages 6 to 24 suggest ways in which this can be done effectively.

To help teachers select appropriate learning experiences for the children, the activities are grouped into sections within the book. However, the activities are not expected to be used in this order unless stated otherwise. The sheets are intended to support, rather than direct, the teacher's planning.

Some activities can be made easier or more challenging by masking or substituting numbers. You may wish to re-use pages by copying them onto card and laminating them.

Teachers' notes

Brief notes are provided at the foot of each page, giving ideas and suggestions for maximising the effectiveness of the activity sheets. These can be masked before copying.

Solutions can be found on pages 215 to 216.

Assessment

Use the completed activities as part of your day-to-day assessment to help you to build a picture of children's learning in order to plan future teaching and learning. Activities can also be used as examples of significant evidence for your periodic assessment. In order to help you to make reliable judgements about your pupils' attainment, the assessment focuses for each activity are given in the grids on pages 6–24.

Some of the activities provide opportunities for children to carry out self assessment. Encourage children to reflect on their learning and discuss with them whether there are areas that they feel they need to practise further.

The CD-ROM

All activity sheets can be found as PDF and Word versions on the accompanying CD-ROM. These can be printed or displayed on an interactive whiteboard. The Word versions can be customised in Microsoft Word in order to assist personalised learning.

They can be accessed through an interface that makes it easy to select worksheets and display them. You can also search for lessons that will meet a particular Assessment Focus for Assessing Pupils' Progress. For more information on system requirements, please see the inside front cover.

If you have any questions regarding the *A Lesson For Every Day* CD-ROM, please email us at the address below. We will get back to you as soon as possible.
educationalsales@acblack.com

Whole class warm-up activities

The following activities provide some practical ideas that can be used to introduce or reinforce the main teaching part of the lesson, or provide an interesting basis for discussion.

Making number sentences

Draw a 4 x 4 square on the board, with a number in each section, for example:

3	22	2	36
16	3	15	8
7	12	19	20
25	6	10	30

Ask the children to create number sentences from the numbers in the square, such as: 3 * 10 = 30, 25 − 15 = 10, 19 + 3 = 22, 20 ÷ 2 * 3 = 30

It can be useful to draw the template on card and laminate it. New numbers can then be written whenever required.

Making decisions

Count the number of children in the class. Choose individuals to sort the children into groups, for example trousers/skirts or hair ribbon/no hair ribbon. Less clear-cut distinctions like fair hair/brown hair, long hair/short hair, tall/short etc. can be used to provoke discussion. Once the children are sorted you can ask questions about the groups such as, 'Who thinks Jess has short hair?' ' Who would put Emma in the 'tall' group?'

What's the question?

Give the children the answer to a question for example, 'Can you give me a question with the answer nineteen?' for example 'twelve add seven' 'Can anyone give me another question with the answer nineteen? Can you think of a subtraction question with the answer nineteen?' Explore the range of calculations that give the answer nineteen etc. and discuss the methods that the children used to find them.

Estimating

Hold up several fingers or pens etc. and quickly hide them. 'How many fingers did you see?' Write several children's estimates on the board. Demonstrate how the real answer can be found by counting in 2s, 5s or 10s and discuss the estimates.

Run-around

Around the walls of the hall or classroom, pin pieces of paper showing zero and the multiples of 10 from 10 to 100. Ask the children to stand in the middle of the room and call out 2-digit numbers. Ask them to round the number to the nearest ten and run to the correct sign. This can be played as a game where children who are standing by incorrect signs are out.

Crocodile

Invite two children to the front of the class and give them each a different number of cubes or items. Invite a third child to be the greedy crocodile and to come to the front and stand facing the child with more cubes, holding arms to represent the crocodile's mouth. Demonstrate how this can be recorded, for example 15 > 12 or 15 < 18. Point out that the mouth is always open towards the larger number.

What's my number

Write a number on a sticky note and place on a child's forehead so they are unable to read it. Ask other children to give clues about the identity of the number, for example: 'It's less than ten', 'It's two more than six' etc.

Pointing the finger

One child begins to count on in ones from zero, and then points to another child. This child now continues the count before pointing to another child. Try counting backwards from 20 or 30, counting on or back in twos, threes, fives or tens.

Block A Counting, partitioning and calculating - Unit 1

Activity name	Strand and learning objectives	Notes on the activities	Assessment Focus	Page number
Animal sorting Triplet trouble: 1 and 2	**Using and applying mathematics** Present solutions to puzzles and problems in an organised way; explain decisions, methods and results in pictorial, spoken or written form, using mathematical language and number sentences	**Animal sorting** Processes: *look for pattern, be systematic, explain, reason, compare, record* Children can work in pairs or small groups to compare and discuss solutions. **Triplet trouble: 1 and 2** Processes: *visualise, test ideas, look for pattern, record, be systematic* This problem-solving activity involves arranging children into the seats in different ways so that those of the same family are kept apart. SUGGESTED QUESTIONS: • Can it be done in a different way? • How could you record this?	Communicating	25 26–7
Hide and seek Odd and even racers	**Counting and understanding number** Read and write two-digit and three-digit numbers in figures and words; describe and extend number sequences and recognise odd and even numbers	**Hide and seek** For this activity, it is important that children have the correct spellings displayed clearly somewhere in the classroom for them to refer to. In the extension activity, four and nine can be found within fourteen and nineteen that the children have already ringed. As a further extension activity, the children could be encouraged to make up their own puzzle on squared paper. SUGGESTED QUESTIONS: • What number does this word say? • How would you write this in figures/using digits? **Odd and even racers** This sheet could be copied onto A3 paper, and a small group of children could play together. The group will need one dice and each child will need a counter. At the start of the lesson, revise odd and even numbers and check that the children know which digit to look at to work out whether a number is even. SUGGESTED QUESTIONS: • How can you recognise an even number? • How can you recognise a multiple of 2? What do you notice about even numbers and multiples of 2?	Numbers and the number system	28 29
At the sweetshop The pirates' library	**Counting and understanding number** Count up to 100 objects by grouping them and counting in tens, fives or twos; explain what each digit in a two-digit number represents, including numbers where 0 is a place holder; partition two-digit numbers in different ways, including into multiples of 10 and 1	**At the sweetshop** Children need to be confident in counting in twos and fives from zero for this activity. SUGGESTED QUESTIONS: • How many would you estimate there are? • Have you checked your answer? **The pirates' library** After revising the multiples of 10 at the start of the lesson, hold up sticks of ten cubes and ask the children to say how many, for example 4 sticks is 40, 7 sticks is 70. Now hold up two more cubes and ask them to say how many (42 or 72). Demonstrate that the first digit shows the number of sticks of 10 and the second digit shows how many loose cubes there are. SUGGESTED QUESTIONS: • How many rows of ten books are there? • How many single books are there? • How many books are there in total?	Numbers and the number system	30 31
Don't get shirty! Woolly jumpers!	**Counting and understanding number** Order two-digit numbers and position them on a number line; use the greater than (>) and less than (<) signs	**Don't get shirty!** This activity involves ordering sets of four numbers up to 100. Note that the numbers are not consecutive. The extension activity then asks the children to order a set of six numbers. SUGGESTED QUESTIONS: • Which of these numbers is the smallest? Which is the largest? • Which numbers come in between them? **Woolly jumpers!** This activity asks the children to choose the 'greater than' or 'less than' sign to complete a statement. Encourage them to say each statement in words using the terms 'greater than' and 'less than' appropriately. SUGGESTED QUESTIONS: • How do you remember which sign means 'greater than' and which means 'less than'? Can you explain to the class? • How would you say this statement aloud?	Numbers and the number system	32 33
Pasta party Seeing spots! Round 'em up!	**Counting and understanding number** Estimate a number of objects; round two-digit numbers to the nearest 10	**Pasta party** The worksheet could be enlarged on a photocopier, stuck onto card, coloured and laminated for a more permanent classroom resource. SUGGESTED QUESTIONS: • Which set of pasta was the easiest to estimate? Why? • Which card has the most/fewest pasta pieces? • How did you estimate the number on this card? Did you count in twos or fives to check? **Seeing spots!** This activity involves estimating 'spots' of different sizes. To prevent the children counting, ask them to write down their three estimates before a buzzer sounds. SUGGESTED QUESTIONS: • Roughly how many large spots are there in this picture? • About how many small spots are there? • Do you think the number of spots is nearer to 100 or to 200? **Round 'em up!** This activity enables children to really begin to appreciate how numbers round up or down to the nearest 10. Use a number line to show the children which numbers round to which multiple of 10. SUGGESTED QUESTIONS: • Which numbers round to 30? • How many numbers greater than 30 round to 30? • How many numbers less than 30 round to 30?	Numbers and the number system	34 35 36
Playful seals	**Calculating** Add or subtract mentally a one-digit number or a multiple of 10 to or from any two-digit number; use practical and informal written methods to add and subtract two-digit numbers	**Playful seals** The children could work in pairs, scoring a point each time they create a question with a ball answer. SUGGESTED QUESTIONS: • How did you work out that total? • How could you work out 41 and 30?	Mental methods Written methods	37

Activity name	Strand and learning objectives	Notes on the activities	Assessment Focus	Page number
Animal magic	**Calculating** Understand that subtraction is the inverse of addition and vice versa; use this to derive and record related addition and subtraction number sentences	**Animal magic** This activity provides practice in recording what is happening in a problem as a subtraction sentence. Remind the children that as well as seeing these contexts as 'take away' subtraction, if they compare the number of letters in the two words then they are 'finding the difference'. **Suggested question/prompt:** • How did you work out the answer to that question? • Tell me that calculation in words	Operations, relationships between them	38

Block A Counting, partitioning and calculating – Unit 2

Activity name	Strand and learning objectives	Notes on the activities	Assessment Focus	Page number
Domino decisions: 1 and 2	**Using and applying mathematics** Present solutions to puzzles and problems in an organised way; explain decisions, methods and results in pictorial, spoken or written form, using mathematical language and number sentences	**Domino decisions: 1 and 2** *Processes: look for pattern, reason, test ideas, be systematic* The following 'domino sets' sheet can be used to provide further opportunities for children to investigate this domino grid. **Suggested questions:** • What are the totals? • Can you explain how you worked this out?	Communicating	39–40
Find Bo-Peep's sheep! Flying high	**Counting and understanding number** Read and write two-digit and three-digit numbers in figures and words; describe and extend number sequences and recognise odd and even numbers	**Find Bo-Peep's sheep!** This activity involves reading numbers in words. It might be useful for children to write the numbers in digits next to the words on the sheep so that they remember the digits they are looking for on the wall. **Suggested questions:** • Read this number to me. Is it more or less than fifty? • How would this number be written in figures/using digits? **Flying high** Watch out for children who write 'fourty' rather than 'forty' and for those who reverse the digits, for example confusing 32 and 23. The extension activity involves finding the seventh letter of each word to spell a new number. **Suggested question:** • Look at the spelling on the board. Can you see any difference between how I have spelt fourteen and how I have spelt it?	Numbers and the number system	41 42
Happy 'tens' families Brainy birds	**Counting and understanding number** Count up to 100 objects by grouping them and counting in tens, fives or twos; explain what each digit in a two-digit number represents, including numbers where 0 is a place holder; partition two-digit numbers in different ways, including into multiples of 10 and 1	**Happy 'tens' families** Children may already be familiar with the card game 'Happy Families' where one must collect all the members of a family. This card game involves collecting four numbers that have the same 'tens' digit. When the children run out of cards, they can turn the discarded cards over and start again. **Suggested question:** • How many tens has this number? **Brainy birds** This activity includes a number with nine tens and no ones, i.e. 90. Children need to begin to appreciate that the 0 means that there are no extra ones. This awareness of zero as a place holder is vital if the children are to understand two- and, more importantly, three-digit numbers. **Suggested question:** • Can you think of other numbers with 9 tens?	Numbers and the number system	43 44
Flower power	**Calculating** Add or subtract mentally a one-digit number or a multiple of 10 to or from any two-digit number; use practical and informal written methods to add and subtract two-digit numbers	**Flower power** The extension activity involves pairs of numbers with a total greater than 100. The children may find it useful to be shown a number line that extends beyond 100, or a 100 square that has been continued up to, perhaps, 200. **Suggested questions:** • What do you notice about the units/ones digit of each answer in a flower? • What happens to the units/ones digit when you add a multiple of 10? Is this always true? Why?	Mental methods Written methods	45

Block A Counting, partitioning and calculating – Unit 3

Activity name	Strand and learning objectives	Notes on the activities	Assessment Focus	Page number
Going potty Storytime	**Using and applying mathematics** Present solutions to puzzles and problems in an organised way; explain decisions, methods and results in pictorial, spoken or written form, using mathematical language and number sentences	**Going potty** Processes: *reason, compare, explain* It is important that children are given the opportunity to explain their thinking and strategies. SUGGESTED QUESTION/PROMPT: • Which calculation would you use? • Why? **Storytime** Processes: *explain, reason, ask own questions* This activity encourages the children to think of their own stories to match given calculations. Provide a range of examples and contexts for the children to think about before beginning this sheet, for example shopping with money, numbers of sweets, vegetables, pieces of fruit, measurement contexts, and so on. SUGGESTED QUESTIONS/PROMPTS: • What could your story be about? • What has to happen?	Communicating	46 47
Hungry puppies Three-digit dominoes	**Counting and understanding number** Read and write two-digit and three-digit numbers in figures and words; describe and extend number sequences and recognise odd and even numbers	**Hungry puppies** It is vital for the children to have the number names available to them in the classroom for this activity. Number names should include numbers to 20, multiples of 10 to 100 and multiples of 100 to 1000. As a further extension activity, ask the children to cover each of the bowls and then write in figures the number names they have written on the right. They can then compare the original bowl number with their new number and see if they are the same. SUGGESTED QUESTION: • Look at the spelling on the board. Can you see any difference between how I have spelt forty-two and how you have spelt it? **Three-digit dominoes** As for the two-digit dominoes sheet, these cards could be copied onto A3 card and laminated for a more permanent place value resource. Ensure that children are familiar with the term 'ones' as meaning 'units' if they have been introduced to the latter term. SUGGESTED QUESTIONS: • How many tens are there in one hundred and thirty-seven? How many ones? • How would you say this number? • Read this number to me. How would you write that number?	Numbers and the number system	48 49
Whose pet? Split decisions Dinner time	**Counting and understanding number** Count up to 100 objects by grouping them and counting in tens, fives or twos; explain what each digit in a two-digit number represents, including numbers where 0 is a place holder; partition two-digit numbers in different ways, including into multiples of 10 and 1	**Whose pet?** SUGGESTED QUESTION: • How many ones has this number? **Split decisions** This activity shows chunks of chocolate and asks the children to split them in different ways. This can be demonstrated at the start of the lesson with cubes that click together in multiple ways, such as Multilink cubes. Make a 'chocolate bar' out of cubes, where each full row has ten cubes. Ask a child to split the bar into two, stressing that the parts do not need to be equal. The term 'partition' could also be introduced. SUGGESTED QUESTION: • How could you split this number into two parts? **Dinner time** Similarly, for this activity children are splitting numbers into parts, but this time they do not have the representation of items to count. If the children experience difficulties with this give them cubes to work with. SUGGESTED QUESTION: • How could you split this number into two parts?	Numbers and the number system	50 51 52
Bird-watching: 1 and 2 Nutty squirrels Reading the signs	**Counting and understanding number** Order two-digit numbers and position them on a number line; use the greater than (>) and less than (<) signs	These worksheets could be enlarged on a photocopier, stuck onto card, coloured and laminated for a more permanent classroom resource. Children find this type of trumping game very entertaining once they are comfortable with the rules. It allows them to compare numbers (comparing two numbers if two play, three numbers if three play, and so on). *Additional rule* When a category is picked, if two players have the same number in that category then a second category should be chosen (as a tie breaker). SUGGESTED QUESTIONS: • What did you like best about the game? • Can we make some more bird cards like this to use? **Nutty squirrels** The extension activity asks the children to choose an appropriate number to make a true inequality statement. Demonstrate this at the start of the lesson by asking three children to stand in a line at the front of the class. Give one child a number card to hold and the middle child a 'greater than' or 'less than' sign. Give the third child a number to make the statement true, but ask him/her to hide the number from the rest of the class. Ask the class to try to guess the number. Explain that there are many answers that will make the statement true. Encourage the children to say each statement in words using the terms 'greater than' and 'less than' appropriately. SUGGESTED QUESTIONS: • How would you say this statement aloud? • What number could go here to make the statement true? **Reading the signs** This activity involves writing two true statements using the same two numbers and the 'greater than' and 'less than' signs. At the end of the activity, ask the children to read each statement in words using the terms 'greater than' and 'less than' appropriately. SUGGESTED QUESTIONS: • Which numbers did you choose? • How would you say this statement aloud?	Numbers and the number system	53–4 55 56
Monster making Round in space	**Counting and understanding number** Estimate a number of objects; round two-digit numbers to the nearest 10	**Monster making** The children will each need a copy of the worksheet, and some coloured pencils and a set of 0 to100 number cards (with the multiples of 10 removed) to share. SUGGESTED QUESTIONS: • Which numbers round to 30? • How many numbers greater than 30 round to 30? • How many numbers less than 30 round to 30? **Round in space** Provide the children with a number line to help them with this activity. Ask them to choose a number on the line that is closer to 30 than it is to 20 or 40 and to write it onto a planet. SUGGESTED QUESTIONS: • What happens to numbers ending in the digit 5? Do they round up or down?	Numbers and the number system	57 58

Activity name	Strand and learning objectives	Notes on the activities	Assessment Focus	Page number
Dixie the pixie	**Calculating** Understand that subtraction is the inverse of addition and vice versa; use this to derive and record related addition and subtraction number sentences	**Dixie the pixie** At the start of the lesson, ask the children to count out a set of cubes, for example 15, and then add seven more to them. Finally, ask the children to take seven away from the answer. Discuss why they end up with the number they started with. Repeat for subtraction. **Suggested questions:** • How do you know that the answer is 34? • What do I have to do to undo 29 + 6?	Operations, relationships between them	59
Cube covering	**Calculating** Use the symbols +, −, ×, ÷ and = to record and interpret number sentences involving all four operations; calculate the value of an unknown in a number sentence (e.g. □ ÷ 2 = 6, 30 − □ = 24)	**Cube covering** At the start of the lesson, show a completed addition and subtraction statement, such as 14 + 7 = 21 and 15 − 5 = 10. Cover each number in the addition statement and discuss how you would find the hidden number, for example if 7 is covered you could find the difference between 14 and 21 by counting up from the smaller number. Show that this is a subtraction: 21 − 14 = 7, even though the question is an addition. Similarly, show that when the first number of a subtraction question is hidden, it can be found by adding, for example □ − 5 = 10 – the missing number is found by adding 5 to 10. **Suggested question/prompt:** • Show me how you worked out that you need to add 8 to 13 to make 21. • Look at this question (□ − 6 = 10). How could you say that in words?	Operations, relationships between them Written methods	60

Block B Securing number facts, understanding shapes - Unit 1

Activity name	Strand and learning objectives	Notes on the activities	Assessment Focus	Page number
Missing digits	**Using and applying mathematics** Describe patterns and relationships involving numbers or shapes, make predictions and test these with examples	**Missing digits** *Processes: look for pattern, compare, be systematic* Encourage the children to work systematically, using patterns within the digits to check their answers. **Suggested questions:** • What patterns did you use to help you? • What patterns did you notice? • How do you know you have found all the solutions?	Communicating	61
Check it out		**Check it out** *Processes: look for pattern, test ideas, predict, reason* Ensure the children provide sufficient answers to prove or disprove each statement. **Suggested questions:** • What examples can you give me? • Is this true or false? • How can you be sure?		62
Cherry time	**Using and applying mathematics** Solve problems involving addition, subtraction, multiplication or division in contexts of numbers, measures or pounds and pence	**Cherry time** *Processes: record, reason, compare, be systematic look for pattern* Encourage the children to look for patterns in the totals they find. **Suggested questions/prompts:** • What patterns do you notice? • What if we reorder the answers?	Problem solving	63
Loop the loop		**Loop the loop** *Processes: reason, make decisions* There are 10 different ways of making totals from 3 bowls. For a further activity children could investigate picking any 4 (or 2) bowls and finding possible totals. **Suggested questions/prompts:** • How many different answers can you find? • How many ways are there of making the total 45? 48? 51? • Are there any other solutions? • Explain why you have set your work out this way.		64
Hoopla	**Knowing and using number facts** Derive and recall all addition and subtraction facts for each number to at least 10, all pairs with totals to 20 and all pairs of multiples of 10 with totals to 100	**Hoopla** Discuss appropriate strategies for adding numbers that involve crossing 10, such as 6 + 7. Encourage the children to use number pairs which total 10 and to partition the number being added, for example partition 7 into 4 and 3, so that the question is 6 + 4 + 3 = 10 + 3 = 13. **Suggested question:** • Can you see patterns in the positions of the totals?	Mental methods	65
Cross out		**Cross out** This activity is useful for helping children to recall and recognise pairs of numbers with given totals. **Suggested question:** • How did you know that you had to cross out that number to make the total of the row correct?		66
Donkey hats		**Donkey hats** In order to successfully add and subtract numbers of different sizes, it is vital that children memorise and know by heart the totals of pairs of one-digit numbers, including those with totals over 10. This activity involves key number facts and encourages the children to quickly recall such pairs. Encourage the children to use doubles to help them derive the facts if not yet memorised, for example 6 + 6 = 12, so 6 + 7 = 13. **Suggested question:** • What would the total have been if I had crossed this number out instead? • Which two numbers have a total of 17?		67
Magic Meg	**Knowing and using number facts** Understand that halving is the inverse of doubling and derive and recall doubles of all numbers to 20, and the corresponding halves	**Magic Meg** For this activity, discuss strategies for working out doubles that are not known, such as partitioning the number first and then doubling each part, for example 17 = 10 + 7, 20 + 14 = 34. **Suggested questions:** • How does knowing that double 7 is 14 help you find half of 14? • Half of 22 is 11. What is double 11?	Operations, relationships between them Mental methods	68

Activity name	Strand and learning objectives	Notes on the activities	Assessment Focus	Page number
Twins	**Knowing and using number facts** Derive and recall multiplication facts for the 2, 5 and 10 times-tables and the related division facts; recognise multiples of 2, 5 and 10	**Twins** This activity links finding doubles of numbers with answers in the 2 times-table. At the start of the lesson you could ask pairs of children to take the roles of pairs of twins. The rest of the class could give them cubes each and say how many they have altogether. SUGGESTED QUESTIONS: • This pair of twins has 8 cubes each. What is double 8? What is 2 lots of 8? **Plastered!** At the start of the lesson revise the multiples of 10 to 100 and demonstrate how the number of tens counted can be written as a multiplication question, for example 3 × 10 can mean that three tens have been counted. For the extension activity, the children could interpret the division as 'how many tens are in 80' etc. SUGGESTED QUESTIONS: • How many tens are in 50? • Can you use counting on in tens from zero to help you?	Mental methods	69
Plastered!				70
Chain reaction		**Chain reaction** This sheet could be used as an assessment activity to see whether children are confident in writing the multiplication facts for the 2, 5 and 10 times-tables in order. SUGGESTED QUESTIONS: • What is 5 × 4? What is 2 × 4? What is 10 × 4? • Tell me two tables facts that have the answer 30. **Weaving** At the start of the lesson, practise saying the 5 times-table together. Then ask the children some of the multiplication facts 'out of order' for example What is 5 × 3? What is 5 × 9? Look out for children who have to count through the table to work out the answer. SUGGESTED QUESTIONS: • What do you notice about the numbers when you count in fives? • What is special about the last digit of each number?		71
Weaving				72
Round to check	**Knowing and using number facts** Use knowledge of number facts and operations to estimate and check answers to calculations	**Round to check** Discuss alternative strategies for answering these questions, such as: • when adding 9, add 10 and subtract 1 • counting on through the next multiple of 10 • partitioning and recombining	Operations, relationships between them	73
Spot the shapes	**Understanding shape** Visualise common 2-D shapes and 3-D solids; identify shapes from pictures of them in different positions and orientations; sort, make and describe shapes, referring to their properties	**Spot the shapes** As the children become more familiar with standard shapes they will begin to recognise them when several shapes overlap. This activity can be used as an assessment to see how visually perceptive the children are in distinguishing overlapping shapes. Encourage them to make their own designs, perhaps by drawing round shapes, and to ask a partner to say which shapes they used. SUGGESTED QUESTIONS: • What shapes can you see here? • Can you draw one for me? • How many sides/corners does this shape have? • What is the name of this shape? • How many sides does it have? **Sticky labels** At the start of the lesson revise the common shape names and their properties, recording the number of sides of pentagons, hexagons, triangles, rectangles, octagons and squares on the board.	Properties of shape	74
Sticky labels				75
True or false?		**True or false?** This activity also addresses the objective 'Describing and locating regions in a grid' where children use letters to describe the column and numbers to describe the row, for example A4 or C2. Watch out for those children who incorrectly answer 'false' to the first question as this suggests that they do not appreciate that 2-D and 3-D shapes can be in any position or orientation and will still be classed as the same shape. SUGGESTED QUESTIONS: • Do you know what this shape is called? • Describe the shape to me. What does it remind you of? • How many sides/corners has it?		76

Block B Securing number facts, understanding shapes – Unit 2

Activity name	Strand and learning objectives	Notes on the activities	Assessment Focus	Page number
Shape mysteries	**Using and applying mathematics** Describe patterns and relationships involving numbers or shapes, make predictions and test these with examples	**Shape mysteries** Processes: visualise, compare, reason Demonstrate this activity with the whole class to help the children appreciate that the hidden part of a shape can take on a range of different forms and not just the expected shape. The children may not be able to name all their four-sided shapes unless they are familiar with the term 'quadrilateral'. As an alternative to the extension activity, the children could cut some shapes from a piece of paper and cover parts of them for a friend to guess what shape it might be. SUGGESTED QUESTIONS/PROMPTS: • Can you imagine what this shape might look like? • How many sides do you think it might have?	Communicating	77
Shape shifting: 1 and 2		**Shape shifting 1 and 2** Processes: visualise, compare, test ideas, trial and improvement In this activity, the children cut out the shapes on Shape shifting: 2 and arrange two of them to make the shapes shown on Shape shifting: 1. To prevent the shapes getting mixed up, you could photocopy the sheets onto different coloured paper so that on each table, individual children have different coloured sets. SUGGESTED QUESTION: • What other shapes could you make? • Tell us about your shapes.		78–9

Activity name	Strand and learning objectives	Notes on the activities	Assessment Focus	Page number
All change!	**Using and applying mathematics** Solve problems involving addition, subtraction, multiplication or division in contexts of numbers, measures or pounds and pence	**All change!** *Processes: reason, explain, record* For this activity, focus on children describing how they worked each answer out. You could discuss the shopkeeper method of giving change with the class, e.g. counting up from the price up to the given amount. Some children might benefit from having coins to work with. Children will require assistance with the Now Try This challenge in recording money in pounds and pence correctly. Ask them to write the whole numbers of pounds with .00 after it, for example £3 being £3.00. Remind the children that £3 and 1p is written as £3.01. **Suggested question:** • How would you write this amount in pounds and pence?	Problem solving	80
Bikers!	**Knowing and using number facts** Derive and recall all addition and subtraction facts for each number to at least 10, all pairs with totals to 20 and all pairs of multiples of 10 with totals up to 100	**Bikers!** Invite the children to answer all the questions for each letter and then use the answers to crack the codes. This idea makes a useful display and can be permanently on the wall with questions altered occasionally. Show the code word made from the answers and see who can find the letters of the word first. This encourages speedy recall. **Suggested question:** • What kind of question could you use in your own code? **Turtlemania!** Ensure the children appreciate the commutative nature of addition, that is, the order of the numbers does not matter as the total is the same, for example 3 + 17 = 20 so 17 + 3 = 20. This can be described as 'learn one, get one free.' It is not necessary for children to know the word 'commutative', rather they should just appreciate this aspect of addition. The children could use stopwatches to time themselves doing the activity and then repeat it to see whether they can better their time. **Suggested prompts/questions:** • Find four turtles that involve the digits 1, 4 and 6. • What can you tell me about those facts? • How are they related? **Can you?** Encourage the children to use suitable checking procedures for this activity, such as adding the answer to the number being subtracted to see if they make the first number.	Mental methods	81
Turtlemania!				82
Can you?		**Creepy crawlies** When completing this activity, the children could be given number ranges appropriate to their ability, for example using start numbers up to 20, or between 30 and 50. Encourage the children to read their questions aloud, using a range of appropriate subtraction vocabulary (to support children who find this difficult, hold up cards showing subtraction words such as minus, take away, subtract). **Suggested question:** • Could you use the word 'subtract' / 'minus' / 'difference' when reading out your question? **Superheroes** Ensure the children understand that when they must write the amount to make £1 and not the amount of money shown. **Suggested question:** • Shout out the amount I would need to make £1 if I had '10p,' '40p' etc.		83
Creepy crawlies				84
Superheroes				85
Tennis game	**Knowing and using number facts** Derive and recall multiplication facts for the 2, 5 and 10 times-tables and the related division facts; recognise multiples of 2, 5 and 10	**Tennis game** Remind the children that when zero is divided by a number the answer is zero. It can help to explain this idea in the context of sharing. If no cubes are to be shared equally between five children, each child will get none! **Suggested questions:** • What is zero divided by 2? • Can you give me another division question with the answer zero?	Mental methods	86
Two-digit dominoes	**Counting and understanding number** Read and write two-digit and three-digit numbers in figures and words; describe and extend number sequences and recognise odd and even numbers	**Two-digit dominoes** The two-digit domino cards could be copied onto A3 card and laminated for a more permanent place value resource. Ensure that the children are familiar with the term 'ones' as meaning 'units' if they have been introduced to the latter term. **Suggested questions:** • How many tens are there in thirty-seven? How many ones? • How would you say this number? • Read this number to me. How would you write that number?	Number and the number system	87
Snail trails		**Snail trails** The focus of this activity is on reading three-digit number names and then writing them in figures. The activity includes numbers where 0 is a place holder, such as 530 and 908. Children require a solid understanding of place value to answer this type of question correctly. **Suggested questions:** • How many hundreds/tens/ones are there in this number? • Read this number to me. How would you write that number?		88
Guess the shape	**Understanding shape** Visualise common 2-D shapes and 3-D solids; identify shapes from pictures of them in different positions and orientations; sort, make and describe shapes, referring to their properties	**Guess the shape** It is important that the children have as much experience with actual solid shapes as possible. Children, in pairs, could be provided with the full set of shapes and asked to match up each card with the correct shape. **Suggested questions:** • Look at the solid shapes. Which has only one curved face? • How many edges has this cylinder? • Can you find a matching card for this shape?	Properties of shape	89

Activity name	Strand and learning objectives	Notes on the activities	Assessment Focus	Page number
Open up: 1 and 2 Flat shape speedway! Mirror mania Snip, snip	**Understanding shape** Identify reflective symmetry in patterns and 2-D shapes and draw lines of symmetry in shapes	**Open up: 1 and 2** At the start of the lesson hold up a symmetrical shape, already folded along its mirror line and explain to the children that you have folded a shape in half to make this one. Ask them to imagine the shape being opened out and invite them to describe the whole shape to you, referring to the numbers of sides, angles and its general shape. Then unfold the shape and discuss it further. Provide the children with Open up: 1 and ask them to imagine these shapes being opened up. Once they have predicted the number of sides for each shape they can be given the solutions on Open up: 2. The children should cut out the full shapes and fold them along the dotted lines to check, before opening out and checking their predictions. SUGGESTED QUESTIONS: • Can you imagine this square being opened out? • How many sides will the whole shape have? **Flat shape speedway!** For this game the children should work in pairs. Each pair will need a dice, a counter each and one sheet (ideally enlarged onto A3 paper). Small mirrors should also be provided so that the children can check lines of symmetry. SUGGESTED QUESTIONS: • Do you know the name of this shape? • How many sides/right angles/lines of symmetry has this shape? **Mirror mania** This activity can be introduced to the class using some birthday cards. Hold them next to a mirror and ask the children to look at the reflection and comment on what they see. Encourage them to notice that any pictures or letters on the card are reflected and so face the other way. Choose a simple design and draw the reflection, asking the children to say which colours go where in the reflection. SUGGESTED QUESTIONS: • Have you checked your reflection? • Hold the mirror next to the card. Lift the mirror and check your colouring underneath. **Snip, snip** This activity involves lines of symmetry (fold lines) in different orientations, including where the lines are diagonal. All shapes have only one line of symmetry. Encourage the children to use a ruler for this activity and to use small mirrors to check their answers. SUGGESTED QUESTIONS: • Where do you think the fold line must be? • Can you use the mirror to check?	Properties of shape	90–1 92 93 94

Block B Securing number facts, understanding shapes – Unit 3

Activity name	Strand and learning objectives	Notes on the activities	Assessment Focus	Page number
Billy's door Amy's seat	**Using and applying mathematics** Describe patterns and relationships involving numbers or shapes, make predictions and test these with examples	**Billy's door** Processes: *look for pattern, compare, reason, predict, test idea, explain* As a further investigation, the children could test every door number between 20 and 30 to see whether it would be open or closed in each pattern. SUGGESTED QUESTIONS: • Can you describe this pattern? • What do you predict? • How could you check? **Amy's seat** Processes: *look for pattern, compare, reason, predict, test ideas, explain* As a further investigation, the children could test every seat number between 20 and 30 to see the colour each number would be for each pattern. SUGGESTED QUESTIONS: • Can you describe this pattern? • What do you predict? • How could you check?	Communicating	95 96
Sandy's sandwich bar Car boot sale	**Using and applying mathematics** Solve problems involving addition, subtraction, multiplication or division in contexts of numbers, measures or pounds and pence	**Sandy's sandwich bar** Processes: *make decisions, record, reason, explain* This activity encourages the children to make their own decisions as to how to answer the questions, whether pictorially, numerically or practically. SUGGESTED QUESTIONS: • How did you work out the answer to this question? • How did you know what to do? • What other similar questions could you ask? **Car boot sale** Processes: *reason, make own decisions* This sheet provides an opportunity for the children to determine which calculation is necessary to solve problems involving money (in pounds). To provide differentiation for less-confident children, you could simplify question 6 to 'Mrs Sellers sold 9 Tshirts, each for £2. How much money did she get?' (9 x 2 = 18) and question 7 to 'Mr Stall spent £4 on a chair and £8 on a table. How much did he spend on both?' SUGGESTED QUESTIONS: • How did you find the answer? • What method did you use to find the answer? • Did you use the same method for each question or did you do anything different on this question?	Problem solving	97 98
Dicey dinosaurs Fairy wings Ski slalom	**Knowing and using number facts** Derive and recall all addition and subtraction facts for each number to at least 10, all pairs with totals to 20 and all pairs of multiples of 10 with totals up to 100	**Dicey dinosaurs** When playing this game, some children experience difficulty in knowing how to read the key. Demonstrate how to call one of the dice 'Dice 1' and the other 'Dice 2' and to place the dice, after rolling, onto the appropriate pictures. The children should then read off the numbers below their dice and add them to see if they make 100. In cases where children are finding this difficult, it can be helpful if the two dice are a different colour from each other. Draw children's attention to the relationship between 4 + 6 = 10, for example, and 40 + 60 = 100. SUGGESTED QUESTION: • Jump up if the two numbers I say have a total of 100. '60 and 30', '40 and 60'... etc. **Fairy wings** This activity encourages the children to record additions and subtractions using the +, – and = signs. Encourage the children to read their questions aloud, using a range of appropriate addition and subtraction vocabulary. Suggested questions: • Is the sum of 40 and 60 one hundred? • How could you write this as a subtraction statement? **Ski slalom** In the main activity, ask the children to write their answers as quickly as they can. The children could use stopwatches to time themselves doing the activity and then repeat it to see whether they can better their time.	Mental methods	99 100 101

Activity name	Strand and learning objectives	Notes on the activities	Assessment Focus	Page number
		SUGGESTED QUESTIONS: • How quickly did you reach the bottom? • What number fact that you know already can you use to help you add 70 and 20? • 3 + 8 = 11. What is 30 + 80?		
Four in a line	**Knowing and using number facts** Understand that halving is the inverse of doubling and derive and recall doubles of all numbers to 20, and the corresponding halves	**Four in a line** This sheet could be enlarged to A3 on a copier to make it easier for children to work in pairs. Remind the children to read carefully whether the instruction they land on says double or halve. Demonstrate strategies for working out doubles that are not known, such as partitioning the number first and then doubling each part, for example 17 = 10 + 7, 20 + 14 = 34. SUGGESTED QUESTIONS: • How could you work out double 17? • Do you notice a link between double 7 and double 17? • How far can you count in twos? Can you go any further? • Which number comes after 12 if you are counting in twos? • What patterns did you notice in the numbers? • Which of these numbers are multiples of 2?	Operations, relationships between them Mental methods	102
Animal races	**Knowing and using number facts** Derive and recall multiplication facts for the 2, 5 and 10 times-tables and the related division facts; recognise multiples of 2, 5 and 10	**Animal races** This activity is more challenging than it seems at first glance. Children need to examine what the numbers in each line have in common, with the exception of one of them. It would be helpful if the children could refer to a list of the multiples of 2, 5 and 10. SUGGESTED QUESTIONS: • Which is the odd number out? • What do all the rest of the numbers have in common?	Mental methods	103
Fact file	**Knowing and using number facts** Use knowledge of number facts and operations to estimate and check answers to calculations	**Fact file** This activity could be used at the start of a term to assess the children's confidence in dealing with numbers in different ways and following instructions requiring doubling, halving and adding or subtracting the numbers. Encourage them to use a range of operations including doubling and halving as part of their own questions, and ask them to share their questions with the class, discussing difficult or interesting ones written. SUGGESTED QUESTIONS: • What were your estimates for questions 6 and 8? • How did you check your answer to question 10?	Operations, relationships between them	104
Crazy colours Solids speedway!	**Understanding shape** Visualise common 2-D shapes and 3-D solids; identify shapes from pictures of them in different orientations; sort, make and describe shapes, referring to their properties	**Crazy colours** Some children experience difficulty in identifying 3-D shapes from pictures of them. Before beginning the activity, discuss the shapes shown on the sheet and ask the children to select them from a set of real solid shapes. Discuss the 2-D shapes of the faces of the 3-D shapes and ensure the children know the meaning of the word 'face' in this context. Be aware of children who do not yet appreciate that 3-D shapes can be in any position or orientation and are still the same shape. Note that technically the cubes could be ticked red and also pink, since squares are types of rectangles. This could be discussed with more confident pupils if thought appropriate. SUGGESTED QUESTIONS: • What shapes are the faces of a cube/cuboid? • Which shapes have one or more curved faces? **Solids speedway!** For this game, the children should work in pairs. Each pair will need a dice, a counter each, and one sheet (ideally enlarged onto A3 paper). Ensure that children are familiar with the term 'vertices' or alter the term before copying to 'corners' if more appropriate. Discuss shapes such as cylinders and spheres that have no vertices and ensure the children appreciate that faces can be curved or flat, for example a sphere has one curved face. The sheet could also be altered to include edges for variety. Provide 3-D shapes for examination. SUGGESTED QUESTIONS: • Do you know the name of this shape? • How many faces/vertices has this shape? • Are its faces curved or straight?	Properties of shape	105 106

Block C Handling data and measures – Unit 1

Activity name	Strand and learning objectives	Notes on the activities	Assessment Focus	Page number
Someone said: 1 and 2 Hold it!	**Using and applying mathematics** Follow a line of enquiry; answer questions by choosing and using suitable equipment and selecting, organising and presenting information in lists, tables and simple diagrams	**Someone said: 1 and 2** *Processes: make decisions, record, cooperate, predict* These activity sheets encourage the children to make decisions and to plan how to follow lines of enquiry by collecting data or (in the Let's measure activity sheets) by using measuring equipment to answer questions. SUGGESTED QUESTIONS: • How did you decide what to do? • What do you think the outcome might be? **Hold it!** *Processes: be systematic, make decisions, look for pattern, record* This activity continues with the idea of working systematically, in order to find different possibilities. Initially, the children could work practically with coins and should then be asked to record different solutions. SUGGESTED QUESTIONS/PROMPT: • How many different ways did you find? • How can you be sure that you have found them all? • Were you systematic?	Reasoning	107–8 109

Activity name	Strand and learning objectives	Notes on the activities	Assessment Focus	Page number
The vet: 1 and 2 Bird spotting In the fridge	**Handling data** Answer a question by collecting and recording data in lists and tables; represent the data as block graphs or pictograms to show results; use ICT to organise and present data	**The vet: 1 and 2** This activity could link in with your home corner/role-play area if you have it set up as a vet's waiting room. The children could collect and organise the data required from the toy animals they have in the play area. Find out if any of the children have had to take a pet to the vet and make a list of their names demonstrating list-making as you do. Ask them to explain what happened when they went. As a further extension activity, the children could research other pets and make up their own vet's activity similar to this. **Suggested questions:** • How did you collect the data? • Is a list a better way to show data than the picture? Why? • Could you have used something other than a list? **Bird spotting** Before beginning the activity, ask the children to tell you the names of any birds they know. Make a list and then discuss which are likely to be found in a wood. Cross out those that would not. If possible, show photos of the birds named in the table and ask the children to identify the pictures on the resource sheet from the photos. During the plenary ask the children to share their questions from the extension activity. **Suggested questions:** • What does this table show you? • How many children were walking in the woods? How do you know? • What do the rows show? What about the columns? **In the fridge** This would fit well with a Science topic on healthy eating. Before you begin, make a list of the healthy foods that the children may have in their fridges at home. This will also give them some ideas for the extension activity. Discuss the rows and columns and what information they will need to hold. In the plenary, invite some children to share the lists they made up. **Suggested questions:** • What does this table need to tell us? • Is there another way you could show the information? • How many dairy items are there in the fridge?	Processing and representing data	110–1 112 113
Longer or shorter? Dice	**Handling data** Use lists, tables and diagrams to sort objects; explain choices using appropriate language, including 'not'	**Longer or shorter?** Before beginning the activity, give each child a ruler and discuss what it shows – for example the number of centimetres, the marks between the centimetres, and how long it is. Discuss the items that the children might find in the classroom and whether they would be shorter or longer than their ruler. During the plenary invite the children to explain how they measured the items in their lists. **Suggested questions:** • Which list would a chair go in? • What about a book? Would all books go in the same list? • What do you think would definitely go in your list? **Dice** For the extension activity, encourage the children to think of questions that involve more complex calculation work, for example what is the total of all your throws? What is the biggest difference you can make? During the plenary invite the children to share their questions and ask the class to answer them. **Suggested questions:** • Why is your list helpful? • What would happen if you did not make one? • What is the difference between the lowest and the highest numbers that you threw?	Interpreting data	114 115
The metre beater game Doggy differences Doggy dilemmas Litre checker	**Measuring** Estimate, compare and measure lengths, weights and capacities, choosing and using standard units (m, cm, kg, litre) and suitable **Measuring** instruments	**The metre beater game** These cards can be used for a range of comparing activities, such as the following: • Working in pairs, the children can pick a card each and say the difference between the two lengths. • Cards can be placed face down. A target length can be chosen and the children pick a card each and see who has the length closer to the chosen target. • More confident children can write the lengths in metres, in centimetres, or in both. **Suggested questions:** • Do you think this is larger or smaller than one metre? • Can you show me with your hands how long you think this length is? **Doggy differences** At the start of the lesson, discuss whether any children have dogs at home and if so what breed they are. Invite a child to describe how heavy their dog is, for example: 'Can you easily lift it up?' 'Is it too heavy to lift up?' Explain that we use kilograms to find out and compare how heavy things are. Pass round a kilogram weight and ask the children to say whether a dog is heavier or lighter than this. Discuss how heavy different breeds are and, where possible, find objects of an equivalent amount, such as: a bag of potatoes, a chair, a pile of books, etc. **Suggested questions:** • How did you work out the difference between those two weights? • Do you think that you weigh more or less than a chihuahua? **Doggy dilemmas** Demonstrate with a set of balance scales how things that balance remain horizontal when let go and things that do not balance tilt, with the heavier going down further. Explain that some of these pictures show things that will balance and others do not. The child's job is to find out which are which, using the information on the 'Doggy differences' cards. **Suggested questions:** • Do these balance? • How heavy are the things in the left-hand pan? • How heavy are the things in the right-hand pan? • Are they equal? So will they balance? **Litre checker** At the start of the lesson, give each group of children a litre container full of water and different containers to compare it with. They could test which of the containers holds more or less than one litre by pouring water into them. If your school has large plant pots and tubs, discuss with the children whether these would hold more than, less than or exactly one litre. **Suggested question:** • Which object do you think holds the most/least?	Measures	116 117 118 119
Scale trail	**Measuring** Read the numbered divisions on a scale, and interpret the divisions between them (e.g. on a scale from 0 to 25 with intervals of 1 shown but only the divisions 0, 5, 10, 15 and 20 numbered); use a ruler and measure lines to the nearest centimetre	**Scale trail** Ensure that children understand the rules for this activity. When the scale is read, the number of kilograms shown becomes the number of positions down the track that the counter is moved. The scale landed on is then read and the activity continues to the winning sections. Different starting points can be explored. **Suggested questions:** • What mass does this scale show? • Which number comes between 2 and 4?	Measures	120

Block C Handling data and measures – Unit 2

Activity name	Strand and learning objectives	Notes on the activities	Assessment Focus	Page number
T-shirt printer	**Using and applying mathematics** Follow a line of enquiry; answer questions by choosing and using suitable equipment and selecting, organising and presenting information in lists, tables and simple diagrams	**T-shirt printer** Processes: *visualise, reason, record, compare* Encourage the children to compare their solutions and to think about how a table could show all the solutions more easily than a list. SUGGESTED QUESTION: • Have you drawn all the apples in the description?	Reasoning	121
Unusual pets Chocolate bars Celebrations Favourite circus acts	**Handling data** Answer a question by collecting and recording data in lists and tables; represent the data as block graphs or pictograms to show results; use ICT to organise and present data	**Unusual pets** Before beginning the activity, together with the children, make a class block graph to show the pets the children have. As you do this, discuss the numbers that go up the vertical axis and explain how to write labels under the columns to show the different pets. Discuss the pets on the sheet and match them to their pictures. SUGGESTED QUESTIONS: • How many people own a chinchilla? • Who would find this graph useful? Why do you think that? • Why is this a good way of showing the data? **Chocolate bars** To simplify this activity, the children could write the missing numbers on the vertical axis and use a ruler to help them read each block. To extend the activity, you could delete the numbers and marks for all the intervals and ask the children to complete this part of the block graph. SUGGESTED QUESTIONS: • Which is the most popular chocolate bar? • Which is the least popular? **Celebrations** You could link this with the celebrations theme in RE. Ask the children to think of what they might celebrate, for example birthdays and weddings. Demonstrate drawing a block graph for the children's birthdays. Highlight the numbering of the vertical axis and the months of the year labels along the horizontal axis. Ask questions from the graph which involve finding totals and differences. SUGGESTED QUESTIONS: • What does the tallest column mean? • What does the shortest column mean? • Which is the best way to show the information, tally, block graph or table? Why? **Favourite circus acts** Before beginning the actual task, discuss the circus, what it is and where the children might have seen one. Invite any children who have been to describe their experiences. Using their ideas, make a list of circus acts on the board. SUGGESTED QUESTIONS: • What is your block graph going to show? • How is this different from the table? • How many clowns voted for their favourite act?	Processing and representing data	122 123 124 125
Clothes: 1 and 2	**Handling data** Use lists, tables and diagrams to sort objects; explain choices using appropriate language, including 'not'	**Clothes: 1 and 2** Before beginning the activity, ask the children to tell you the different clothes that they wear. Make a list of about 10. Ask them to think of ways to sort them, for example things you wear on your feet, things you wear on your legs. During the plenary look at the children's ideas for sorting the clothes a second time. SUGGESTED QUESTIONS: • Where would you put a thick, chunky cardigan? Why? • How else could you sort the clothes? Is there another way?	Interpreting data	126–7
Crunchy carrots Marble mania	**Measuring** Estimate, compare and measure lengths, weights and capacities, choosing and using standard units (m, cm, kg, litre) and suitable **Measuring** instruments	**Crunchy carrots** For more variety of lengths, the sheet could be enlarged through various percentages, for example enlarging by 50% or onto A3. SUGGESTED QUESTIONS: • How many centimetres long do you think this carrot is? • Can you explain to me how you estimated that? • Which of these two do you think is longer? **Marble mania** Children should be given practical experience of weighing marbles and jars to reinforce this activity. Once the weights of objects are known, the total weight of items can be easily calculated. The extension activity involves the children beginning to appreciate that 500 g is half a kilogram and that 1000 g is one kilogram. SUGGESTED QUESTIONS: • How many grams is the same as a kilogram? • How many grams is the same as half a kilogram? • Which pictures show things that are heavier/lighter than half a kilogram?	Measures	128 129
Monster weights Spaghetti spikes	**Measuring** Read the numbered divisions on a scale, and interpret the divisions between them (e.g. on a scale from 0 to 25 with intervals of 1 shown but only the divisions 0, 5, 10, 15 and 20 numbered); use a ruler to draw and measure lines to the nearest centimetre	**Monster weights** This activity contains scales with numbered divisions going up in 5s. The arrows could be masked and altered to provide more variety or the numbers could be changed as appropriate, for example going up in 10s. SUGGESTED QUESTIONS: • Which monster is the heaviest/lightest? • How much heavier is this monster than this one? **Spaghetti spikes** Provide small pieces of string for the extension activity and demonstrate how string and a ruler can be used to find the length of non-straight lengths. SUGGESTED QUESTIONS: • Where do you place your ruler when you measure a line? • Is your little finger longer or shorter than the shortest line on the page?	Measures	130 131

Block C Handling data and measures – Unit 3

Activity name	Strand and learning objectives	Notes on the activities	Assessment Focus	Page number
Let's measure: 1 and 2	**Using and applying mathematics** Follow a line of enquiry; answer questions by choosing and using suitable equipment and selecting, organising and presenting information in lists, tables and simple diagrams	**Let's measure: 1 and 2** Processes: make decisions, record, cooperate, predict These activity sheets encourage the children to make decisions and to plan how to follow lines of enquiry by collecting data or (in the Let's measure activity sheets) by using measuring equipment to answer questions. SUGGESTED QUESTIONS: • How did you decide what to do? • What do you think the outcome might be?	Reasoning	132–3
Wheels	**Handling data** Answer a question by collecting and recording data in lists and tables; represent the data as block graphs or pictograms to show results; use ICT to organise and present data	**Wheels** This activity would link well with a topic that you might be covering in Design and Technology to do with vehicles. Before the children begin, discuss the importance of wheels with vehicles and ask them to tell you as many different vehicles with wheels that they can think of. Make a list of some or all. To simplify, delete two of the columns. To extend, encourage a reasoned argument as to why the village should or should not win the award for the least amount of traffic. SUGGESTED QUESTIONS: • What does this block graph tell us? • Can you tell us some facts? • What does the graph tell us about the village?	Processing and representing data	134
Macy and her kittens		**Macy and her kittens** As this is the first activity for pictograms, review the children's knowledge by making one about Buster and the number of tins of dog food he eats in a week. Throw a dice to generate the numbers. Ask questions that refer to the data. During the plenary, ask questions from their pictograms that involve finding totals and differences. Also discuss the children's responses to the extension activity in the Teachers' Note. SUGGESTED QUESTIONS: • What does this pictogram tell you? What else? • On which day did they eat the least food? • How many more tins did they eat on Sunday than on Thursday?		135
In the garden		**In the garden** Ask the children to tell you some flowers that they might find growing in gardens or fields. Make a list and then choose four. Draw a basic frame for a pictogram on the board with space along the horizontal axis to write the names of the four flowers. You will need two dice and Post-It notes. Invite a child to throw the dice and together find the total. Place that number of Post-It notes in a column to represent the first flower. Repeat for the other three. Ask questions that involve reading the pictogram and finding totals and differences. After their activity, during the plenary, invite the children to share their statements. SUGGESTED QUESTIONS: • How many snowdrops and pansies did Adam plant altogether? • How many more snowdrops than crocuses did he plant? • If he planted two more of each plant, how would the pictogram be different?		136
Goal!		**Goal!** Before beginning this activity, show examples of completed pictograms such as those from previous activities and discuss how they have been made up. As they work on their task, give pairs of children a copy of one to help them visualise what their result should look like. During the plenary, discuss the children's answers to the extension activity. SUGGESTED QUESTIONS: • If Saturn had scored 5 more goals, how many would they have scored in total? • Who scored the same number of goals? • What is the difference between the number of goals scored by Pluto and Venus?		137
Multiples	**Handling data** Use lists, tables and diagrams to sort objects; explain choices using appropriate language, including 'not'	**Multiples** Before you begin, rehearse counting in steps of 5 to 50 and back. Take the opportunity to rehearse the 5 times-table as well. Discuss what numbers a multiple of 5 always ends with. For the extension activity, encourage the children to think of alternative ways to sort the numbers, for example odd or even, multiples of 2 or 3. Discuss any other ways the children have thought of during the plenary. SUGGESTED QUESTIONS: • How do you know which numbers will go in your list of multiples of 5? • How do you know you have them all?	Interpreting data	138
Numbers		**Numbers** This is a diagram for sorting numbers similar in many ways to a Venn diagram (which is not in the Year 2 objectives of the Primary Framework for mathematics). You could begin the lesson by sorting objects into hoops and asking the children to write labels for each hoop. SUGGESTED QUESTIONS: • What can you tell me about the numbers in the hoops? • Where would the number 60 go? • Can you tell me another number that will go in the middle?		139
Pets: 1 and 2		**Pets: 1 and 2** SUGGESTED QUESTIONS: • How many children on your diagram have pets? • If I had a dog, where would you put my name?		140–1
Toys		**Toys** Discuss the different sorting diagrams that the children have been working on with one criterion and then two criteria. Demonstrate how to use a sorting diagram for two criteria by carrying out a class survey of children's eye and hair colour. SUGGESTED QUESTIONS: • What does this sorting diagram show? • If Sally and Steve had another toy that had blue eyes and blonde hair, how many would go in that section?		142
Right angles: 1 and 2		**Right angles: 1 and 2** Before beginning the activity, review right angles. Ask the children to tell you what a right angle is, to show you with their fingers and to tell you some shapes that have them. Discuss where they can see them in the classroom and make a list of these places, for example: table, window, door. During the plenary, invite the children to share the criteria they picked for their own sorting diagram. SUGGESTED QUESTIONS: • Where will you put this shape? How do you know? • If we added this shape (draw a right-angled triangle on the board) where would it go? • What other headings could we use to sort the shapes?		143–4

Activity name	Strand and learning objectives	Notes on the activities	Assessment Focus	Page number
Going to great lengths	**Measuring** Estimate, compare and measure lengths, weights and capacities, choosing and using standard units (m, cm, kg, litre) and suitable measuring instruments	**Going to great lengths** Children need to appreciate when it is best to use centimetres (for measuring smaller lengths) and when it is best to use metres (for measuring longer lengths). Where the children give different answers from those below, discuss how long they think the item is and encourage them to estimate it in metres or centimetres. SUGGESTED QUESTION/PROMPT: • About how wide do you think a butterfly is? • Show me with your fingers. Now measure with a ruler to check your answer.	Measures	145
Deep water	**Measuring** Read the numbered divisions on a scale, and interpret the divisions between them (e.g. on a scale from 0 to 25 with intervals of 1 shown but only the divisions 0, 5, 10, 15 and 20 numbered); use a ruler to draw and measure lines to the nearest centimetre	**Deep water** This sheet explores some of the vocabulary related to nonexact readings on a simple scale. SUGGESTED QUESTIONS: • Does your picture show more or less than 3 litres? Is either correct?	Measures	146

Block D Calculating, measuring and understanding shape – Unit 1

Activity name	Strand and learning objectives	Notes on the activities	Assessment Focus	Page number
Rick's restaurant London Eye	**Using and applying mathematics** Solve problems involving addition, subtraction, multiplication or division in contexts of numbers, measures or pounds and pence	**Rick's restaurant** *Processes: record, reason, explain* This activity provides the children with an opportunity to focus on what to do, rather than the answer. Provide several similar examples at the start of the lesson to ensure that the children understand what is being asked of them. SUGGESTED QUESTIONS: • How would you work out the answer to this question? • How could you write this as a number sentence? **London Eye** *Processes: record, reason, make decisions* These word problems involve the range of different operations. The children should be encouraged to explain how they worked out each answer and to record it as a number fact. SUGGESTED QUESTIONS: • How did you find the answer? • What method did you use to find the answer? • How could you write this as a number sentence?	Problem solving	147 148
Beaver away I 'eight' a cucumber	**Calculating** Add or subtract mentally a one-digit number or a multiple of 10 to or from any two-digit number; use practical and informal written methods to add and subtract two-digit numbers	**Beaver away** Provide number lines to support children who find this activity difficult. Then model how to draw an empty number line and count back to the previous multiple of 10, and beyond, recording each step. SUGGESTED QUESTIONS: • How do you know that 31 – 5 is 26? • Which number facts did you use to help you work out that 72 – 9 is 63? **I 'eight' a cucumber** The children will need green pencils or crayons for this activity. SUGGESTED QUESTIONS: • How can you use the facts at the top of the page to help you find the green cucumbers? • What is the answer to this subtraction question? • How did you work it out?	Mental methods Written methods	149 150
Flea party Frog tongues!	**Measuring** Estimate, compare and measure lengths, weights and capacities, choosing and using standard units (m, cm, kg, litre) and suitable measuring instruments Read the numbered divisions on a scale, and interpret the divisions between them (e.g. on a scale from 0 to 25 with intervals of 1 shown but only the divisions 0, 5, 10, 15 and 20 numbered); use a ruler to draw and measure lines to the nearest centimetre	**Flea party** For this activity, the children can draw lines between any pair of fleas and measure and record the length. Demonstrate how to use a ruler to measure the length of a line, positioning the ruler correctly at one end of the line. Encourage the children to compare answers with a partner and see if they have measured any of the same lines. Use a range of vocabulary when discussing the distances between fleas such as in the questions below. SUGGESTED QUESTIONS: • How far is flea A from flea D? Are the fleas close together or far apart? • How many centimetres away from flea G is flea D? • Is flea E more than 10 centimetres from flea B? • How far would flea F need to walk in a straight line to reach flea C? **Frog tongues!** Provide small pieces of string for the extension activity and demonstrate how string and a ruler can be used to find the length of non-straight lengths. Children could check each other's work by measuring the lengths of all the frog tongues on a partner's sheet. SUGGESTED QUESTIONS: • How much longer does this line have to be to reach the fly? • What is the longest tongue that your ruler could measure?	Measures	151 152

Activity name	Strand and learning objectives	Notes on the activities	Assessment Focus	Page number
Fun time Charlie and Chester	**Measuring** Use units of time (seconds, minutes, hours, days) and know the relationships between them; read the time to the quarter hour; identify time intervals, including those that cross the hour	**Fun time** Provide some similar oral activities before the children begin this sheet. Discuss classroom activities and say whether they take seconds, minutes or hours. Ask them to make an estimate as to exactly how long each activity takes, for example: taking the register – 4 minutes. SUGGESTED QUESTION: • Do you think it will take 5 seconds, 5 minutes or 5 hours? **Charlie and Chester** This activity involves appreciating the relationship between seconds, minutes and hours. Following a class discussion, write a list of the relationships on the board for children to refer to, for example: 1 minute = 60 seconds 1 hour = 60 minutes 1 day = 24 hours SUGGESTED QUESTIONS: • How can you work out whether 1 hour or 65 minutes is longer? • How many seconds are there in 2 minutes?	Measures	153 154
Pirate map	**Understanding shape** Follow and give instructions involving position, direction and movement	**Pirate map** This activity helps to develop using and applying skills such as trial and improvement, perseverance and visualisation. Children should cut out the cards and move them into position so that every statement is true. SUGGESTED QUESTIONS: • Where is the cave? • Is the parrot above or below the cannon? • What is to the left of the bridge? • What is under the anchor?		155

Block D Calculating, measuring and understanding shape – Unit 2

Activity name	Strand and learning objectives	Notes on the activities	Assessment Focus	Page number
Let's swim again	**Using and applying mathematics** Solve problems involving addition, subtraction, multiplication or division in contexts of numbers, measures or pounds and pence	**Let's swim again** *Processes: explain, reason* These questions can be copied onto thin card and laminated and used as a more permanent classroom resource. The cards could be picked at random and used for whole class problem solving activities in spare moments. Watch out for children who find the distracting words such as 'times' and automatically multiply the numbers or 'fewer' and automatically subtract even though the context does not require this. SUGGESTED QUESTIONS/PROMPTS: • Do you agree on this answer? Read the question again. • Who has swum further? Is that what your answer suggests?	Problem solving	156
Hopping frog Calendar puzzle	**Calculating** Add or subtract mentally a one-digit number or a multiple of 10 to or from any two-digit number; use practical and informal written methods to add and subtract two-digit numbers	**Hopping frog** This activity encourages children to begin to use number lines as an informal jotting to help them reach an answer to a calculation. SUGGESTED PROMPT: • Explain how you used the number line to help you work out the answer. **Calendar puzzle** This activity could be used as a means of introducing the children to adding numbers in columns. For more information, see Stage 2, page 5 of the Primary National Strategy Guidance Paper on Calculation. SUGGESTED QUESTIONS/PROMPT: • How could you work out this answer on paper? • Can you partition both numbers for me? Add the multiples of 10 first, then add the one-digit numbers. What is the total of your two answers?	Mental methods Written methods	157 158
Dizzy the baker: 1 and 2	**Measuring** Read the numbered divisions on a scale, and interpret the divisions between them (e.g. on a scale from 0 to 25 with intervals of 1 shown but only the divisions 0, 5, 10, 15 and 20 numbered); use a ruler to draw and measure lines to the nearest centimetre	**Dizzy the baker: 1 and 2** Hold up a real kitchen timer and discuss what it is used for. These two activity sheets show scales with intervals of 1 but only the divisions 0, 5, 10, 15 and 20 are numbered. The first sheet shows times up to 25 minutes and the second sheet shows times up to 1 hour (60 minutes). SUGGESTED QUESTIONS: • How many minutes does this timer show? • Which cake matches which timer?	Measures	159-60

Activity name	Strand and learning objectives	Notes on the activities	Assessment Focus	Page number
Wally's wonder watch: 1 and 2 Carol's classy clock: 1 and 2	**Measuring** Use units of time (seconds, minutes, hours, days) and know the relationships between them; read the time to the quarter hour; identify time intervals, including those that cross the hour	**Wally's wonder watch: 1 and 2** These two sheets involve analogue clocks (clock-faces). The first involves reading the time in words and drawing it on the clock-face. The second involves reading the time on the clockface and writing the time shown in words. Discuss with the children that the time in words are all correct, for example three-fifteen or quarter past three, and that these are all correct, for example three-fifteen or quarter past three. SUGGESTED QUESTIONS: • What time does this clock show? • Which number is the short hand, the hour hand, pointing to? • How could you show 5 o'clock? • Which number would the short hand be pointing to? **Carol's classy clock: 1 and 2** These two sheets explore digital clocks and time. The first involves reading the time in words and writing it on the digital clock. The second involves reading the time on the digital clock and writing the time shown in words. Encourage the children to use the words 'quarter to/ past', 'o'clock' and 'half past' for the latter activity. At the start of the activities show how 'o'clock' times are represented by :00 on digital clocks and that :30 represents half past, or 30 minutes past: :15 quarter past and :45 quarter to, and so on. Explain also that the hour always comes first in digital clock times, for example 6:30 means half past 6. It is common for children to reverse these times, showing it as 30:6 as this more closely matches the way 30 minutes past 6 or half past 6 is written and spoken. SUGGESTED QUESTIONS: • What time does this clock show? • Which number tells you the hour? • What does :45 mean? • How could you show 5 o'clock? Half past 4?	Measures	161–2 163–4
Rotating pictures In a spin	**Understanding shape** Recognise and use whole, half and quarter-turns, both clockwise and anticlockwise; know that a right angle represents a quarter-turn	**Rotating pictures** This activity is best introduced using software on an interactive whiteboard, for example by rotating a picture using drawing tools in a word-processing package or by rotating using image editing software. By continuously clicking the rotate button (turning the picture through 90° each time) the children can see that four quarter turns return the picture to its original orientation. SUGGESTED QUESTIONS: • If we make two quarter turns is this the same as a half turn? • The picture is the right way up. What will it look like after a half turn? How could we describe the picture now? (upside down) **In a spin** This activity should be introduced practically. Place a letter on each of the four walls of the classroom, for example A, D, R, E. Call out instructions like those on the sheet to spell words such as DARE, DEAR, READ, ARE, EAR, RED, etc. The activity sheet can then be used as an assessment to see which children can successfully follow instructions involving half and quarter turns both clockwise and anticlockwise. Remind the children of the directions of clockwise and anticlockwise. As a further extension activity, the children could also be given their own letters, such as T, R, A, E and asked to write their own similar instructions to spell out simple words for others to solve, such as RATE, TEAR, TARE, ATE, EAR, TEA, RAT, ART, ARE, TAR, etc. SUGGESTED QUESTION: • What do you notice about making a half turn clockwise and making a half turn anticlockwise?	Properties	165 166
School play Avoid the zombies The hamster run	**Understanding shape** Follow and give instructions involving position, direction and movement	**School play** This activity is enhanced if the children are introduced to it practically. Arrange some chairs in the hall and ask several children to sit in some positions. Ask other children to explain the position of those children and how they got there from a fixed point, for example the entrance. The sheet can be used as an assessment activity to see whether the children can follow simple sets of instructions involving direction and distance. SUGGESTED QUESTIONS/PROMPT: • Can you follow this set of instructions? • Where would you end up? • Remember to start at the entrance each time. **Avoid the zombies** As children work in pairs to describe routes, they should be encouraged to record them accurately. There are different ways that the routes could be described, such as referring to turning and moving forwards or in relation to the whole grid, for example move up 1, then left 2, etc. Either approach is valid and the children could be encouraged to discuss which way of directing they find easier. SUGGESTED QUESTIONS: • Can you follow another group's instructions? • Where would you end up? **The hamster run** This sheet can be used as a stimulus for children making up their own escaped pet story. This could be linked to writing activities and the children could use the wordbank from this sheet to include in their story. SUGGESTED QUESTIONS: • Can you describe where the hamster went? • Can anyone think of a better way of saying 'The hamster went along there…'? • Which direction did the hamster go? Did it go under/over or between anything?	Properties	167 168 169

Block D Calculating, measuring and understanding shape – Unit 3

Activity name	Strand and learning objectives	Notes on the activities	Assessment Focus	Page number
Cubs and Brownies	**Using and applying mathematics** Solve problems involving addition, subtraction, multiplication or division in contexts of numbers, measures or pounds and pence	**Cubs and Brownies** *Processes:* explain, ask own questions, reason This activity can help the children to see how many different questions can be asked about a context and encourages them to make up their own questions about the context. SUGGESTED QUESTION/PROMPT: • How many different questions have we asked in our class? • How did you answer your friend's question? Identify and record the information or calculation needed to solve a puzzle or problem; carry out the steps or calculations and check the solution in the context of a puzzle or problem. Carry out the steps or calculations and check the solution in the context of the problem.	Problem solving	170

Activity name	Strand and learning objectives	Notes on the activities	Assessment Focus	Page number
Hop, skip and jump	**Calculating** Add or subtract mentally a one-digit number or a multiple of 10 to or from any two-digit number; use practical and informal written methods to add and subtract two-digit numbers	**Hop, skip and jump** This activity encourages the children to use number lines as an informal jotting to help them reach an answer to a calculation. Here, the subtraction solution is found by counting up from the smaller number to the larger number. Ensure the children realise that the answer is the total of all the jumps made along the line. **SUGGESTED PROMPT:** • Explain how you used the number line to help you work out the answer.	Mental methods	171
Ant trail	**Measuring** Estimate, compare and measure lengths, weights and capacities, choosing and using standard units (m, cm, kg, litre) and suitable measuring instruments Read the numbered divisions on a scale, and interpret the divisions between them (e.g. on a scale from 0 to 25 with intervals of 1 shown but only the divisions 0, 5, 10, 15 and 20 numbered); use a ruler to draw and measure lines to the nearest centimetre	**Ant trail** As children become more confident in measuring the lengths of straight lines they can begin to explore early ideas of perimeter, found by measuring each side and then finding the total of all the lengths. **SUGGESTED QUESTIONS:** • How far around the whole shape will the ant travel? • What is the length/width of this rectangle? • What do you notice about how long these two opposite sides are? Is this always true?	Measures	172
TV times: 1 and 2 Time quiz	**Measuring** Use units of time (seconds, minutes, hours, days) and know the relationships between them; read the time to the quarter hour; identify time intervals, including those that cross the hour	**TV times: 1 and 2** Provide the children with clocks with moveable hands to help them with the following activities. They should move the hands from one time to the other and work out how long has passed. **SUGGESTED QUESTIONS:** • How long do you have to wait until the cartoons begin? How could you say that in a different way? • How many minutes are between 2 o'clock and quarter past 2? **Time quiz** The times on this sheet could be altered before copying to provide further practice. If the children are experiencing difficulty with this sheet showing digital times, give small analogue clocks to the children and ask them to make the correct time and then turn the hand backwards or forwards to answer the question. Note that it is preferable to have clocks where the hour hand correctly moves as the minute hand is turned. **SUGGESTED QUESTIONS:** • What time does this clock show? • Can you show me this time on the clock-face?	Measures	173–4 175
Feeding time Hexagon handiwork Power-robots!	**Understanding shape** Recognise and use whole, half and quarter-turns, both clockwise and anticlockwise; know that a right angle represents a quarter-turn	**Feeding time** At the start of the lesson, show how the angles between scissor blades link turning with static angles. Demonstrate using a pair of scissors how the blades can be turned to create larger or smaller angles. Show a right angle and encourage children to identify when you are holding the blades at right angles to each other. This can be made into a game, where you keep moving the scissors and the children put their hands on their heads when it shows right angles. When the children play the game with the cards from the sheet, encourage them to think about scissor angles to help them compare the angles. **SUGGESTED QUESTIONS:** • A right angle is a quarter turn. True or false? • Is this angle larger or smaller than a right angle? • How can you check? **Hexagon handiwork** There are many different hexagons that can be drawn on a 4 by 4 dotted grid. Examples of hexagons that contain right angles include the following: **Power-robots!** This activity involves static pictures where the children must identify right angles. They should cut out and use the right angle gobbler to check the angles. **SUGGESTED QUESTION:** • If you twist the paper can you see whether there are any other right angles that you have missed? **SUGGESTED QUESTIONS:** • How many sides does a hexagon have? • Does this hexagon have any right angles? • Can you mark them?	Properties	176 177 178

Block E Securing number facts, calculating, identifying relationships – Unit 1

Activity name	Strand and learning objectives	Notes on the activities	Assessment Focus	Page number
What a match: 1 and 2 Make 26 Hide the cakes	**Using and applying mathematics** Identify and record the information or calculation needed to solve a puzzle or problem; carry out the steps or calculations and check the solution in the context of the problem	**What a match: 1 and 2** Processes: *explain, record, reason* These two sheets provide children with the opportunity to consider and identify which operations are necessary in solving each question. SUGGESTED QUESTION: • Which calculation would you use? **Make 26** Processes: *explain, look for pattern, record, test ideas, trial and improvement* This problem-solving activity requires children to take account of not only the numbers of faces but also the shapes of the pieces. Tell the children to begin by choosing the corner pieces and then to find all the other outside pieces. SUGGESTED QUESTIONS: • Did you manage to find a solution? • What was difficult about this task? • How could you record the solution for someone else to be able to work it out? **Hide the cakes** Processes: *visualise, make decisions, reason, be systematic, test ideas* Ask the children to cover one of the cakes with a counter. Initially, ask them to say how many buns and how many doughnuts they can see in each row. Then ask them to see how many they can see in each column. Once the children have understood this concept they can attempt the problem-solving activities, trying to place counters in such a way that the number of buns and doughnuts in each row and column matches the description at the top. Draw attention to those children who try a systematic approach and explain that many different solutions are possible. Children could be given plain paper or a second photocopied sheet to record solutions. Explain that there are many different possible solutions. SUGGESTED QUESTIONS: • How did you find this solution? • Have you checked each row and column? • If you were to do this again, would you try a different way?	Reasoning Problem solving	179–80 181 182
Building bricks	**Calculating** Represent repeated addition and arrays as multiplication, and sharing and repeated subtraction (grouping) as division; use practical and informal written methods and related vocabulary to support multiplication and division, including calculations with remainders	**Building bricks** Encourage the children to see how an array can represent two multiplication facts. Draw a 3 × 4 array and explain that this shows three rows of four. Draw a ring around each row to explain what you mean. Then show that the same array can represent another fact by drawing a ring around each column and telling them that this shows four columns of three. SUGGESTED QUESTION: • Why do these shapes have only one multiplication fact?	Operations, relationships between them	183
Market stall	**Calculating** Use the symbols +, −, ×, ÷ and = to record and interpret number sentences involving all four operations; calculate the value of an unknown in a number sentence (e.g. □ ÷ 2 = 6, 30 − □ = 24)	**Market stall** This context can be used to introduce the activity through other oral questions, for example: 'I have 15 apples and I sell 4 of them. How many have I now?' Invite the children to say what they would do to find the answer to each question and then ask them to give the question and answer as a number sentence, using the appropriate signs. SUGGESTED QUESTIONS: • I have 15 apples and I sell 4 of them. How many have I now? • There are 4 pears in each bag. I have 5 bags. How many pears do I have? • How could you write these as number sentences?	Operations, relationships between them Written methods	184
Fraction webs Quarter shapes Crazy custard machine	**Counting and understanding number** Find one-half, one-quarter and three-quarters of shapes and sets of objects	**Fraction webs** Children tend to become familiar with the shapes created when a half or a quarter of a shape is shaded. It is important, however, that they appreciate that the number on the bottom of a fraction indicates the number of equal parts into which the whole has been split. SUGGESTED QUESTIONS: • Why do you think this is a quarter? • What is special about a quarter? **Quarter shapes** This activity can follow on nicely from the children's own experiences of folding pieces of paper in half and then in half again. Cutting along the edge with the four exposed sides can create symmetrical patterns that can be coloured when opened out. This task can also help the children to appreciate that two quarters is one-half and that three-quarters is three lots of one quarter. An understanding of four-quarters as 'one whole' can also be developed. SUGGESTED QUESTION: • Can the fraction of this shape be described in more than one way? **Crazy custard machine** Make sure the children understand that it is the shaded area of the circle that they are describing as a fraction of a full turn. SUGGESTED QUESTIONS: • Why do you think this is one-quarter? • What is special about one-quarter?	Numbers and the number system	185 186 187

Block E Securing number facts, calculating, identifying relationships – Unit 2

Activity name	Strand and learning objectives	Notes on the activities	Assessment Focus	Page number
Wheels away	**Using and applying mathematics** Identify and record the information or calculation needed to solve a puzzle or problem; carry out the steps or calculations and check the solution in the context of the problem	**Wheels away** *Processes: estimate, reason, predict, test ideas, trial and improvement* The numbers can be changed before copying to provide further investigations. If the numbers are changed to the following, more than one solution is possible for each question: **Q1** 20 **Q2** 22 **Q3** 35 **Q4** 26	Reasoning Problem solving	188
Triangle tricks: 1 and 2		**Triangle tricks: 1 and 2** *Processes: visualise, be systematic, test ideas, trial and improvement* This activity requires perseverance and trial and improvement strategies. Note which children use reasoning strategies and those who give up quickly. **SUGGESTED QUESTIONS:** • How could you work this out? • Why did you decide to record it like this? • Did you use pictures or another way? **SUGGESTED QUESTION:** • How many different ways did you find?	Reasoning Problem solving	189–90
Wendy's window box Traffic jam Marching mummies Farmer Palmer's diary: 1 and 2 Sponsored spell	**Using and applying mathematics** Solve problems involving addition, subtraction, multiplication or division in contexts of numbers, measures or pounds and pence	**Wendy's window box** *Processes: reason, compare, record, ask own questions* Allow the children to make their own decisions about what to do and encourage them to use number sentences to record the operation they chose to use. **SUGGESTED QUESTIONS:** • How did you find this solution? • How could you write this as a number sentence? **Traffic jam** *Processes: visualise, look for pattern, reason, record* Observe the methods children use to find the answers, for example noting which children use the picture, their fingers, equipment or a mental method. For the extension activity, ask the children to present their solution clearly in a way that others could understand. **SUGGESTED QUESTIONS/PROMPTS:** • How did you find this solution? • Did you use the picture or your fingers or a mental method? • Can you see a pattern? • How many people? **Marching mummies** *Processes: reason, make decisions, look for pattern* Children could work together in pairs on this activity to promote discussion. Once the children have completed the sheet, ask them to look for patterns in their answers, to notice, for example, that the answer to each part of question 3 is half the number in the question. In the extension activity, watch out for children who give the answer 15 steps, incorrectly halving rather than doubling the number. **Farmer Palmer's diary: 1 and 2** *Processes: record, reason, be systematic, compare, test ideas* These two activity sheets begin with some information about the farmer's chickens or cows. Read through the information together and encourage the children to imagine a farm and the number of items mentioned. Sometimes, when facing word problems, the children fail to engage with the context and merely look at the numbers and do something with them. By presenting the information first, the children are encouraged to focus on the context rather than the questions. The numbers can be altered before copying to provide differentiation. **SUGGESTED QUESTIONS:** • How easy did you find this? • Did you find the answer straight away? • How did you work it out? **Sponsored spell** *Processes: reason, make decisions, explain* Discuss strategies that the children chose to work out the answers, drawing attention to use of equipment such as number lines, 100 squares, materials or other methods or known number facts. **SUGGESTED QUESTIONS:** • How did you find the answer? • What method did you use to find the answer? • Did you use the same method for each question or did you do anything different on this question? • Could you have used a tables fact?	Problem solving	191 192 193 194–5 196
Hungry as a horse Monkey tricks Playful kittens Pirate gold	**Calculating** Represent repeated addition and arrays as multiplication, and sharing and repeated subtraction (grouping) as division; use practical and informal written methods and related vocabulary to support multiplication and division, including calculations with remainders	**Hungry as a horse** Provide the children with practical equipment such as cubes, bricks or counters to help them with this activity. Encourage the children to read their questions aloud and to use appropriate vocabulary, for example '14 shared between 2', '14 divided by 2'. **SUGGESTED QUESTIONS:** • Can you read me this question? • What if there had been five horses to share the 20 carrots between? • Can you make up some more division questions of your own? **Monkey tricks** For this activity, encourage the children to interpret the division sign as meaning 'shared between'. Provide practical equipment such as cubes, bricks or counters to help the children. **SUGGESTED QUESTIONS:** • Can you read me this question? • How could you work out the answer? **Playful kittens** At the start of the lesson, practise counting forwards and backwards in steps of two, five and ten, from and back to zero. As the children count, encourage them to use their fingers to keep track of how many twos, fives or tens they have counted. **SUGGESTED QUESTIONS:** • How did you work out that there are 9 groups of 2 in 18? • There are 6 groups of 5 in 30. How could you use that answer to work out how many groups of 5 there are in 60? **Pirate gold** Begin the lesson by demonstrating how to use cubes to work out the answer to the first question, i.e. sorting the 18 cubes into equal groups of two and then counting the number of groups to find the number of pirates. **SUGGESTED QUESTIONS:** • How do you know that this ship has seven pirates? • These ships both have 24 gold coins. Tell me how you know that this ship has more pirates than this ship?	Operations, relationships between them	197 198 199 200

Activity name	Strand and learning objectives	Notes on the activities	Assessment Focus	Page number
Counter covering	**Calculating** Use the symbols +, −, ×, ÷ and = to record and interpret number sentences involving all four operations; calculate the value of an unknown in a number sentence (e.g. □ ÷ 2 = 6, 30 − □ = 24)	**Counter covering** At the start of the lesson, show a completed multiplication and division fact, such as 3 × 5 = 15 and 20 ÷ 5 = 4. Cover each number in the multiplication and then the division statement and discuss how you would find the hidden number each time. At this stage, the children will probably need to refer to lists of tables and division facts to help them find the missing numbers. **SUGGESTED QUESTIONS:** • What number fact did you use to help you work out that the missing number in 2 × □ is 4? • How can you use your 5 times-table to help you work out the answer to 5 × □ = 40?	Operations, relationships between them Written methods	201
Cake calculations	**Counting and understanding number** Find one-half, one-quarter and three-quarters of shapes and sets of objects	**Cake calculations** At the start of the lesson, demonstrate how the cake shown on the worksheet can be used to help you find one-quarter of a set of cubes. Show how 24 cubes can be arranged into four equal groups and ask the children to count one group, to give the answer to the question: 'What is one-quarter of 24?' Before asking the children to complete the activity, ensure they appreciate that three-quarters is three lots of one-quarter and can be found by counting the number of cubes in three of the equal sets. **SUGGESTED QUESTION:** • What is three-quarters of 40/80?	Numbers and the number system	202

Block E Securing number facts, calculating, identifying relationships – Unit 3

Activity name	Strand and learning objectives	Notes on the activities	Assessment Focus	Page number
Cross out	**Using and applying mathematics** Identify and record the information or calculation needed to solve a puzzle or problem; carry out the steps or calculations and check the solution in the context of the problem	**Cross out** *Processes: reason, test ideas, trial and improvement* The second puzzle is more difficult as there are several numbers the same in a row or column and so it is less clear about which of those should be crossed out. **SUGGESTED QUESTIONS:** • How could you work this out? • What problems did you encounter?	Reasoning Problem solving	203
Soldiers on parade Jumping Jack How? These lines of mine	**Using and applying mathematics** Present solutions to puzzles and problems in an organised way; explain decisions, methods and results in pictorial, spoken or written form, using mathematical language and number sentences	**Soldiers on parade** *Processes: visualise, test ideas, trial and improvement, record* Encourage the children to find different ways of recording the activity so that others can follow the instructions and repeat the steps. Explain that the other soldiers can shuffle along the line once the soldiers have moved. Note that there is a different investigation that could also be explored, where the soldiers move in the same way, but where there are 10 boxes with one soldier in each and no shuffling along is allowed. **SUGGESTED QUESTIONS:** • How many different ways did you find? • How could you show this so that someone else can follow the instructions? **Jumping Jack** *Processes: explain, compare, reason* Introduce the activity, by demonstrating how to use a number line and show the children various strategies for working out the answer. The numbers can be altered before copying to provide differentiation. **SUGGESTED QUESTIONS:** • What calculation do these arrows represent? • How can you be sure? • Do you agree? **How?** *Processes: explain, reason, ask own questions* This activity encourages children to describe the strategies they would use to answer a calculation and to consider the different ways this could be done. Calculations can be altered before copying. Suggested questions: • What would you do? • Would you use any equipment? • Could you show me this on a number line/a 100 square? • What other ways could it be done? **These lines of mine** *Processes: explain, reason, ask own questions* Allow the children to choose from different equipment and then record what they do on the number lines. For example, they might use a hundred square for 13 + 9: add 10 by going down one square to 23 and then going back one square to 22. They would record this method on the number line like this: +10 −1 13 14 15 16 17 18 19 20 21 22 23 **SUGGESTED QUESTIONS:** • What would you do? • How can addition be shown on a number line? • What about multiplication or division?	Communicating	204 205 206 207

Activity name	Strand and learning objectives	Notes on the activities	Assessment Focus	Page number
Going crackers! Cross-number puzzles Special sheep Grape remainders	**Calculating** Represent repeated addition and arrays as multiplication, and sharing and repeated subtraction (grouping) as division; use practical and informal written methods and related vocabulary to support multiplication and division, including calculations with remainders	**Going crackers!** At the beginning of the lesson, talk with the children about how it can be much quicker to know a multiplication or doubling fact, rather than adding a number repeatedly. SUGGESTED QUESTIONS/PROMPT: • How do you know that this addition gives the same answer as this multiplication? • I add another 3 to this addition. What is the multiplication now? **Cross-number puzzles** These cross-number puzzles could be used as an assessment to check the children's knowledge of times-tables facts. SUGGESTED QUESTIONS: • Can you tell me a question that could have been set for the answer in 6 across (35)? • How could you check your answer to 9 × 5? **Special sheep** To make the L shapes for this activity, cut sheets of A4 paper or card in half to make two sheets of A5. Cut a piece out of each A5 sheet measuring approximately 10 cm × 17cm, as shown below: 10cm 17 cm SUGGESTED QUESTIONS: • Which of these answers are tables facts that you know already? • How could you use what you know about 3 rows of 4 sheep to help you work out the answer to 4 rows of 4 sheep? **Grape remainders** At the end of the game, the completed cards could be glued onto paper or into books as evidence of the activity. SUGGESTED QUESTIONS: • How many grapes does each person get? • How many are left over?	Operations, relationships between them	208 209 210 211
Ghostly grids	**Calculating** Use the symbols +, −, ×, ÷ and = to record and interpret number sentences involving all four operations; calculate the value of an unknown in a number sentence (e.g. ☐ ÷ 2 = 6, 30 − ☐ = 24)	**Ghostly grids** Use this grid to introduce the activity: | 10	+	10	=	
+		+		
5	×	2	=	
=		=		
	×		=	| Work across the first two rows, asking the children to divide first and then multiply to find the answers. Then show how questions are formed working down each column. Fill in the missing numbers and finally check that the last row is correct: 2 × 5 = 10. SUGGESTED QUESTIONS: • What multiplication and division facts can you work out from 12 ÷ 2 = 6? • What multiplication and division facts can you work out from 35 ÷ 5 = 7?	Operations, relationships between them Written methods	212
Group survey Wilma and Thelma	**Counting and understanding number** Find one-half, one-quarter and three-quarters of shapes and sets of objects	**Group survey** This activity encourages the children to describe fractions of a set of four, in this case, using themselves. Discuss that two out of four of their group can be described as ½ or ¼. This activity can promote some interesting display work, where children write their true statements onto cards and draw a picture of the children in their group. As an extension, ask the children to find some more facts about the children in their groups and write three more true statements using ¼, ½ or ¾. **Wilma and Thelma** This activity can be introduced practically using coins or cubes. SUGGESTED PROMPT: • Four out of four of you like football. So we can say that four quarters, or all of you, like football. SUGGESTED QUESTIONS: • How do you find one-quarter using the answer to one-half? • What does the 2 (or 4) at the bottom of the fraction stand for?	Numbers and the number system	213 214

Animal sorting

- **Cut out the animals below.**
- **Sort them into the fields so that each sign is** `true`.
- **There must be the** `same number` **of animals in each field.**

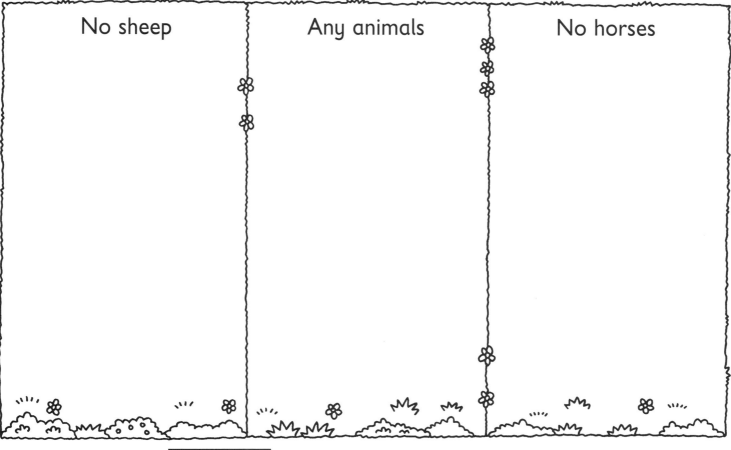

| No sheep | Any animals | No horses |

- **How many** `different` **ways can you find to sort them?**

Teachers' note The focus of this activity should be on finding and recording the different possible ways of placing the animals into the three fields. Provide a separate piece of paper for the children to record their answers, using any appropriate method they choose.

A Lesson for Every Day
Maths
6-7 Years
© A&C Black

The triplets in each family always argue and need to be kept apart.

- Cut out the cards and sort them so that none of each family is next to each other.

You need:
'Triplet trouble: 2'.

Teachers' note Ensure children understand that triplets from each family cannot be next to each other vertically or horizontally in the grid. Encourage them to find and record the different possible ways of placing the children into the grid. Children record their answers on 'Triplet trouble: 2'. Encourage them to use letters A, A, A, B, B, B; C, C, C to represent the triplets or to use a colouring method.

A Lesson for Every Day
Maths
6-7 Years
© A&C Black

• **Use this sheet to record different ways you have found.**

Teachers' note Use in conjunction with 'Triplet trouble: 1'. Draw attention to solutions that are the same, but rotated or reflected.

A Lesson for Every Day
Maths
6–7 Years
© A&C Black

Hide and seek

- **Ring the number names hidden in this wordsearch.**

s	n	e	e	t	r	u	o	f
i	e	i	g	h	t	s	t	t
x	e	m	f	k	r	e	w	z
t	t	q	i	s	e	v	e	n
y	r	p	f	t	b	e	l	y
s	i	x	t	e	e	n	v	x
i	h	c	e	n	o	t	e	w
x	t	d	e	g	w	e	v	a
i	n	i	n	e	t	e	e	n
h	j	d	t	w	e	n	t	y
t	h	i	r	t	y	b	c	e

- **Write the 'teen' numbers you have found in figures.**

14					

- **Which 'teen' number is missing?** [ ]

NOW TRY THIS!

- **Write the twelve other numbers in the wordsearch in figures.**

Teachers' note Ensure that somewhere on the classroom wall or board are the numbers to 20 and multiples of 10 to 100 written in figures and words. Discuss which numbers are 'teen' numbers. Explain that the numbers can be read horizontally (forwards and backwards), and vertically (up or down) in the grid.

A Lesson for Every Day
Maths
6–7 Years
© A&C Black

Odd and even racers

• **Play this game with a partner.**

☆ Take turns to roll the dice and move your counter forward.

☆ Score points for an **odd** or **even** number.

☆ The winner is the player with the most points after five laps.

You need a counter each and a dice.

| Even number | 2 points |
| Odd number | 1 point |

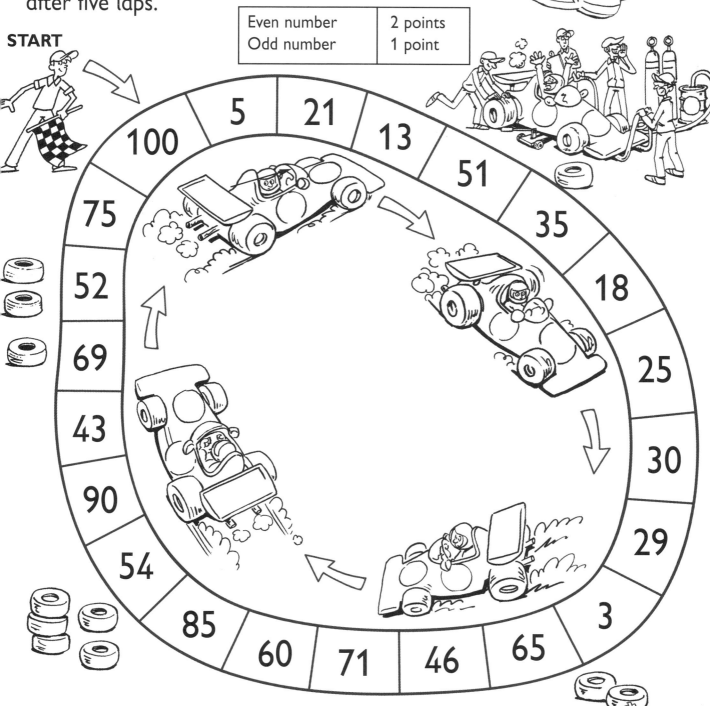

START

100 5 21 13 51 35 18 25 30 29 3 65 46 71 60 85 54 90 43 69 52 75

Teachers' note Before playing the game, ensure that the children understand how to recognise odd and even numbers. The players should record on scrap paper the points they score.

A Lesson for Every Day
Maths
6-7 Years
© A&C Black

At the sweetshop

- ## How many sweets in each tray?
- ## Count them in ⬚twos⬚ .

30

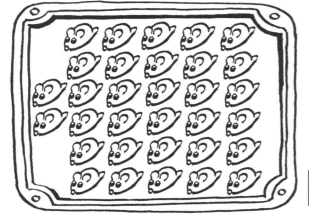

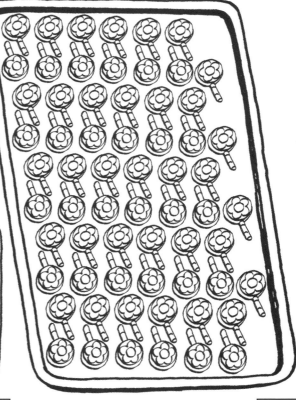

NOW TRY THIS!

- ## Check your answers by counting them in ⬚fives⬚ .

Teachers' note Demonstrate how to count in twos, fives or tens at the start of the lesson. The children could be asked to draw rings around pairs of items before counting in twos.

A Lesson for Every Day
Maths
6–7 Years
© A&C Black

The pirates' library

Exactly ten books fit on a shelf.

• How many books in each bookcase? Count in $\boxed{\text{tens}}$ **.**

NOW TRY THIS!

• Count the books on a bookshelf in your classroom.

Teachers' note At the start of the lesson, practise counting in tens from 0 to 100. For the extension activity, it may be more appropriate for you to provide a large pile of cubes for children to estimate and count, by grouping in tens. Ensure the children realise that after grouping in tens, the number left is the number of units/ones.

A Lesson for Every Day
Maths
6–7 Years
© A&C Black

31

Don't get shirty!

• **Write the numbers in order.**

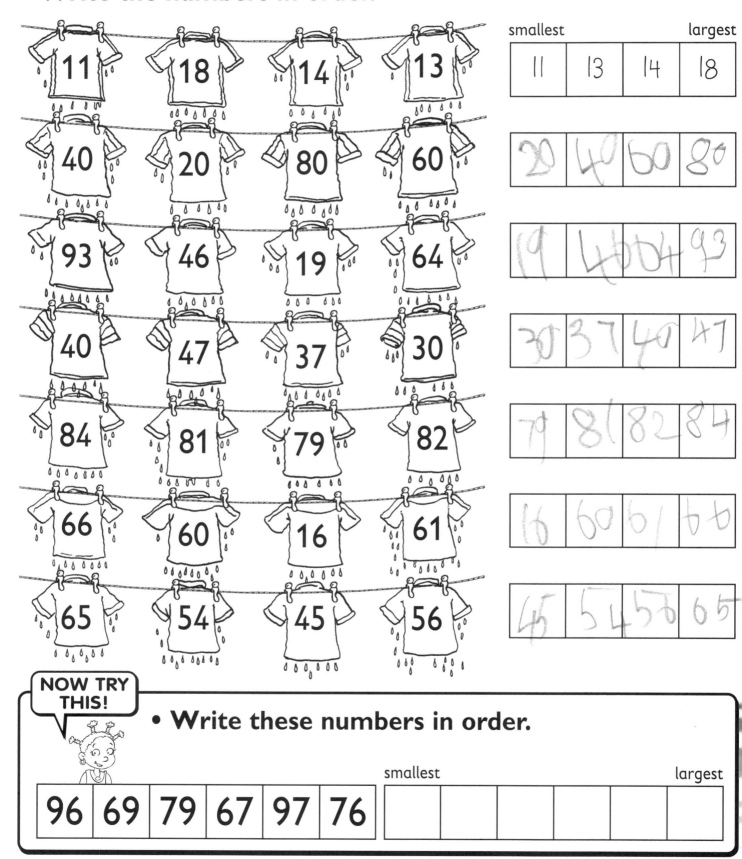

smallest			largest
11	13	14	18

20	40	60	80

19	40	64	93

30	37	40	47

79	81	82	84

16	60	61	66

45	54	56	65

NOW TRY THIS!

• **Write these numbers in order.**

96	69	79	67	97	76

smallest					largest

Teachers' note At the start of the lesson, give groups of four children number cards from a set of 0 to 100. Ask the children to rearrange themselves in order, starting with the smallest number. Use the vocabulary 'least' and 'most' and 'largest' and 'smallest' to compare and order other small sets of numbers. When completing the sheet, some children may need to refer to a number line.

A Lesson for Every Day
Maths
6–7 Years
© A&C Black

Woolly jumpers!

- Use the greater than $>$ or less than $<$ sign to show which ball of wool is longer.

55 m $>$ 47 m   35 m ☐ 53 m

95 m ☐ 98 m   84 m ☐ 79 m   63 m ☐ 36 m

40 m ☐ 39 m   76 m ☐ 74 m   66 m ☐ 88 m

NOW TRY THIS!

- Use $<$ or $>$ to show which is longer.

105 m ☐ 104 m   140 m ☐ 130 m   167 m ☐ 176 m

Teachers' note At the start of the lesson, revise the meaning of the 'greater than' and 'less than' signs. It can sometimes be helpful for children to think of the signs as the open mouth of a greedy crocodile, always about to eat the larger number. When first introduced, a picture of the crocodile with large jaws can be used, before progressing to the jaws only, i.e. the symbol.

A Lesson for Every Day
Maths
6-7 Years
© A&C Black

33

Pasta party

- **Play this game with a partner.**

☆ Cut out the cards and place them face down.

☆ Take turns to pick a card.

☆ Each **estimate** the number of pasta pieces, then count to check. The closest estimate wins the card.

☆ Collect the most cards to win the game.

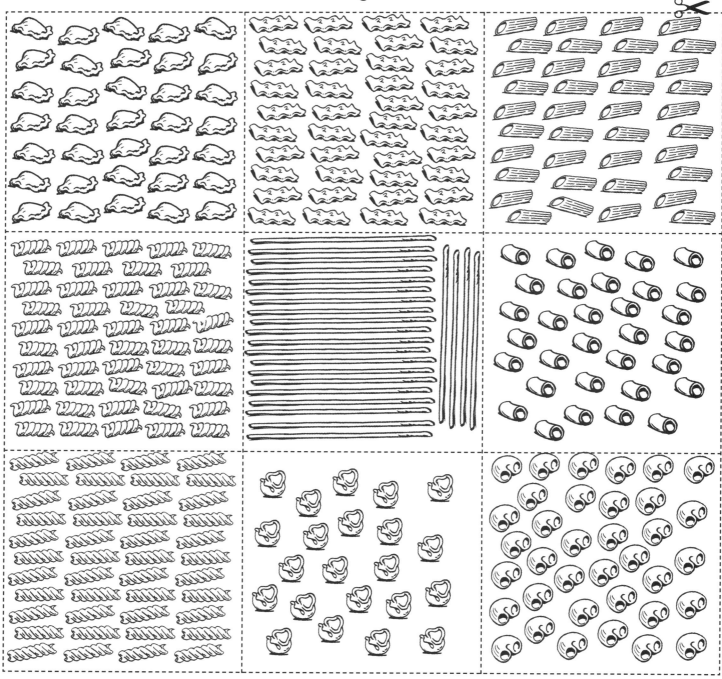

Teachers' note Ensure the children realise that, when estimating, they should not actually count the pasta. You may wish to appoint a third child as an adjudicator. As an extension, the children could make their own version of the game by drawing up to 100 items on each card.

A Lesson for Every Day
Maths
6-7 Years
© A&C Black

Seeing spots!

- Estimate the number of 'spots' in each picture.

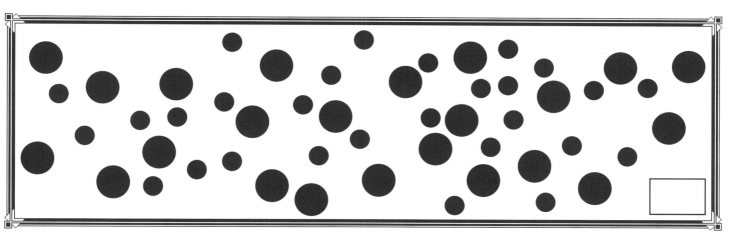

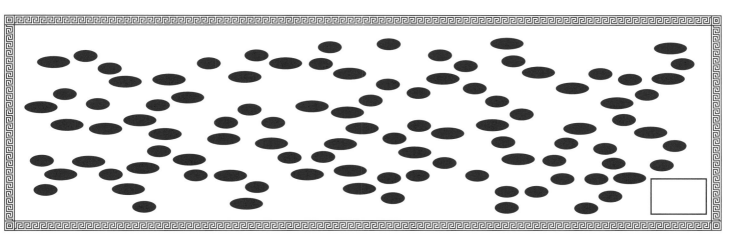

 **NOW TRY THIS!**

- **Group the spots into tens, then count them. Write the numbers here:** ☐ ☐ ☐

Teachers' note Encourage the children to develop strategies for estimating, such as asking: 'Is the number nearer to fifty or one hundred?' or by mentally grouping the 'spots' into fives or tens.

A Lesson for Every Day
Maths
6-7 Years
© A&C Black

Round 'em up!

- **Round** each number to the **nearest 10**.
- **Using the key, draw the correct shape around each number.**

Key ⟨10⟩ ▭20 △30 ◯40 ▢50 ✿60 ★70 ⬡80 ♡90 ☁100

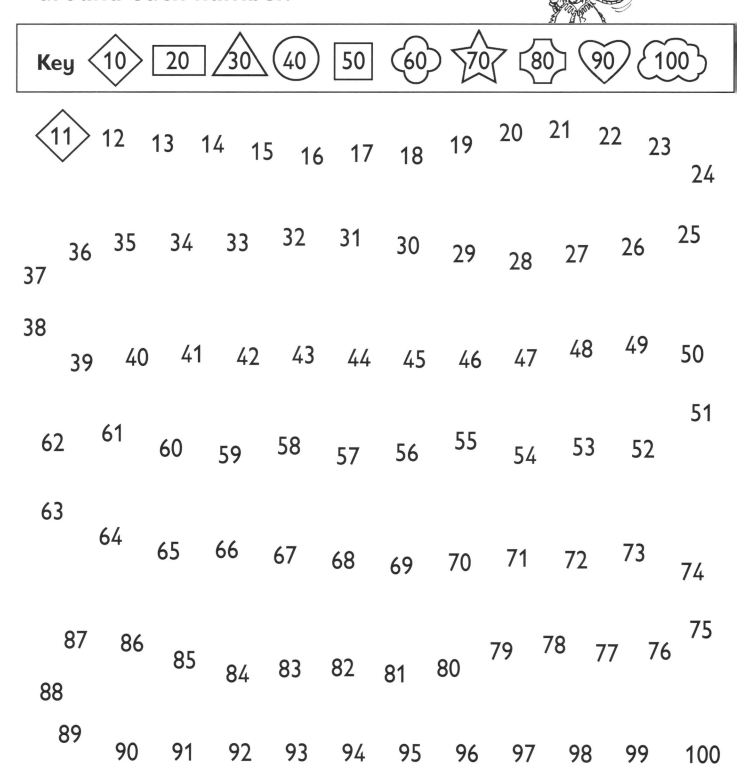

⟨11⟩ 12 13 14 15 16 17 18 19 20 21 22 23 24

37 36 35 34 33 32 31 30 29 28 27 26 25

38 39 40 41 42 43 44 45 46 47 48 49 50

51

62 61 60 59 58 57 56 55 54 53 52

63 64 65 66 67 68 69 70 71 72 73 74

75

87 86 85 84 83 82 81 80 79 78 77 76

88

89 90 91 92 93 94 95 96 97 98 99 100

Teachers' note Throughout this activity, remind the children that numbers ending with the digit 5 round up to the next multiple of 10 and thus the shape change occurs at 15, 25, 35, etc. At the end of the activity, call out two-digit numbers and ask the children to round the numbers to the nearest 10. As an extension, ask the children to find out how many numbers round to 80.

A Lesson for Every Day
Maths
6-7 Years
© A&C Black

Playful seals

☆ Choose a seal from each side.

☆ Add the numbers and write the addition sentence on a separate piece of paper.

☆ Keep going. Can you make all of the answers on the balls?

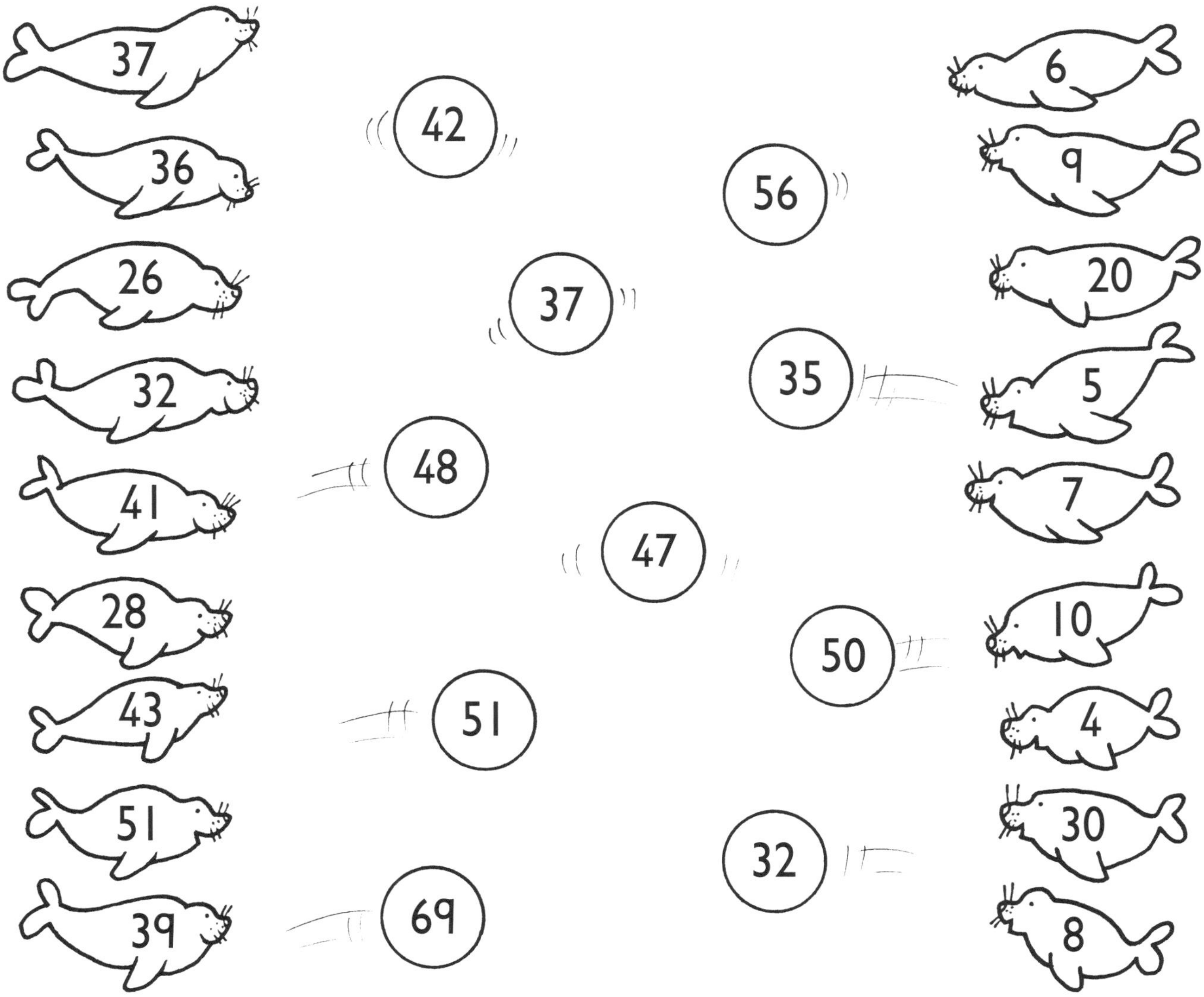

37
36
26
32
41
28
43
51
39

42
37
48
47
51
69

56
35
50
32

6
9
20
5
7
10
4
30
8

NOW TRY THIS!

• **Write four addition sentences for this ball.**

45

_____   _____

_____   _____

Teachers' note Discuss different strategies for adding the numbers, such as using a number line and counting on from the two-digit number or partitioning and adding the units digits of both numbers first, for example 43 + 8: 3 + 8 = 11, 11 + 40 = 51. Suggest that the children tick off a ball once they have made that total.

A Lesson for Every Day
Maths
6-7 Years
© A&C Black

Animal magic

- **Count the letters in the animal name.**
Some of the letters disappear!
- **Write the subtraction sentence.**

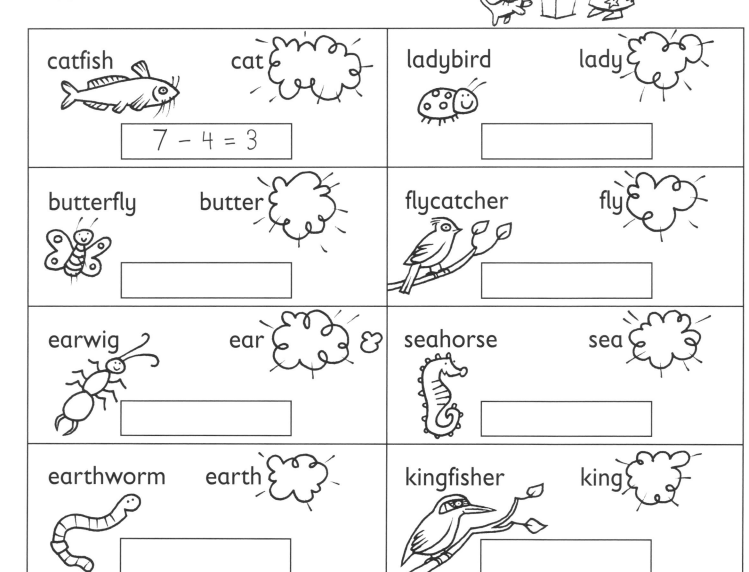

catfish   cat

$$7 - 4 = 3$$

ladybird   lady

butterfly   butter

flycatcher   fly

earwig   ear

seahorse   sea

earthworm   earth

kingfisher   king

NOW TRY THIS!

- **Write a subtraction to show how each animal name can be changed.**

caterpillar   hippopotamus

Teachers' note As a further extension, ask the children to look again at the animal names in the main activity. Can they write a different subtraction sentence by making the beginning of the name disappear, for example 'catfish' will become 'fish' (7 – 3 = 4). Is the subtraction sentence always different? Why not?

A Lesson for Every Day
Maths
6-7 Years
© A&C Black

Domino decisions: 1

- **Cut out the dominoes at the bottom of the sheet.**
- **Arrange the dominoes so that each of the four** totals **marked is the same.**

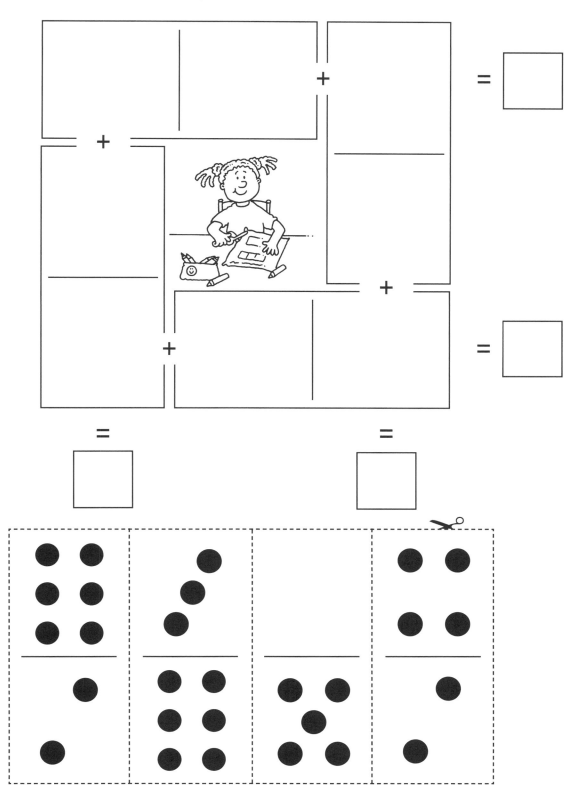

A Lesson for Every Day
Maths
6-7 Years
© A&C Black

Teachers' note Ask the children to compare their answers and to find out if there is more than one solution. Other sets of four dominoes, such as those on 'Domino decisions: 2', can be provided for further experience of this type.

• **Use each set to solve the problem.**

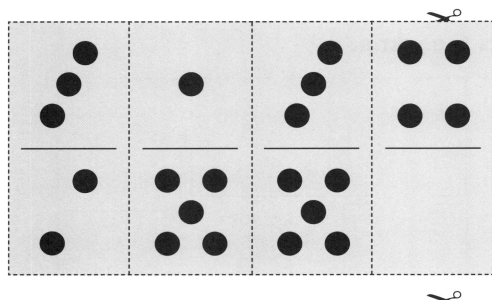

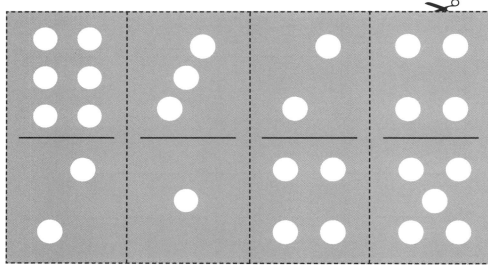

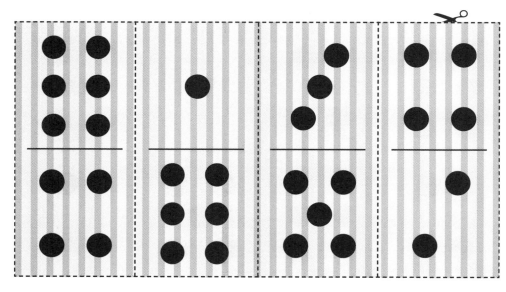

Teachers' note Use this sheet in conjunction with 'Domino decisions: 1'.

A Lesson for Every Day
Maths
6–7 Years
© A&C Black

Find Bo-Peep's sheep!

- **Find each sheep's number on the wall.**
- **Draw a ring around it.**

> The numbers may be vertical or horizontal.

twenty-three

eighty-one

seventy-two

thirty-six

ninety-four

forty-seven

fourteen

sixty-three

seventy-four

fifty-eight

ninety-seven

twenty-nine

seventy

sixty

sixty-nine

0	8	1	3	0	5	3	6	8	5
7	5	0	7	1	8	2	0	7	2
4	6	4	0	9	2	3	8	3	9
1	9	7	6	3	0	1	4	0	4

NOW TRY THIS!

- **Choose six** three-digit numbers **on the wall.**
- **Write the numbers in words.**

Teachers' note Ensure the children understand that the numbers on the wall should be found horizontally (reading from left to right) or vertically (reading downwards), and not diagonally. Before starting the extension activity, ensure the children understand the term 'three-digit number' and that they should ignore the rings already drawn on the wall.

A Lesson for Every Day
Maths
6–7 Years
© A&C Black

Flying high

• **Write the number in words on each banner.**

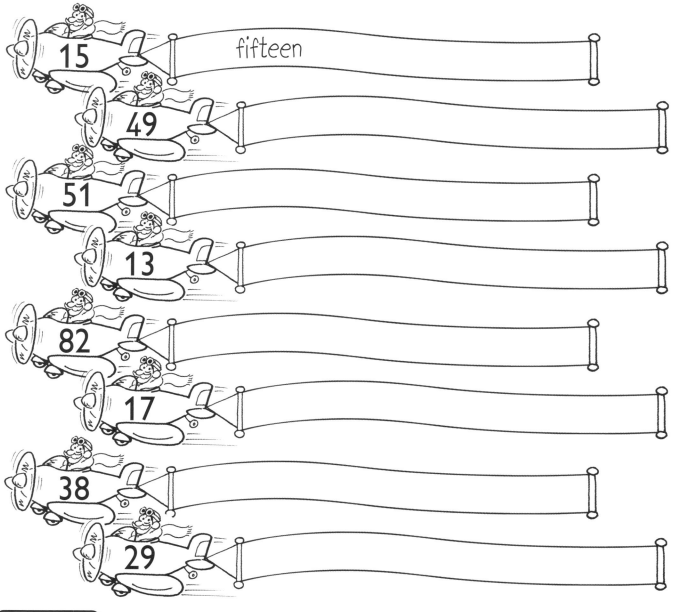

15   *fifteen*

49

51

13

82

17

38

29

• **Find the** seventh **letter of each of the numbers to spell a new number.**
• **Write it in figures and words.**

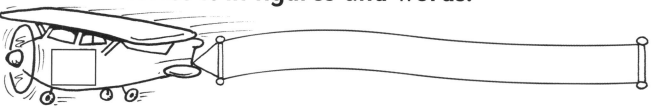

Teachers' note Ensure that somewhere on the classroom wall or board are the numbers to 20 and multiples of 10 to 100 written in figures and words, for children to refer to.

A Lesson for Every Day
Maths
6–7 Years
© A&C Black

Happy 'tens' families

- **Play this game with a partner.**

☆ Cut out the cards and place them face down in a pile.

☆ Each player takes four cards and tries to collect a 'family' of four cards with the same number of tens.

☆ Take turns to turn over a card from the pile. You can throw away the card or keep it and throw one of yours away instead.

☆ Collect a 'family' and put the cards in order to win the game.

42	**32**	**22**	**55**
35	**47**	**27**	**57**
25	**37**	**45**	**52**
48	**28**	**58**	**38**

Teachers' note When putting numbers in order of size, ask the children to order them from smallest to largest. As an extension activity, the children could make families of 'ones' where they try to collect numbers with the same units digits.

A Lesson for Every Day
Maths
6-7 Years
© A&C Black

43

Brainy birds

• **Write the number on each bird in figures and in words.**

three tens — six ones
36
thirty-six

four tens — seven ones

five tens — no ones

six tens — eight ones

seven tens — five ones

nine tens — no ones

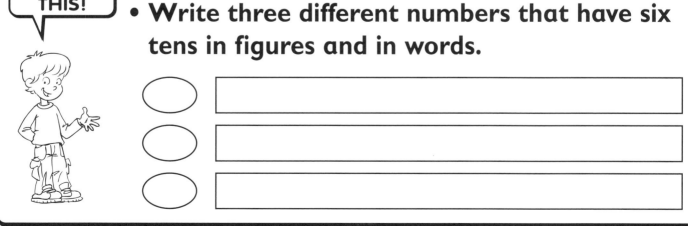

NOW TRY THIS!

• **Write three different numbers that have six tens in figures and in words.**

Teachers' note This activity encourages the children to begin to realise the different values of a digit in a two-digit number. Ensure the children understand, for example, that the two fives in 55 represent different values depending on their position in the number.

A Lesson for Every Day
Maths
6–7 Years
© A&C Black

Flower power

- **Find the total of the middle number and the multiple of 10.**
- **Write the answer in the outer petal.**

Flower 1 (middle **26**): petals 30, 10, 36, 20, 40, 50

Flower 2 (middle **24**): petals 60, 30, 50, 70, 10

Flower 3 (middle **11**): petals 70, 60, 40, 50, 80

Flower 4 (middle **33**): petals 20, 60, 10, 40, 50

Flower 5 (middle **18**): petals 70, 80, 30, 40, 60

Flower 6 (middle **42**): petals 30, 10, 20, 40, 50

Flower 7 (middle **49**): petals 30, 10, 20, 40, 50

Flower 8 (middle **37**): petals 40, 10, 60, 50, 20

NOW TRY THIS!

- **Answer these.**

The answers are all over 100.

$46 + 60 = \boxed{}$ $78 + 40 = \boxed{}$

$27 + 90 = \boxed{}$ $89 + 20 = \boxed{}$

Teachers' note At the start of the lesson, practise counting in tens from zero, up to and beyond 100. Then count on in tens from any number, such as 42, 52, 62, 72. Point out that the units/ones digit remains the same when counting in tens.

A Lesson for Every Day
Maths
6–7 Years
© A&C Black

45

Going potty

- **Ring** one of the **4** options to show what you would use to work out the answer to the question.

1 Mrs Jones's class had six pots with four pencils in each pot. How many pencils altogether?

6 + 4   4 + 4   6 × 4   4 + 6

2 Miss Wood has five more pencils in a blue pot than in a red pot. She has eight pencils in the red pot.
How many in the blue pot?

5 + 5   8 − 5   8 + 5   5 × 8

3 Mr Miller has three more pencils in a yellow pot than in a green pot. He has six pencils in the yellow pot.
How many in the green pot?

6 − 3   6 + 6   6 × 3   6 + 3

4 Mr Smith has 27 pencils. He put 3 in each pot.
How many pots did he need?

27 − 3   27 + 3   3 × 27   27 ÷ 3

 **NOW TRY THIS!**

- **Write a pencil pot question for 4 × 5.**

_____

_____

Teachers' note This activity helps children to consider which operation to use to solve a problem. Discuss the children's answers, explaining why some are not correct and draw attention to the fact that the word 'more' in question 3 does not mean that the calculation is an addition.

A Lesson for Every Day
Maths
6–7 Years
© A&C Black

Storytime

- **Make up a story for each calculation.**

25 + 14

7 × 5

100 − 75

20 ÷ 5

NOW TRY THIS!

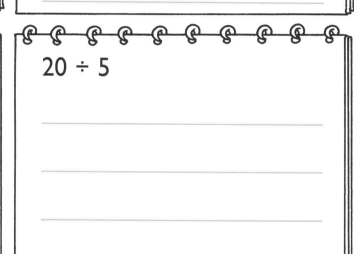

- **Try this one.**

3 × 5 + 8

Teachers' note Give the children some story contexts to think about before beginning this sheet, for example shopping with money, sharing out sweets, etc. Invite the children to read out their stories for others to listen to and ask the other children to guess the calculation. Calculations can be altered before copying.

A Lesson for Every Day
Maths
6-7 Years
© A&C Black

47

Hungry puppies

- **Write each number in words.**

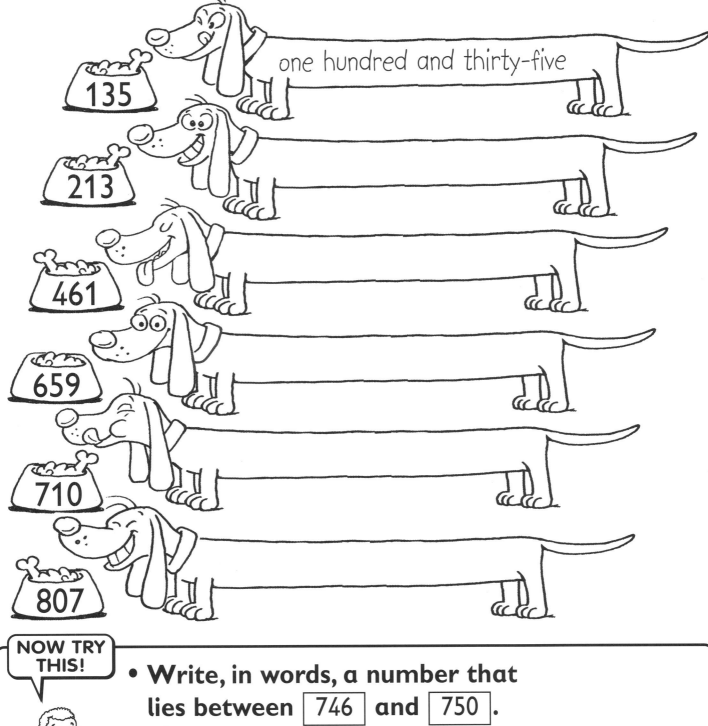

135 one hundred and thirty-five

213

461

659

710

807

NOW TRY THIS!

- **Write, in words, a number that lies between** 746 **and** 750 .

Teachers' note Ensure that somewhere on the classroom wall or board the following are shown in figures and words for the children to refer to: numbers to 20, multiples of 10 to 100, and multiples of 100 to 1000.

A Lesson for Every Day
Maths
6-7 Years
© A&C Black

Three-digit dominoes

- **Cut out the dominoes and play a game with a partner.**
- **You can match numbers in figures, words or with the number of** hundreds , tens **and** ones .

439	five hundred and twenty-one	521	two hundreds, three tens and seven ones	237	five hundreds, one ten and four ones
five hundred and fourteen	608	six hundreds, no tens and eight ones	185	one hundred and eighty-five	seven hundreds, six tens and no ones
760	nine hundred and fifty-three	nine hundreds, five tens and three ones	472	four hundred and seventy-two	106
one hundred and six	815	eight hundreds, one ten and five ones	seven hundred and ninety-six	796	eight hundreds, no tens and no ones
eight hundred	905	nine hundreds, no tens and five ones	six hundred and twenty	620	765
seven hundreds, six tens and five ones	five hundred and eight	508	six hundreds, no tens and two ones	six hundred and two	500
five hundreds, no tens and no ones	294	two hundred and ninety-four	three hundreds, six tens and two ones	362	seven hundred and sixty-nine
769	nine hundred and ninety	nine hundreds, nine tens and no ones	839	eight hundreds, three tens and nine ones	four hundred and thirty-nine

Teachers' note Some dominoes have 0 as a place holder, for example 500 where the digits represent five hundreds, no tens and no ones. Explain how to play the game. Share out the dominoes. Place one on the table. Each player should try to place a domino on one side or other of the domino so that the numbers match, or else miss a turn. The winner is the first to use up all his/her dominoes.

A Lesson for Every Day
Maths
6-7 Years
© A&C Black

Whose pet?

- **Look at the digits of the numbers.**
- **Mark trails from one side of the grid to the other to find who owns which pet.**

Use a different-coloured pencil to show each trail.

9 ones	6 tens		5 ones		same tens and ones digits		
89	64	60	75	8	11	18	53
49	69	58	61	55	5	51	52
56	59	17	54	66	57	15	34
73	23	29	77	31	68	98	95
20	16	79	22	93	97	63	45
42	91	99	90	21	62	85	26
94	88	14	39	28	65	24	27
36	17	33	13	19	25	68	13
10	44	81	30	35	9	67	12

5 tens → (row 3)

2 tens → (row 5)

9 tens → (row 7)

NOW TRY THIS!

- **Write all the two-digit numbers that have 3 ones.** _____
- **Which can you find in the grid?**

_____

Teachers' note For the extension activity, ensure that the children understand what the term 'two-digit numbers' means. The children can also be encouraged to recognise that the trail with numbers that have '5 ones' has different numbers from those in the '5 tens' trail, with the exception of 55, which has both 5 tens and 5 ones.

A Lesson for Every Day
Maths
6-7 Years
© A&C Black

Split decisions

- ## List ten different ways that these chunks of chocolate can be split between Ben and Alia.

36 chunks

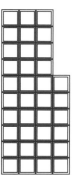

10 + 26	
1 + 35	
15 + 21	

49 chunks

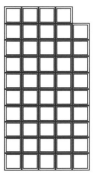

52 chunks

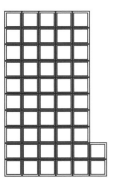

NOW TRY THIS!

- ## Split 99 chunks in ten different ways. List the ways on the back of this sheet.

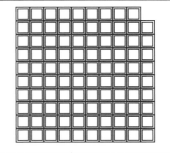

Teachers' note Begin the lesson by holding up 32 cubes in the form of three ten-rods and two cubes. Show that this represents 32 cubes and write this number on the board. Ask a child to put the cubes into two groups, splitting a ten if they so choose. Record how the cubes have been split, for example 31 and 1 or 25 and 7. List different ways that this can be done, including 30 and 2.

A Lesson for Every Day
Maths
6-7 Years
© A&C Black

Dinner time

- **Write numbers on the bowls to show different ways that each amount can be split.**

Teachers' note This activity can be used as a more abstract follow-on activity from the previous page. Again, begin the lesson by holding up some cubes which have been grouped together in tens. Ask a child to put the cubes into two groups, splitting a ten if they so choose.

A Lesson for Every Day
Maths
6–7 Years
© A&C Black

Bird-watching: 1

• **Cut out the cards.**

Goldfinch

Mass (g)	17
Length (cm)	12
Length of egg (mm)	17
Number of eggs laid	4

Linnet

Mass (g)	20
Length (cm)	14
Length of egg (mm)	18
Number of eggs laid	5

Greenfinch

Mass (g)	28
Length (cm)	15
Length of egg (mm)	20
Number of eggs laid	5

House sparrow

Mass (g)	31
Length (cm)	15
Length of egg (mm)	22
Number of eggs laid	4

Starling

Mass (g)	80
Length (cm)	22
Length of egg (mm)	30
Number of eggs laid	4

Magpie

Mass (g)	220
Length (cm)	45
Length of egg (mm)	34
Number of eggs laid	6

Jay

Mass (g)	180
Length (cm)	35
Length of egg (mm)	32
Number of eggs laid	4

Blue tit

Mass (g)	11
Length (cm)	12
Length of egg (mm)	16
Number of eggs laid	11

Great tit

Mass (g)	18
Length (cm)	14
Length of egg (mm)	17
Number of eggs laid	10

Teachers' note The children play in pairs. Each child has a pile of nine cards. Both players turn a card. Player 1 chooses a category s/he thinks most likely to win, for example the number of eggs. Both players say how many eggs their bird lays. The player with the highest number wins the cards. Players pick a new card and player 2 chooses the category, and so on.

A Lesson for Every Day
Maths
6-7 Years
© A&C Black

Bird-watching: 2

• **Cut out the cards.**

Blackbird

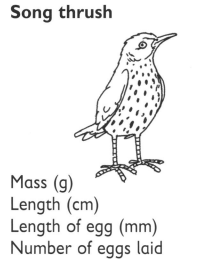

Mass (g)	100
Length (cm)	25
Length of egg (mm)	30
Number of eggs laid	4

Song thrush

Mass (g)	83
Length (cm)	23
Length of egg (mm)	27
Number of eggs laid	4

Robin

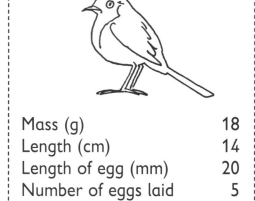

Mass (g)	18
Length (cm)	14
Length of egg (mm)	20
Number of eggs laid	5

Wren

Mass (g)	9
Length (cm)	10
Length of egg (mm)	16
Number of eggs laid	6

Swallow

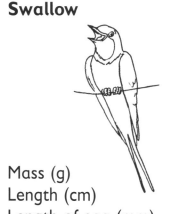

Mass (g)	19
Length (cm)	18
Length of egg (mm)	20
Number of eggs laid	5

Swift

Mass (g)	44
Length (cm)	17
Length of egg (mm)	25
Number of eggs laid	2

Little owl

Mass (g)	175
Length (cm)	22
Length of egg (mm)	36
Number of eggs laid	4

Wood pigeon

Mass (g)	500
Length (cm)	42
Length of egg (mm)	41
Number of eggs laid	2

Kestrel

Mass (g)	200
Length (cm)	34
Length of egg (mm)	39
Number of eggs laid	5

Teachers' note This sheet should be used in conjunction with 'Bird-watching: 1'.

A Lesson for Every Day
Maths
6–7 Years
© A&C Black

Nutty squirrels

- Use the greater than ⟨>⟩ or less than ⟨<⟩ sign to show which squirrel has more nuts.

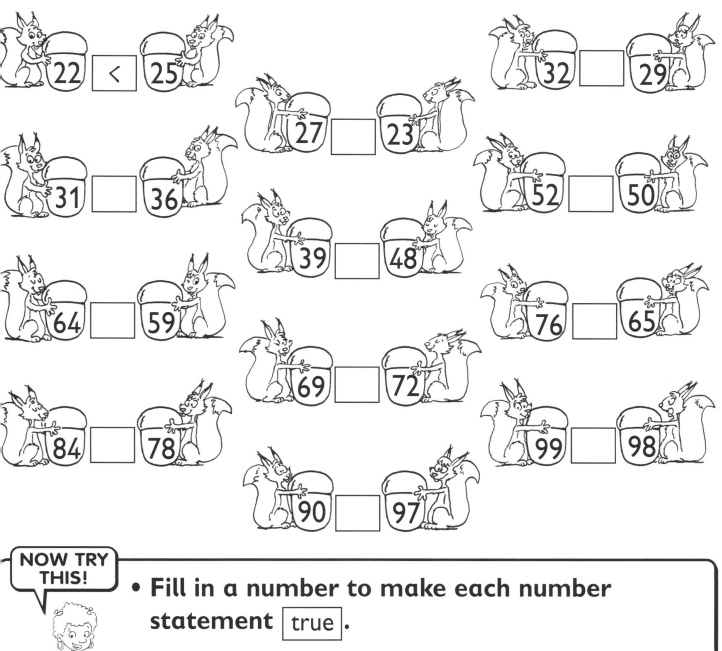

22 < 25

32 ☐ 29

27 ☐ 23

31 ☐ 36

52 ☐ 50

39 ☐ 48

64 ☐ 59

76 ☐ 65

69 ☐ 72

84 ☐ 78

99 ☐ 98

90 ☐ 97

NOW TRY THIS!

- Fill in a number to make each number statement ⟨true⟩.

 < 34  89 >   75 <

Teachers' note If necessary, revise the meaning of the 'greater than' and 'less than' signs. The image of 'the greedy crocodile' whose mouth always eats the larger amount can be helpful.

A Lesson for Every Day
Maths
6–7 Years
© A&C Black

Reading the signs

- **Mark the two numbers on the line.**
- **Use the ⬚ > and ⬚ < signs to make the statements ⬚ true .**

One has been done for you.

To the monster →

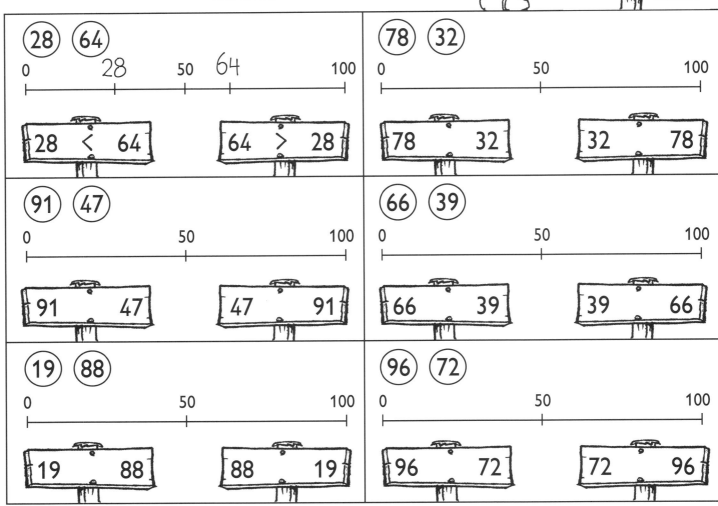

Box 1 (done): ㉘ ㉞
0 — 28 — 50 — 64 — 100
28 < 64   64 > 28

Box 2: ㉑ ㉜
0 — 50 — 100
78 ⬚ 32   32 ⬚ 78

Box 3: �91 ㊸
0 — 50 — 100
91 ⬚ 47   47 ⬚ 91

Box 4: ㊻ ㊴
0 — 50 — 100
66 ⬚ 39   39 ⬚ 66

Box 5: ⑲ �
0 — 50 — 100
19 ⬚ 88   88 ⬚ 19

Box 6: ㊱ ㊲
0 — 50 — 100
96 ⬚ 72   72 ⬚ 96

NOW TRY THIS!

- **Choose your own two-digit numbers.**

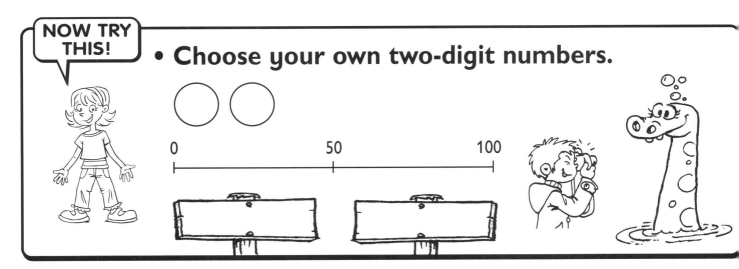

0 — 50 — 100

Teachers' note Children sometimes find it difficult to know which sign to use. If this is still the case, remind them that a good way to remember is to think of the 'greater than' and 'less than' signs as the open mouth of a greedy crocodile, always eating the larger number.

A Lesson for Every Day
Maths
6-7 Years
© A&C Black

Monster making

- **Play this game with a partner.**
- **You need coloured pencils and 0 to 100 number cards.**

☆ Shuffle the cards.

☆ Take turns to pick a card and round the number to the **nearest 10**.

☆ Record your answer and colour the body part on your monster.

☆ The player who colours the most body parts is the winner.

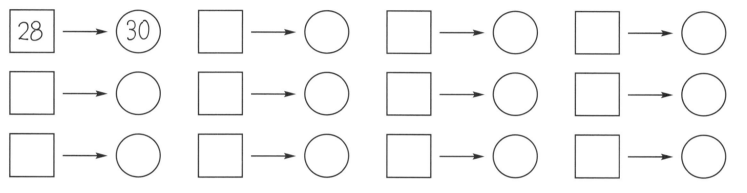

Teachers' note Before giving the set of 0 to 100 number cards to the children, remove all the multiples of 10.

A Lesson for Every Day
Maths
6–7 Years
© A&C Black

Round in space

- ## Write numbers that round to the planet numbers.

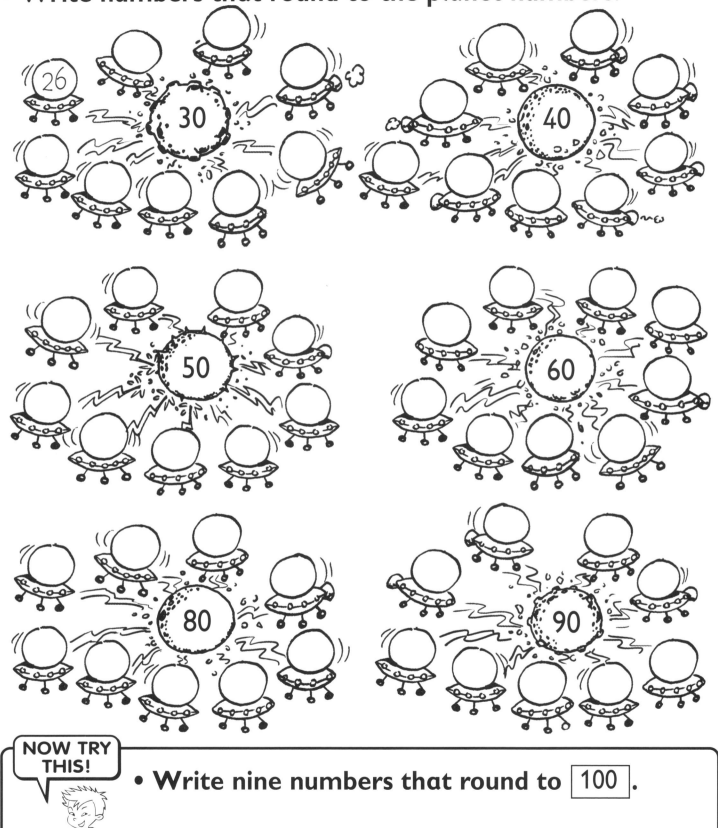

- ## Write nine numbers that round to 100 .

_____

Teachers' note Ensure the children understand that numbers with a units digit of 5 round up to the nearest 10, so 65 rounds to 70.

A Lesson for Every Day
Maths
6–7 Years
© A&C Black

Dixie the pixie

Every time Flynn does a calculation,
Dixie the pixie undoes it!
So, if Flynn $\boxed{\text{adds } 8}$, Dixie $\boxed{\text{takes away } 8}$
and undoes the calculation.

• Write the answer to each calculation.

$10 + 8 - 8$ = $\underline{10}$

$12 + 7 - 7$ = _____

$30 - 9 + 9$ = _____

$24 - 6 + 6$ = _____

$16 + 7 - 7$ = _____

$34 - 5 + 5$ = _____

NOW TRY THIS!

• **Write what Dixie will do to undo Flynn's work.**

$60 + 4$ = 60

$42 + 9$ = 42

$50 - 9$ = 50

$54 - 5$ = 54

$19 + 8$ = 19

$36 - 7$ = 36

Teachers' note This activity encourages the children to appreciate the inverse nature of addition and subtraction. The children could be given a calculator to check their answers.

A Lesson for Every Day
Maths
6-7 Years
© A&C Black

59

Cube covering

A cube is covering one number in each addition or subtraction sentence.

• Write the number on the cube.

$12 +$  8 $= 20$

$12 -$ ☐ $= 8$

$17 +$ ☐ $= 25$

$28 -$ ☐ $= 21$

$16 +$ ☐ $= 30$

$13 +$ ☐ $= 21$

$14 -$ ☐ $= 9$

$18 +$ ☐ $= 24$

$29 -$ ☐ $= 19$

$18 +$ ☐ $= 32$

NOW TRY THIS!

• **Try these in the same way.**

☐ $- 6 = 10$

☐ $+ 19 = 26$

☐ $- 12 = 8$

☐ $- 8 = 7$

☐ $+ 17 = 27$

☐ $- 18 = 5$

Teachers' note Demonstrate to the children how the inverse operation can sometimes be used to find a missing number, for example ☐ − 4 = 9 can be solved by adding 9 and 4 together.

A Lesson for Every Day
Maths
6–7 Years
© A&C Black

Missing digits

- **Write digits to make each statement correct.**
- **Find** 4 **different ways to do this each time.**

◯◯ + ◯1◯ = ②②   ◯◯ + ◯1◯ = ②②

◯◯ + ◯1◯ = ②②   ◯◯ + ◯1◯ = ②②

◯②+ ◯◯ = ③⑤   ◯②+ ◯◯ = ③⑤

◯②+ ◯◯ = ③⑤   ◯②+ ◯◯ = ③⑤

◯⑤+ ◯◯ = ④③   ◯⑤+ ◯◯ = ④③

◯⑤+ ◯◯ = ④③   ◯⑤+ ◯◯ = ④③

NOW TRY THIS!

- **Write all the possible ways of making this statement** true .

◯◯ + ◯1◯ = ③①

How many ways can you find?

Teachers' note This activity encourages the children to notice patterns in digits. Ensure the children realise that some of the calculations could be answered with a mix of one-digit and two-digit numbers. For the extension activity, encourage children to list all the numbers that have a tens digit of 1, preferably listing them in order and using this to help them find the other number in each pair.

A Lesson for Every Day
Maths
6–7 Years
© A&C Black

61

Check it out

- **Is the statement** | true | **or** | false |**?**
- **Colour the correct answer.**
- **Write examples to prove it.**

1 There are exactly 5 odd numbers between 10 and 20.

_____

| true |

_____

| false |

2 There are exactly 4 multiples of 10 between 25 and 75.

_____

| true |

_____

| false |

3 If you double any odd number the answer is always even.

_____

| true |

_____

| false |

4 If you halve any even number the answer is always odd.

_____

| true |

_____

| false |

5 There are exactly 6 multiples of 5 between 24 and 51.

_____

| true |

_____

| false |

6 There are exactly 5 multiples of 3 between 17 and 29.

_____

| true |

_____

| false |

NOW TRY THIS!

- **Write** | 2 | **statements of your own and find out whether they are** | true | **or** | false |**.**

Teachers' note Ask the children to make predictions before checking and finding examples to prove or disprove it. As a further extension activity, the children could amend the statements to make them true.

A Lesson for Every Day
Maths
6–7 Years
© A&C Black

Cherry time

Sam is going to put some cherries into each bowl to match each number.

- Choose any 3 bowls and find how many cherries altogether.

 14  15  16  17  18

- What different totals can you make?

NOW TRY THIS!

- What is the: largest possible total? _____

  smallest possible total? _____

Teachers' note Encourage the children to work systematically and to notice patterns in the totals. Ask them to consider whether bowls contain 'one more' or 'one less' than other bowls and how this might affect the totals. To simplify the activity, reduce the number of bowls.

A Lesson for Every Day
Maths
6–7 Years
© A&C Black

Loop the loop

- **Cut out the cards.**
- **Answer the 'start' card. Find the answer on one of the other cards. Then answer that question and so on.**
- **Put the cards in a loop on the table.**

Start **25 cm** Jo has a piece of ribbon 12 cm long. She cuts it in half. How long is each half? **O**	**170 cm** Mr Li has 4 lengths of wood, each 2 m. He puts them end to end in a line. How long is it? **N**
160 cm A door was 2 m and 10 cm tall. Jim cut off 5 cm. How tall is the door now? **D**	**1 m** A field is half as wide as it is long. It is 16 m wide. How long is it? **F**
32 m Sally is 138 cm tall. Her mum is 32 cm taller. How tall is her mum? **I**	**6 cm** A worm grows 4 cm a week. Last week it was 9 cm. How long is it now? **N**
17 m A dog is 50 cm. The dog is twice as tall as a cat. How tall is the cat? **Y**	**205 cm** A ball of string has 20 m of string. Dev cuts off 3 m. How much string is left on the ball **A**
13 cm A brick is 25 cm long. What is the length of four bricks in a line? **E**	**8 m** Sam is 25 cm taller than Pete. Sam is 185 cm tall. How tall is Pete? **E**

Teachers' note As a quick way of checking the children's answers, use the letters at the bottom right of each card. If correctly in order they should spell a phrase. Remind the children that 'm' stands for 'metres' and 'cm' stands for 'centimetres'.

A Lesson for Every Day
Maths
6–7 Years
© A&C Black

Hoopla

• Add together the numbers above and across from each hoop. Write the total in the hoop.

+	2	3	4	5	6	7	8	9
2	-	-	⊙ 6	-	◯	-	-	-
3	-	◯	-	-	-	-	◯	-
4	-	-	-	◯	-	-	-	◯
5	-	-	-	-	-	◯	-	-
6	-	◯	-	◯	-	-	-	◯
7	-	-	◯	-	◯	◯	-	-
8	-	-	-	◯	-	-	◯	-
9	◯	-	◯	-	-	◯	-	◯

NOW TRY THIS!

• **Write addition sums to show all the ways you could find the total 14 on this board.**

Teachers' note Ensure that children understand how the row and column headings are added together to find the total for each hoop. As a further extension activity, the children could copy the column and row headings onto squared paper and write all the totals possible on the board. In doing this, the children would begin to see patterns in the totals.

A Lesson for Every Day
Maths
6-7 Years
© A&C Black

Cross out

- **Cross out one number from each row so that the total of each row is correct.**
- **Write the total of the numbers in each column.**

8	7	☒	= 1
6	☒	9	= 1
☒	5	8	= 1

14 12 17

7	9	4	= 13
5	9	4	= 14
7	5	9	= 16

_____ _____ _____

6	8	7	= 1
5	4	8	= 12
8	6	5	= 14

_____ _____ _____

5	7	6	= 11
8	4	6	= 10
8	7	5	= 15

_____ _____ _____

7	5	9	= 12
5	9	8	= 13
4	7	6	= 13

_____ _____ _____

8	3	9	= 12
4	5	8	= 12
6	9	8	= 15

_____ _____ _____

6	7	6	= 12
9	6	8	= 14
7	8	3	= 15

_____ _____ _____

NOW TRY THIS!

- **Draw your own cross-out grid for a partner to try.**

Teachers' note Discuss strategies for helping the children to remember these key addition facts involving pairs of numbers from 3 to 9, such as using near-doubles, adding 10 and subtracting 1 etc. Call out questions orally to encourage a quick response. Remind children doing the extension activity that they should use numbers from 3 to 9.

A Lesson for Every Day
Maths
6-7 Years
© A&C Black

Donkey hats

- **Which two donkeys have numbers that total to the numbers on the suns? Draw hats on them.**

NOW TRY THIS!

- **Write sets of three numbers with a total of 19.**

Teachers' note This activity can help children to memorise the totals of pairs of single-digit numbers. Remind the children to use doubles to help them remember other totals, for example 8 + 7 is one more than double 7 or one less than double 8.

A Lesson for Every Day
Maths
6-7 Years
© A&C Black

Magic Meg

Magic Meg can double and halve numbers.

- **Fill in the missing numbers.**

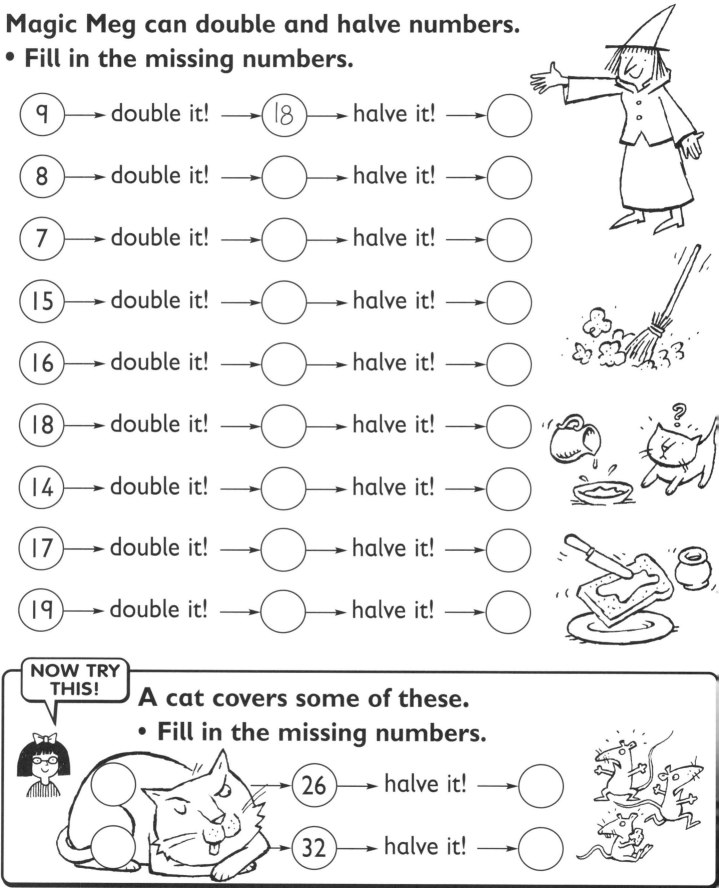

(9) → double it! → (18) → halve it! → ( )

(8) → double it! → ( ) → halve it! → ( )

(7) → double it! → ( ) → halve it! → ( )

(15) → double it! → ( ) → halve it! → ( )

(16) → double it! → ( ) → halve it! → ( )

(18) → double it! → ( ) → halve it! → ( )

(14) → double it! → ( ) → halve it! → ( )

(17) → double it! → ( ) → halve it! → ( )

(19) → double it! → ( ) → halve it! → ( )

NOW TRY THIS!

A cat covers some of these.

- **Fill in the missing numbers.**

( ) → (26) → halve it! → ( )

( ) → (32) → halve it! → ( )

Teachers' note This activity helps the children to appreciate that halving and doubling are inverses. Encourage them to learn their doubles of numbers to 20 by heart and derive quickly the related halving facts.

A Lesson for Every Day
Maths
6–7 Years
© A&C Black

Twins

The twins in each pair have the same number of cubes.
- How many cubes have each pair got altogether?

We have 3 cubes each.   6

We have 6 cubes each.   ___

We have 4 cubes each.   ___

We have 5 cubes each.   ___

We have 2 cubes each.   ___

We have 9 cubes each.   ___

We have 8 cubes each.   ___

We have 10 cubes each.   ___

We have 1 cube each.   ___

We have 7 cubes each.   ___

- **Write all the answers in order.**

2, _____

NOW TRY THIS!

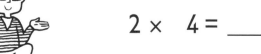

The numbers above are in the 2 times-table.
- **Fill in the missing numbers.**

$2 \times 4 =$ ___ $2 \times 6 =$ ___ $2 \times 3 =$ ___

$2 \times 2 =$ ___ $2 \times 7 =$ ___ $2 \times 1 =$ ___

$2 \times 9 =$ ___ $2 \times 10 =$ ___ $2 \times 5 =$ ___ $2 \times 8 =$ ___

Teachers' note Describe each question using vocabulary such as *What is double 5? What is twice 5? How many is 5 add 5? What is two lots of 5? How many is 2 times 5? 2 multiplied by 5?* Invite the children to describe how they worked out the answers or whether they have learnt the doubles by heart.

A Lesson for Every Day
Maths
6-7 Years
© A&C Black

Plastered!

Plasters come in packs of 10.

● **Write how many plasters are in each set.**

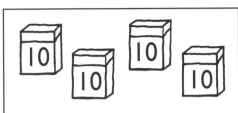

$4 \times 10 = \boxed{40}$

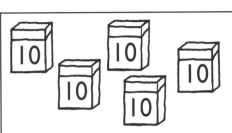

$5 \times 10 = \boxed{}$

$3 \times 10 = \boxed{}$

$1 \times 10 = \boxed{}$

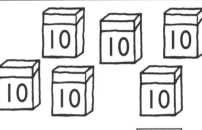

$6 \times 10 = \boxed{}$

$8 \times 10 = \boxed{}$

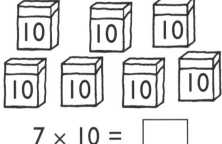

$7 \times 10 = \boxed{}$

$2 \times 10 = \boxed{}$

$9 \times 10 = \boxed{}$

NOW TRY THIS!

Some plasters are put into packs of 10.

● **How many full packs can be made?**

$80 \div 10 = \boxed{8}$ $\qquad$ $50 \div 10 = \boxed{}$ $\qquad$ $70 \div 10 = \boxed{}$

$40 \div 10 = \boxed{}$ $\qquad$ $90 \div 10 = \boxed{}$ $\qquad$ $20 \div 10 = \boxed{}$

$60 \div 10 = \boxed{}$ $\qquad$ $30 \div 10 = \boxed{}$ $\qquad$ $100 \div 10 = \boxed{}$

Teachers' note The extension activity involves seeing division as equal grouping rather than sharing, that is where children find how many equal groups of 10 are in each set.

A Lesson for Every Day
Maths
6-7 Years
© A&C Black

Chain reaction

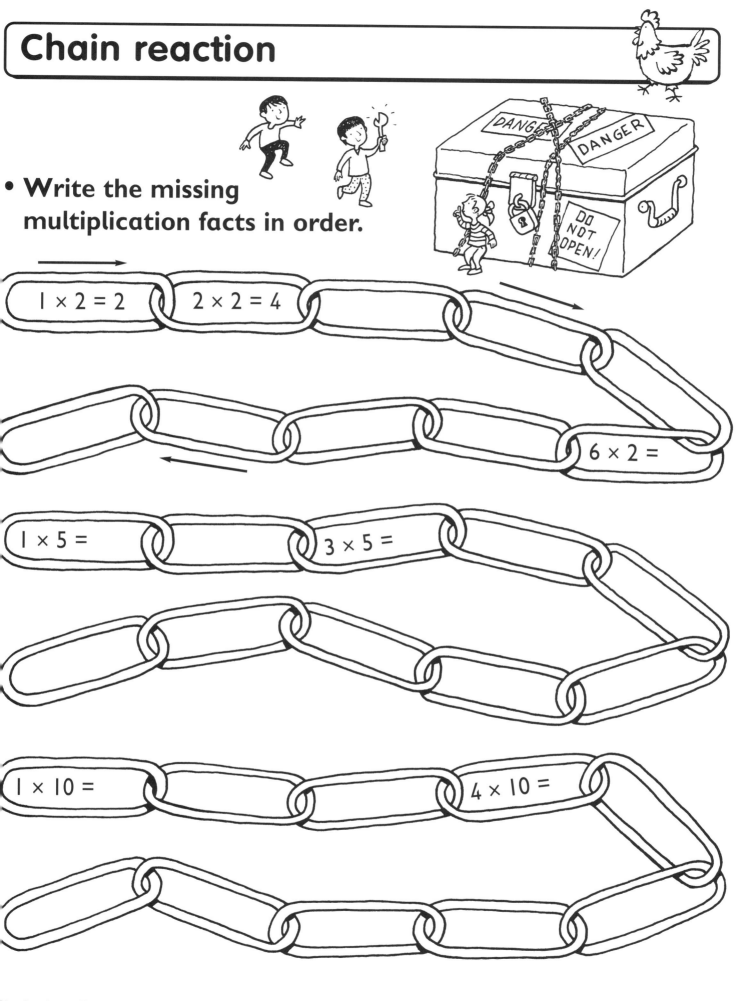

- **Write the missing multiplication facts in order.**

$1 \times 2 = 2$ $2 \times 2 = 4$

$6 \times 2 =$

$1 \times 5 =$ $3 \times 5 =$

$1 \times 10 =$ $4 \times 10 =$

Teachers' note Encourage the children to say the facts aloud using a range of vocabulary, for example three lots of two is six, three times two is six, three multiplied by two equals six. As an extension activity, ask the children to shade three links with the answer 10 in one colour, and three with the answer 20 in another colour.

A Lesson for Every Day
Maths
6-7 Years
© A&C Black

Weaving

- **Use different-coloured pencils to join the related questions and answers.**

5 × 4	6 × 5	15
5 × 3	4 × 5	30
5 × 6	7 × 5	5
5 × 7	1 × 5	20
5 × 1	3 × 5	35
5 × 9	9 × 5	45
5 × 5	5 × 5	10
5 × 8	2 × 5	40
5 × 2	10 × 5	25
5 × 10	8 × 5	50

5 × 7	2 × 5	50
5 × 2	10 × 5	45
5 × 8	9 × 5	10
5 × 9	7 × 5	40
5 × 10	8 × 5	35
5 × 3	5 × 5	25
5 × 6	6 × 5	15
5 × 5	3 × 5	5
5 × 1	4 × 5	30
5 × 4	1 × 5	20

NOW TRY THIS!

- **Write the answers to these multiplications.**

5 × 3	6 × 5	7 × 5	4 × 5	5 × 9	8 × 5	5 × 10
3 × 5	5 × 6	5 × 7	5 × 4	9 × 5	5 × 8	10 × 5
15						

Teachers' note The children will need coloured pencils for this activity. It encourages them to see that once they know one multiplication fact they know a second made by swapping the order of the numbers being multiplied.

A Lesson for Every Day
Maths
6-7 Years
© A&C Black

Round to check

- **Answer the questions, then check your answer by rounding each number and finding the total.**

8 + 29 = ☐ 37

10 + 30 = 40

38 + 8 = ☐

61 + 7 = ☐

52 + 9 = ☐

9 + 78 = ☐

6 + 43 = ☐

82 + 6 = ☐

75 + 8 = ☐

57 + 7 = ☐

NOW TRY THIS!

- **Try these in the same way.**

21 + 37 = ☐

48 + 46 = ☐

Teachers' note At the start of the lesson revise rounding numbers to the nearest ten and show how this can help you to check answers to calculations.

A Lesson for Every Day
Maths
6–7 Years
© A&C Black

73

Spot the shapes

- **Colour the 3** ⬚shapes⬚ **that have been used to make each design.**

NOW TRY THIS!

- **Make up one of your own for a partner to try.**

Teachers' note This activity helps the children to become more visually perceptive and to identify several shapes overlapping. This is an important skill that some children find difficult. Once they have identified the shapes in the designs, discuss their properties, making reference to numbers of sides, whether they are straight or curved, number of right angles and so on.

A Lesson for Every Day
Maths
6-7 Years
© A&C Black

Sticky labels

- **Use the price list to find the cost of each pack of sticky labels.**
- **You may use a price more than once.**

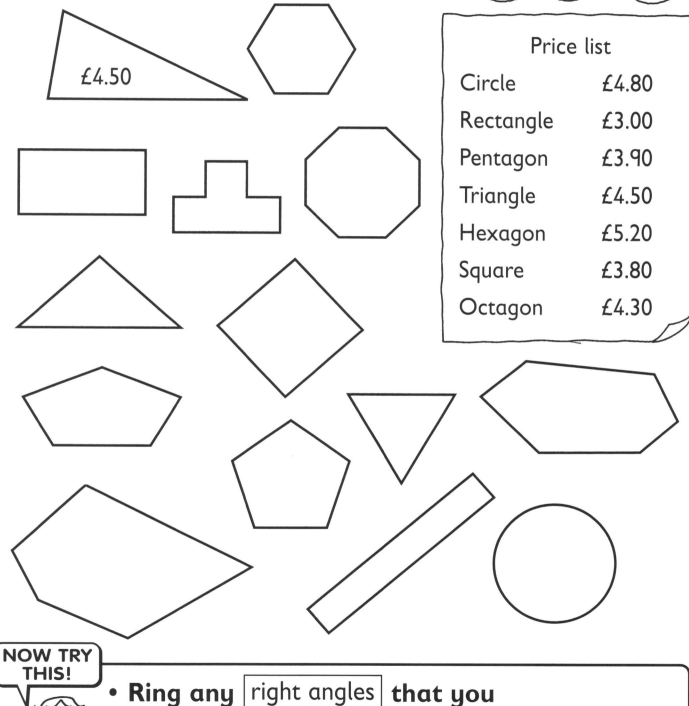

£4.50

Price list	
Circle	£4.80
Rectangle	£3.00
Pentagon	£3.90
Triangle	£4.50
Hexagon	£5.20
Square	£3.80
Octagon	£4.30

NOW TRY THIS!

- **Ring any** right angles **that you can see on the stickers above.**

Teachers' note Discuss the names and properties of the 2-D shapes before beginning this activity. Encourage the children to count the number of straight sides making up the shapes and to find the name of the shape in the list that has that number of sides.

A Lesson for Every Day
Maths
6–7 Years
© A&C Black

True or false?

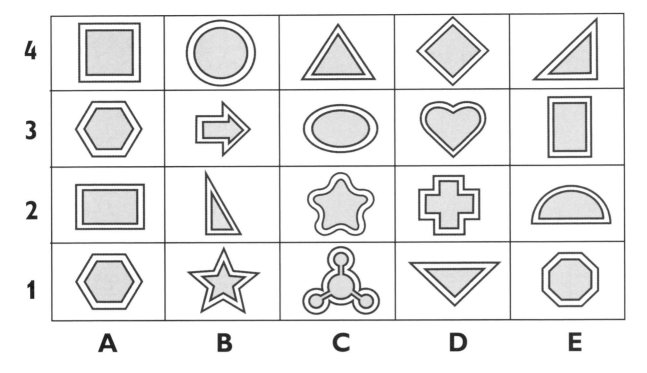

| | A | B | C | D | E |

- **Tick** ⬚ true ⬚ **or** ⬚ false ⬚ **for each statement.**

D4 contains a square.
✔ true ☐ false

Row 3 contains a triangle.
☐ true ☐ false

Column A contains two hexagons.
☐ true ☐ false

B2 contains a triangle.
☐ true ☐ false

A2 and **E3** are the same shape.
☐ true ☐ false

E1 contains a pentagon.
☐ true ☐ false

B4 contains a shape with 1 side.
☐ true ☐ false

B3 contains a hexagon.
☐ true ☐ false

NOW TRY THIS!

- **Write 4 true statements of your own.**

Teachers' note This activity provides revision of shape names and properties and also explores using letters and numbers to represent positions of items in a grid formation.

A Lesson for Every Day
Maths
6–7 Years
© A&C Black

Shape mysteries

- **Part of a shape is hidden.**
- **It has** $\boxed{3}$, $\boxed{4}$, $\boxed{5}$ **or** $\boxed{6}$ **straight sides.**
- **Draw a different shape each time.**

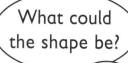

What could the shape be?

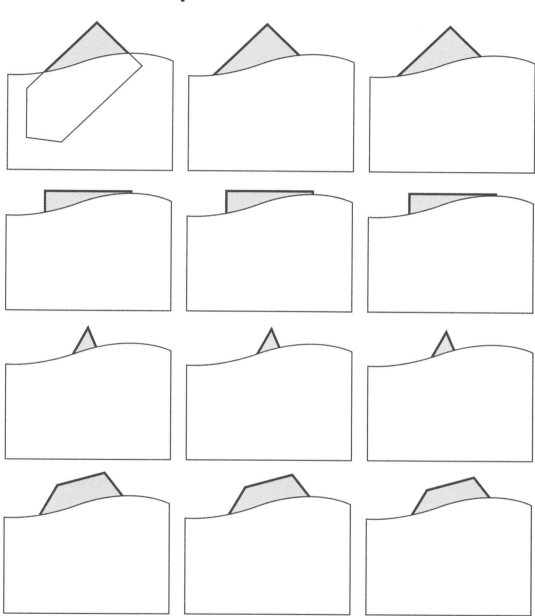

- **Write the name of each shape you have drawn.**

NOW TRY THIS!

- **On the back of this sheet draw some partly hidden shapes of your own.**

Teachers' note Emphasise that the children must draw straight lines and make a shape with up to six sides. Encourage them to imagine that the lines continue behind the screen, rather than just assuming that the points on the shape that touch the edge of the paper are vertices of the shape. Demonstrate this idea with the whole class using paper and plastic shapes.

A Lesson for Every Day
Maths
6-7 Years
© **A&C Black**

Shape shifting: 1

- **You need the shapes from 'Shape shifting: 2'.**

- **Arrange** 2 **of the shapes without overlapping them, to make these:**

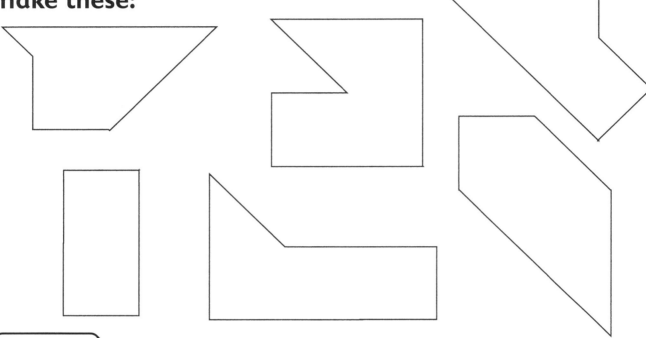

NOW TRY THIS!

- **Arrange** 3 **of the shapes to make these:**

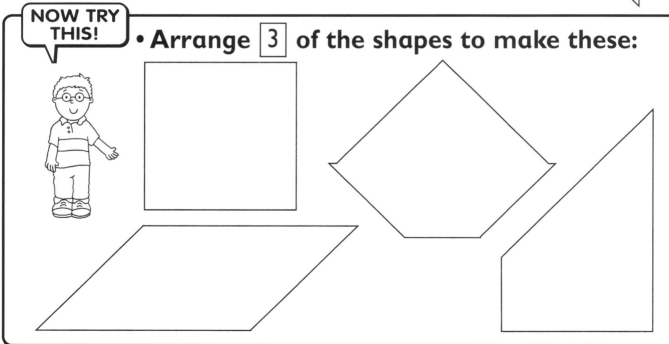

Teachers' note Provide the children with scissors and encourage them to carefully cut the shapes from 'Shape shifting: 2'. Explain that pieces can be turned over if necessary. The pieces could be copied onto card and laminated for a more permanent resource.

A Lesson for Every Day
Maths
6-7 Years
© A&C Black

Shape shifting: 2

- **Cut out the shapes.**

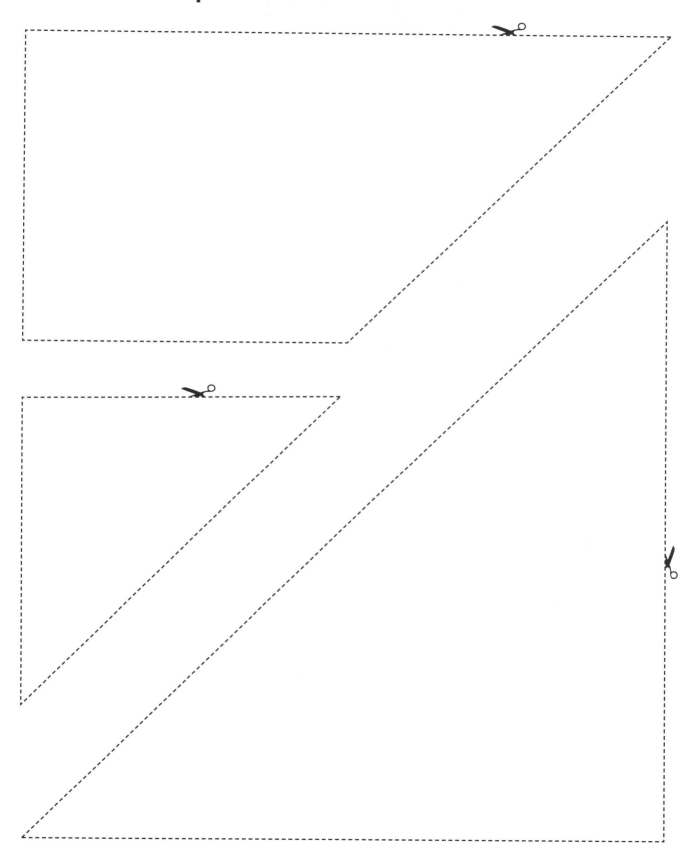

Teachers' note Use this sheet in conjunction with 'Shape shifters: 1'.

A Lesson for Every Day
Maths
6-7 Years
© A&C Black

All change!

• Draw a ☐ ring ☐ around each coin given in change.

1 Jo has a £5 note. She spends £1.99. 	**2** Li has a £5 note. She spends £3.98. 
3 Dan has a £5 note. He spends £2.95. 	**4** Al has a £5 note. He spends £4.89. 

NOW TRY THIS!

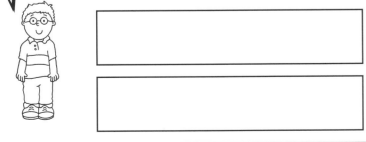

• **Record each situation above using numbers.**

Teachers' note The numbers can be altered before copying to provide differentiation. For the extension activity, the children could use either addition or subtraction and should be encouraged to justify their decisions.

A Lesson for Every Day
Maths
6-7 Years
© A&C Black

Bikers!

Use this code to help you find parts of a bicycle.

a	b	c	d	e
11 + 11	10 – 2	8 + 4	2 + 3	15 + 15
___	___	___	___	___

f	g	h	i	j
4 + 3	16 + 3	9 + 6	13 + 13	8 – 2
___	___	___	___	___

k	l	m	n	o
6 + 10	1 + 2	3 + 7	17 + 1	20 + 20
___	___	___	___	___

p	q	r	s	t
10 – 6	20 – 7	14 – 0	10 – 8	14 + 6
___	___	___	___	___

u	v	w	x	y
50 + 50	20 – 3	17 – 6	20 – 19	15 + 6
___	___	___	___	___

2, 30, 22, 20   ___ ___ ___ ___

8, 30, 3, 3   ___ ___ ___ ___

4, 30, 5, 22, 3   ___ ___ ___ ___ ___

20, 21, 14, 30, 2   ___ ___ ___ ___ ___

8, 14, 22, 16, 30, 2 ___ ___ ___ ___ ___ ___

11, 15, 30, 30, 3, 2 ___ ___ ___ ___ ___ ___

15, 30, 3, 10, 30, 20 ___ ___ ___ ___ ___ ___

Teachers' note As an extension activitiy, ask the children to make their own alphabet questions, ensuring that each letter has a question with a different answer. They can then write their own fruit or animal code using the answers and give them to a partner to solve. This can also make an interesting display, where a new word could be put up each day to encourage quick calculating.

A Lesson for Every Day
Maths
6-7 Years
© A&C Black

Turtlemania!

- **Make each turtle total** $\boxed{20}$.
- **Write as quickly as you can.**

5 | 15

10 | ☐

19 | ☐

4 | ☐

0 | ☐

8 | ☐

1 | ☐

14 | ☐

3 | ☐

11 | ☐

9 | ☐

16 | ☐

6 | ☐

13 | ☐

7 | ☐

2 | ☐

18 | ☐

15 | ☐

12 | ☐

17 | ☐

Teachers' note At the start of the lesson, revise number pairs which total 10 and show the link between these facts and those that total 20, for example 4 + 6 = 10 so 14 + 6 = 20 and 4 + 16 = 20. As an extension activity, ask the children to write all the facts in order as addition sentences, continuing the pattern: 0 + 20, 1 + 19, 2 + 18, etc.

A Lesson for Every Day
Maths
6-7 Years
© A&C Black

Can you?

- **Continue the patterns on each can.**

18 − 3 = [15]

18 − 4 = [ ]

18 − 5 = [ ]

− = [ ]

− = [ ]

− = [ ]

16 − 5 = [ ]

16 − 6 = [ ]

16 − 7 = [ ]

− = [ ]

− = [ ]

− = [ ]

19 − 7 = [ ]

19 − 8 = [ ]

19 − 9 = [ ]

− = [ ]

− = [ ]

− = [ ]

17 − 7 = [ ]

17 − 8 = [ ]

− = [ ]

− = [ ]

− = [ ]

− = [ ]

NOW TRY THIS!

- **Draw your own cans.**
- **Make up subtraction patterns for 13, 14 and 15.**

Teachers' note Provide the children with a number line to help them count backwards from the first number or to count up from the number being subtracted.

A Lesson for Every Day
Maths
6–7 Years
© A&C Black

Creepy crawlies

- **Write a subtraction fact with the answer 7 in each creepy crawly.**

$10 - 3 = 7$

- **Write subtraction facts with the answer 4.**

- **Write subtraction facts with the answer 8.**

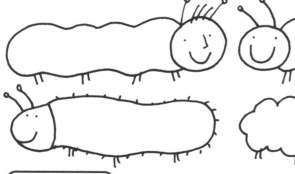  

NOW TRY THIS!

- **Use the numbers 17, 21, 15, 22, 9, 12 to make three subtraction questions with these answers.**

_____ = 7   _____ = 8   _____ = 9

Teachers' note Remind the children that subtraction is the inverse of addition and so they can choose another number to add to the answer to make the first number of the subtraction, for example to make a subtraction with the answer 7 they can add 5 to 7 to make 12 and use this to make the related subtraction 12 − 5 = 7.

A Lesson for Every Day
Maths
6-7 Years
© A&C Black

Superheroes

A packet of Superhero cards costs £1.

0p 10p 20p 30p 40p 50p 60p 70p 80p 90p 100p

£1

- **How much more do you need to buy a packet?**

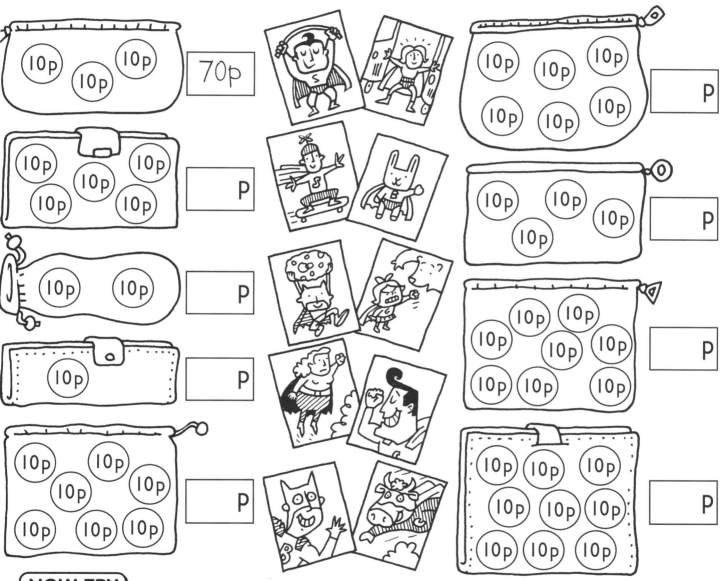

70p

P

P

P

P

P

P

P

P

P

NOW TRY THIS!

- **Write the facts as addition sentences.**

30p + 70p = £1 _____ _____

_____ _____ _____

Teachers' note Practise counting forwards and backwards in tens from zero to 100. Encourage the children to use their fingers when counting and draw attention to the link between single-digit numbers with the total 10 and the multiples of 10 with the total 100, for example 3 + 7 = 10 and 30 + 70 = 100. Demonstrate how to start at an amount on the number line and count up to £1.

A Lesson for Every Day
Maths
6-7 Years
© A&C Black

Tennis game

- **Play this game with a partner.**

☆ Cut out the cards and place them face down.

☆ Take turns to pick a card and, if you can, colour the answer on your racquet. Then replace the card face down.

☆ The first player to colour all their numbers wins the game.

Player 1   **Player 2**

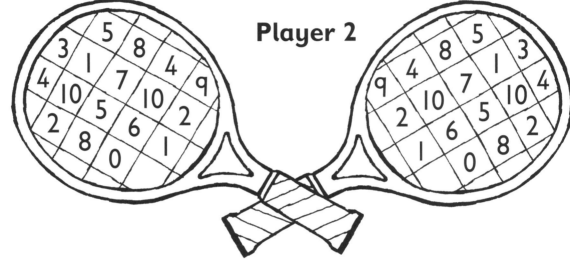

90 ÷ 10	0 ÷ 10	50 ÷ 10	40 ÷ 5	14 ÷ 2
35 ÷ 5	12 ÷ 2	30 ÷ 5	20 ÷ 2	100 ÷ 10
45 ÷ 5	25 ÷ 5	18 ÷ 2	5 ÷ 5	0 ÷ 2
20 ÷ 10	6 ÷ 2	30 ÷ 10	2 ÷ 2	80 ÷ 10
15 ÷ 5	60 ÷ 10	16 ÷ 2	10 ÷ 5	50 ÷ 5
4 ÷ 2	40 ÷ 10	20 ÷ 5	8 ÷ 2	70 ÷ 10

Teachers' note Ensure that a list of the tables facts from the 2, 5 and 10 times-tables is available. Ensure that children know how to use the tables facts to help them answer division facts, for example 7 × 2 is 14 so 14 ÷ 2 = 7.

A Lesson for Every Day
Maths
6-7 Years
© A&C Black

Two-digit dominoes

- **Cut out the dominoes and play a game with a partner.**
- **You can match numbers in figures, words or with the number of** tens **and** ones **.**

17	twenty-six	**26**	three tens and seven ones	thirty-seven
14	one ten and four ones	thirty-two	**32**	fifty-one
five tens and one	eighty-three	**83**	four tens and nine ones	forty-nine
75	seventy-five	**53**	five tens and three ones	twenty-two
22	one ten and three ones	thirteen	**88**	eighty-eight
34	three tens and four ones	sixty-four	**64**	**93**
nine tens and three ones	twenty-nine	**29**	seven tens and seven ones	seventy-seven
four tens and nine ones	**49**	fifty	**50**	eight tens and no ones
80	ninety-eight	nine tens and eight ones	thirty	three tens and no ones
19	one ten and nine ones	**70**	seventy	eighty-six
eight tens and six ones	**99**	ninety-nine	one ten and seven ones	

Teachers' note Some dominoes have 0 as a place holder, for example 70, where the digits represent 7 tens and no ones. Explain how to play the game. Share out the dominoes. Place one on the table. Each player should try to place a domino on one side or other of the domino so that the numbers match, or else miss a turn. The winner is the first to use up all his/her dominoes.

A Lesson for Every Day
Maths
6–7 Years
© A&C Black

Snail trails

- ## Write each number in figures.

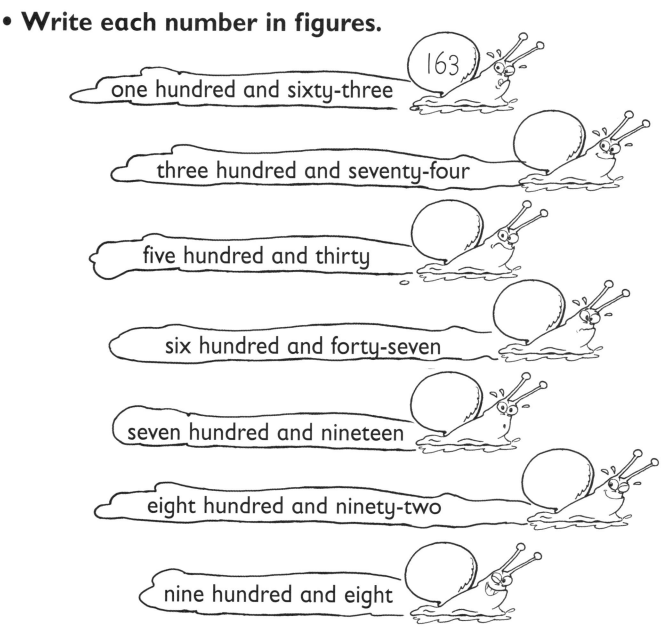

one hundred and sixty-three — 163

three hundred and seventy-four

five hundred and thirty

six hundred and forty-seven

seven hundred and nineteen

eight hundred and ninety-two

nine hundred and eight

NOW TRY THIS!

- ## Write in figures, three numbers that lie between four hundred and fifty and four hundred and sixty.

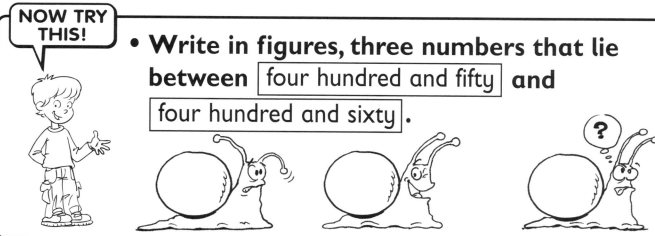

Teachers' note Ensure that somewhere on the classroom wall or board the following are shown in figures and words for children to refer to: numbers to 20, multiples of 10 to 100, and multiples of 100 to 1000.

A Lesson for Every Day
Maths
6–7 Years
© **A&C Black**

Guess the shape

- **Cut out the cards.**
- **Use the clues to help you guess each 3-D shape.**
- **Draw a picture of the shape on the back of the card.**

It has 8 corners.

It has 1 face.
It is curved.

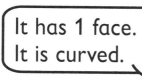

It has 12 edges all the same length. Its faces are square.

All of its faces are triangles.

One of its faces is square. The rest are triangles.

It has 1 corner and 1 edge.

It has 2 curved edges.

All of its faces are rectangles.

NOW TRY THIS!

- **Make up new clues for these shapes.**

 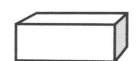 

Teachers' note Provide the children with a set of 3-D shapes, including sphere, cone, cylinder, cube, cuboid, square-based pyramid and tetrahedron (triangular-based pyramid).

A Lesson for Every Day
Maths
6–7 Years
© A&C Black

These shapes have been folded in half along the dotted line.

- **Write how many sides you think each shape will have when opened out.**

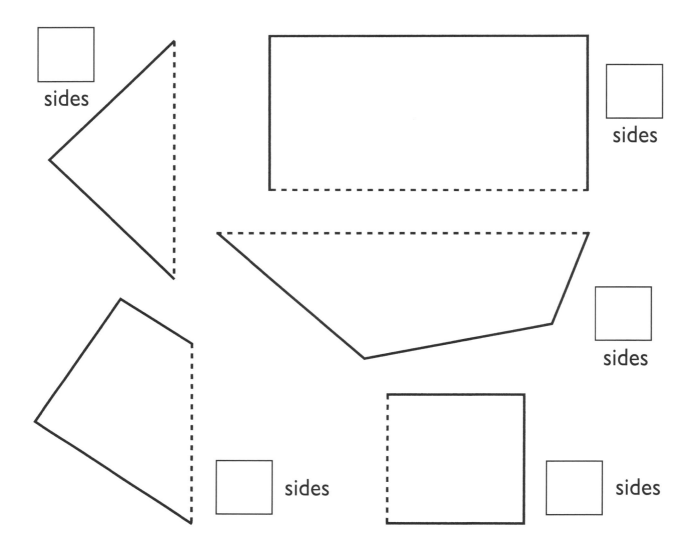

sides

sides

sides

sides

sides

sides

- **Fold a piece of paper and cut out your own shape.**
- **Ask a partner to guess how many sides the shape has when opened out.**

Teachers' note This sheet should be used in conjunction with the following sheet. First give out this sheet and ask children to predict the number of sides of the shapes when opened out. Then provide the solutions on the following page and ask children to cut out the shapes and to fold and open them to check their own answers.

A Lesson for Every Day
Maths
6-7 Years
© A&C Black

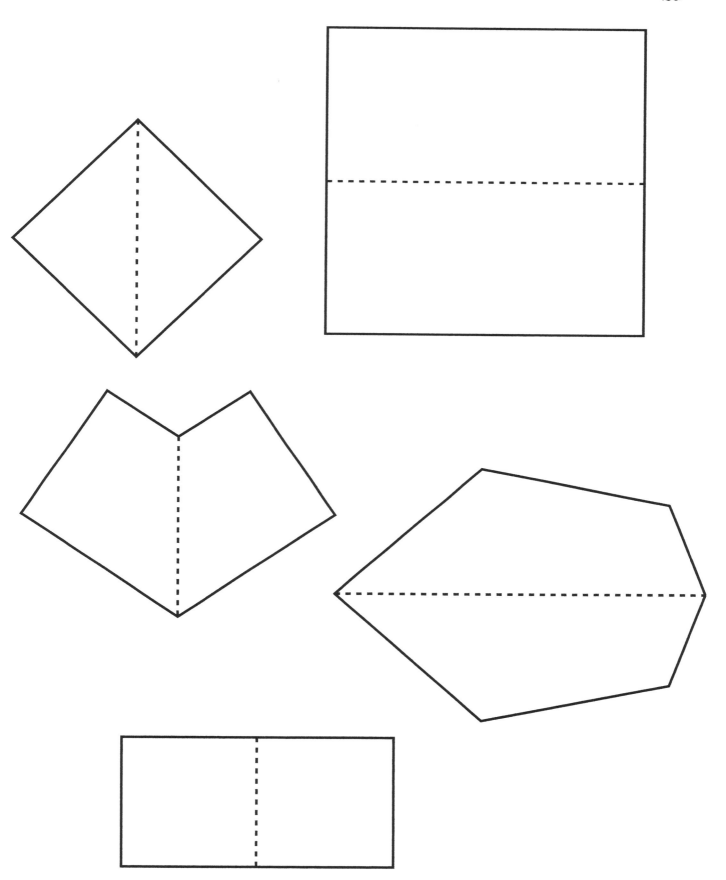

Teachers' note This sheet should be used in conjunction with the previous sheet. First give out that sheet and ask children to predict the number of sides of the shapes when opened out. Then provide the solutions on this page and ask children to cut out the shapes and to fold and open them to check their own answers.

A Lesson for Every Day
Maths
6-7 Years
© A&C Black

Flat shape speedway!

- Play this game with a partner. You need a dice, a counter and a small mirror each.

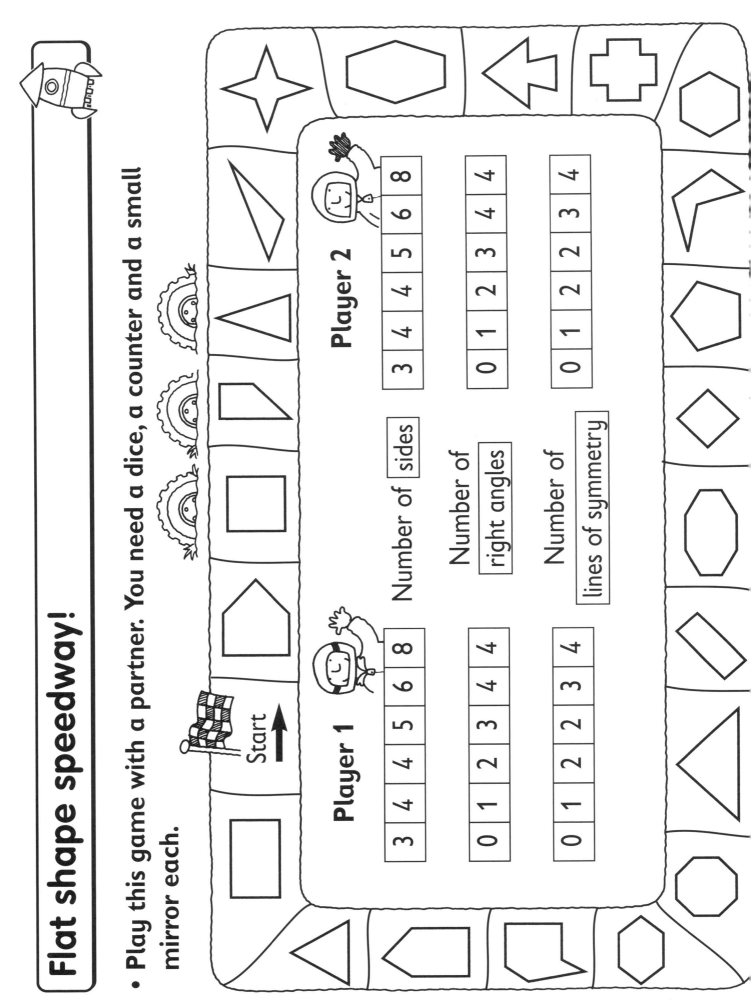

Start →

Player 1

3	4	5	6	8

0	1	2	3	4

0	1	2	3	4

Number of sides

Number of right angles

Number of lines of symmetry

Player 2

3	4	4	5	6	8

0	1	2	3	4	4

0	1	2	2	3	4

Teachers' note The children take turns to roll the dice and move their counter. The shape landed on should be examined for numbers of sides, right angles and lines of symmetry. The children should colour any numbers that they can in the centre. The game ends after a given number of laps. The winner is the player with the most coloured at the end of the game.

A Lesson for Every Day
Maths
6-7 Years
© A&C Black

Mirror mania

Ella holds some cards next to a mirror.

- **Colour the cards using at least 3 different colours so that the mirror shows the reflection each time.**

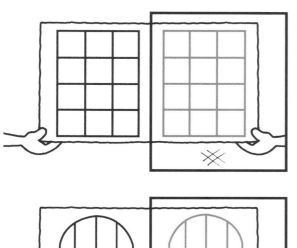
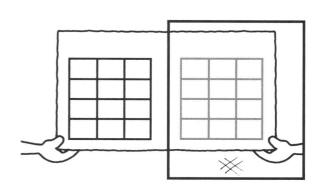

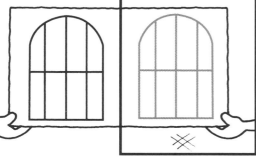
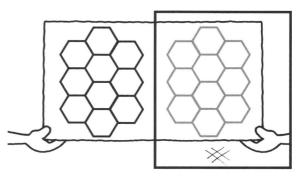

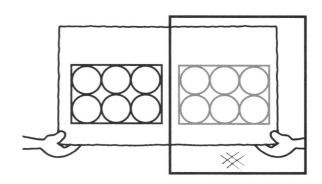

NOW TRY THIS!

- **Draw the reflection of the shape of this card and colour it.**

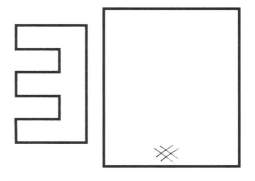

Teachers' note Provide the children with mirrors of their own to test and check their reflections. Demonstrate how to hold the mirror next to the shape and then how to lift it to check whether their answer underneath is correct.

A Lesson for Every Day
Maths
6–7 Years
© A&C Black

Snip, snip

Josh has made these ⌐symmetrical⌐ shapes by folding and cutting paper.

• Draw a line on each shape to show where he folded them.

NOW TRY THIS!

• Make 4 shapes of your own by folding and cutting paper.

Teachers' note Demonstrate how to fold a piece of paper in half and then how to cut and open it out to make a complete shape. Explain that the fold line is known as the 'mirror line' or the 'line of symmetry'.

A Lesson for Every Day
Maths
6-7 Years
© A&C Black

Billy's door

There are ⟨50⟩ rooms on a hotel corridor.
Billy lives in room number ⟨24⟩.

- **Look at the patterns. Predict whether Billy's door is open or shut. Tick ✓ the box. Check if you were correct.**

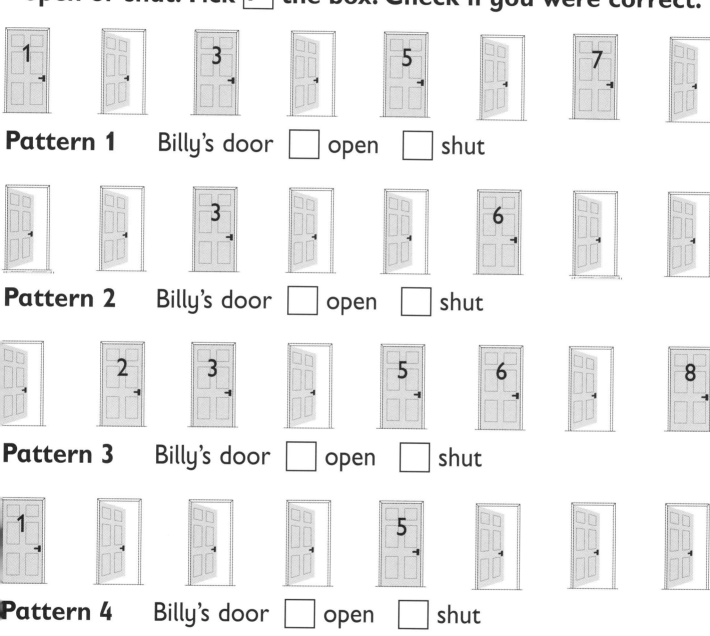

Pattern 1   Billy's door ☐ open ☐ shut

Pattern 2   Billy's door ☐ open ☐ shut

Pattern 3   Billy's door ☐ open ☐ shut

Pattern 4   Billy's door ☐ open ☐ shut

 **NOW TRY THIS!**

- **Make up a pattern of your own that would mean Billy's door was open.**

Teachers' note Ask the children to explain how they came to their decisions and observe the strategies used for checking, for example whether using knowledge of multiples or working practically with suitable equipment or using diagrams or letters as code. Billy's room number can be changed to create variety.

A Lesson for Every Day
Maths
6–7 Years
© A&C Black

Amy's seat

The seats in a stadium are red , white or blue .
The colour of the seats in each row follow a pattern.

- **Look at the patterns. Predict the colour of Amy's seat.**
- **Check to see if you were correct.**

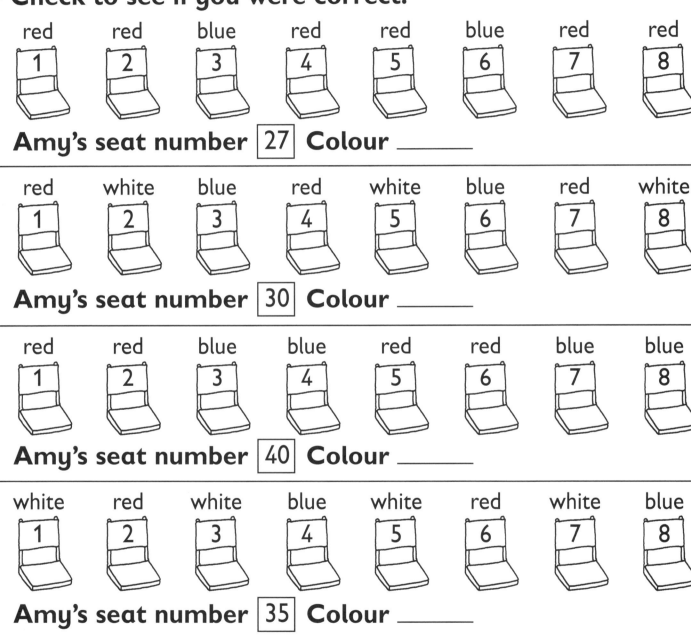

red	red	blue	red	red	blue	red	red
1	2	3	4	5	6	7	8

Amy's seat number 27 Colour _____

red	white	blue	red	white	blue	red	white
1	2	3	4	5	6	7	8

Amy's seat number 30 Colour _____

red	red	blue	blue	red	red	blue	blue
1	2	3	4	5	6	7	8

Amy's seat number 40 Colour _____

white	red	white	blue	white	red	white	blue
1	2	3	4	5	6	7	8

Amy's seat number 35 Colour _____

NOW TRY THIS!

- **Make up a pattern of your own that would mean Amy's seat was red .**

Teachers' note Provide red and blue coloured pencils. The children could start by colouring in the chairs in each pattern so that they can see clearly what is happening, and then make their predictions before checking by continuing the patterns. Ask them to explain how they came to their decisions and observe the strategies used for checking such as using knowledge of multiples.

96

A Lesson for Every Day
Maths
6-7 Years
© A&C Black

Sandy's sandwich bar

Sandy is making sandwiches.
Help her decide what she needs.

She makes 3 ham and cucumber sandwiches.
Each has 2 slices of ham and 3 pieces of cucumber.

- **How many of these does Sandy need?**

slices of bread ☐   slices of ham ☐   pieces of cucumber ☐

She makes 4 bacon and lettuce sandwiches.
Each has 2 pieces of bacon and 3 leaves of lettuce.

- **How many of these does Sandy need?**

slices of bread ☐   pieces of bacon ☐   leaves of lettuce ☐

NOW TRY THIS!

- **Make up 2 of your own sandwich questions for a partner to solve.**

eachers' note The numbers can be altered before copying to provide differentiation. Ensure the
nildren appreciate that each sandwich is made from 2 slices of bread. Once completed, discuss
pproaches used by the children to answer the questions, such as drawing the sandwiches or using
umber sentences. Children can use the space in each question to record their methods.

A Lesson for Every Day
Maths
6-7 Years
© A&C Black

Car boot sale

- **Solve these problems. What calculations are needed? How did you decide?**

1 Mr Deal buys 2 CDs. One costs £5 and the other costs £7. How much did he spend?

2 Mr Thrifty sold 10 books, each for £3. How much did he get?

3 Mrs Gready bought a lampshade. It was £5 more than she hoped to pay. She hoped to pay £12. How much did she pay?

4 Mr Bargain bought 2 chairs. They cost £16 altogether. How much did each chair cost?

5 Mr Broke went with £25. He spent all his money on a guitar and a mirror. The guitar cost £17. How much was the mirror?

6 Mrs Sellers sold 9 T-shirts, each for £2. Before leaving, she spent £6 on an ornament. How much money did she have when she left?

7 Mr Stall spent £4 on a chair and twice as much on a table. How much did he spend on both?

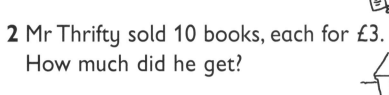

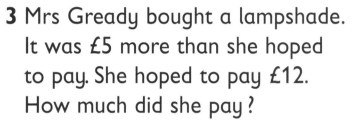

Teachers' note Encourage the children to use number sentences to show what they have decided to do for each calculation and ask them to describe their methods for answering each question. As an extension activity, ask the children to make up two of their own car boot sale questions for a friend to solve.

98

A Lesson for Every Day
Maths
6–7 Years
© A&C Black

Dicey dinosaurs

- **Play this game with a partner. Your teacher will show you how to play the game.**

Dice 1

| 20 | 50 | 0 | 10 | 40 | 30 |

Dice 2

| 60 | 80 | 100 | 50 | 90 | 70 |

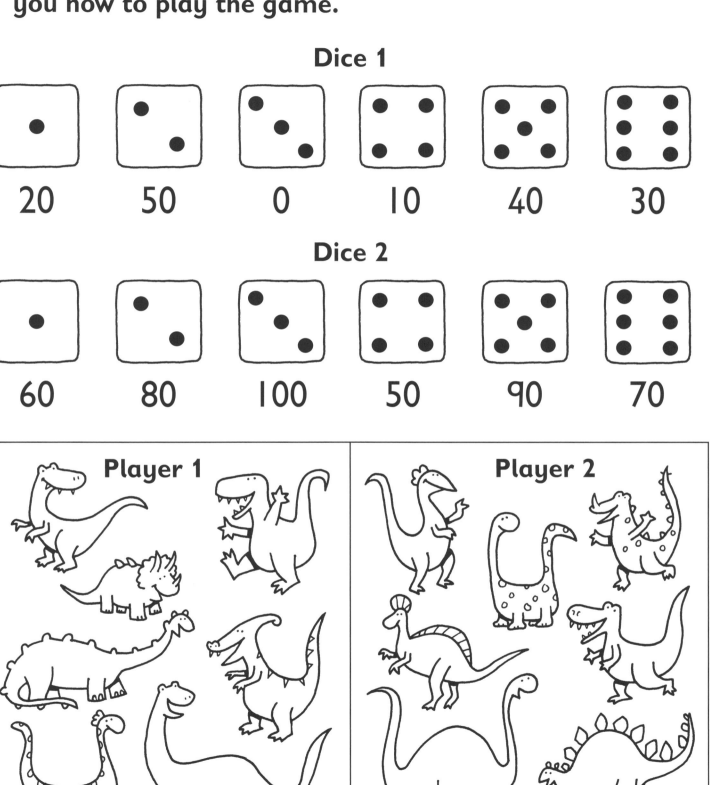

Player 1

Player 2

Teachers' note Begin the lesson by counting on and back in tens to 100 and remind the children of the pairs that total 100. Provide the children with two dice. Tell them to take turns to roll both dice and find the matching number for each dice. If the total of the two numbers is 100, they should cross off a dinosaur. The first player to cross off all their dinosaurs is the winner.

A Lesson for Every Day
Maths
6-7 Years
© A&C Black

Fairy wings

- **On each wing, write an addition question with the answer 100.**

Use multiples of 10.

40 + 60 = 100

- **On each wing, write a subtraction question starting with the number 100.**

100 – 30 = 70

- **Fill in the missing numbers.**

$100 - \boxed{} = 75$ $95 + \boxed{} = 100$ $100 - \boxed{} = 15$

Teachers' note Ensure the children make each fact different. Remind them that for addition the numbers can be swapped around to make a new fact with the same total.

A Lesson for Every Day
Maths
6–7 Years
© A&C Black

Ski slalom

• **Start at the top and write the answers as you go.**

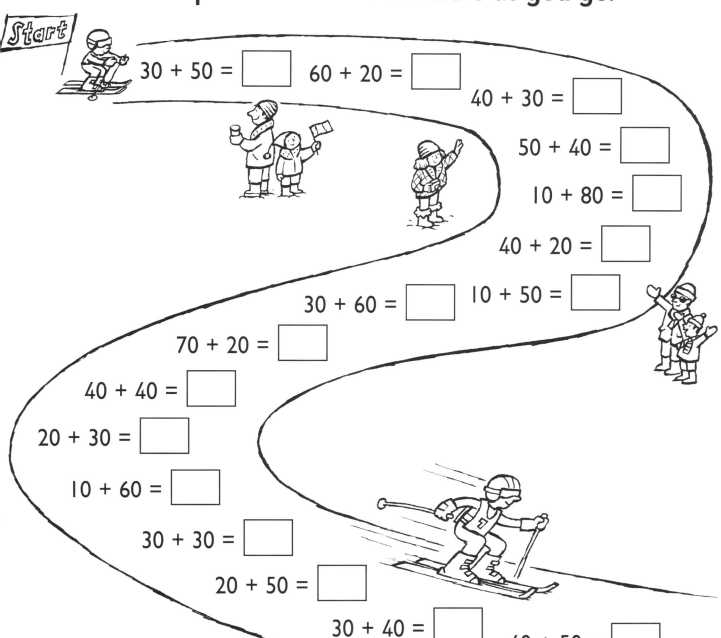

Start

30 + 50 = ☐   60 + 20 = ☐

40 + 30 = ☐

50 + 40 = ☐

10 + 80 = ☐

40 + 20 = ☐

30 + 60 = ☐   10 + 50 = ☐

70 + 20 = ☐

40 + 40 = ☐

20 + 30 = ☐

10 + 60 = ☐

30 + 30 = ☐

20 + 50 = ☐

30 + 40 = ☐   40 + 50 = ☐

NOW TRY THIS!

• **Answer these questions in the same way.**

70 + 60 = ☐   90 + 30 = ☐   80 + 50 = ☐

80 + 70 = ☐   60 + 90 = ☐   40 + 70 = ☐

Teachers' note Encourage the children to see the link between the addition facts for totals to 10 and the addition facts of multiples of 10 with totals to 100, for example. 4 + 5 = 9 so 40 + 50 = 90. Discuss alternative strategies for finding answers, such as counting on from the larger number in tens, or using a number line.

A Lesson for Every Day
Maths
6–7 Years
© A&C Black

Four in a line

• Play this game with a partner.

☆ Take turns to roll the dice and move your counter around the path.

☆ Answer the question and find the answer on a flower.

☆ If it is not coloured, shade it in your colour.

☆ The first player to colour four flowers in a line is the winner.

You need a dice and a different-coloured pencil and counter each.

Start →	Double 15	Halve 4	Double 5	Double 7	Double 20	Double 2

Flowers (grid):

Row 1: 11, 4, 34, 22, 13

Row 2: 20, 17, 2, 16, 28

Row 3: 10, 8, 6, 40, 18

Row 4: 9, 14, 3, 30, 38

Row 5: 24, 15, 36, 5, 32

Left column (top to bottom): Double 17, Double 19, Halve 34, Double 12, Double 3, Halve 30, Double 11, Halve 36

Right column (top to bottom): Halve 6, Double 14, Double 10, Halve 10, Halve 12, Double 18, Halve 16, Halve 32

Bottom row (left to right): Halve 26, Double 8, Double 9, Halve 22, Halve 18, Double 16, Halve 20

Teachers' note Tell the children that the lines can be vertical, horizontal or diagonal. At the start of the lesson revise doubles of all whole numbers to 20 and their corresponding halves. Provide the children with practical equipment if necessary. As an extension activity, ask the children to write twenty doubles facts and twenty halving facts.

A Lesson for Every Day
Maths
6–7 Years
© A&C Black

Animal races

Each row contains multiples of either 2, 5 or 10.

• Colour the odd one out in each row.

A Lesson for Every Day
Maths
6-7 Years
© A&C Black

NOW TRY THIS!

• Put a circle around multiples of 2,
a square around multiples of 5 and
a triangle around multiples of 10.

| 5 | 6 | 7 | 8 | 9 | 10 | 11 | 12 |
| 13 | 14 | 15 | 16 | 17 | 18 | 19 | 20 |

eachers' note For the extension activity ensure that the children realise that some numbers will
ave more than one shape around it.

Fact file

Name _____

My age _____

My favourite even number _____

My favourite odd number _____

Number of:

    letters in my first name _____

    letters in my last name _____

Number of:

    people in my family _____

    children in our class _____

    tables in our classroom _____

• **Now answer these using the numbers in your fact file.**

Double my age. _____   Add 10 to my age. _____

Halve my favourite even number. _____

Double my favourite odd number. _____

Add the number of letters in my first name to the number of letters in my last name. _____

Subtract the number in my family from 50. _____

Double the number in my family. _____

Add 25 to the number in our class. _____

Subtract 10 from the number in our class. _____

Double the number of tables in our class. _____

NOW TRY THIS!

• **Make up ten more questions using the numbers in your fact file and answer them.**

Teachers' note Before starting the lesson, discuss the usefulness of estimating answers before carrying out a calculation. Help the children to fill in their fact file, encouraging them to estimate the number of tables and children in the class before counting to check. Some children may require assistance in reading the questions.

A Lesson for Every Day
Maths
6–7 Years
© A&C Black

Crazy colours

You need coloured pencils for this activity.

Tick red: any cubes

Tick blue: any shape with a circular face

Tick green: shapes that have triangular faces

Tick yellow: shapes that have no flat faces

Tick pink: any shapes with only rectangular faces

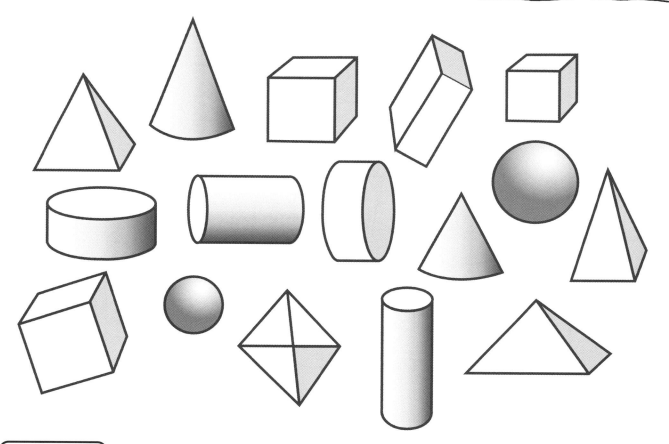

NOW TRY THIS!

- **Draw a ring around any shapes above that have 8 corners.**

Teachers' note Ensure that the children have coloured pencils to match the colours shown. (These can be altered before copying.) Provide the children with matching solid shapes to enable them to count and examine the properties.

A Lesson for Every Day
Maths
6-7 Years
© A&C Black

Solids speedway!

- Play this game with a partner. You need a dice and a counter each.

Start →

Player 1

cone	cube	sphere
cylinder	cuboid	square-based pyramid

Number of faces

1	2	3	5	5	6

Number of corners

0	0	1	5	6	8

Player 2

cone	cube	sphere
cylinder	cuboid	square-based pyramid

1	2	3	5	5	6

0	0	1	5	6	8

Teachers' note The children take turns to roll the dice and move the counter. The shape landed on should be named and examined for number of faces and vertices (corners). The children should colour any names and numbers that they can in the centre. The game ends after a given number of laps. The winner is the player with the most coloured at the end of the game.

A Lesson for Every Day
Maths
6-7 Years
© A&C Black

- **Work with a partner.**
- **Read through the questions and choose one of them to work with.**
- **You need a copy of 'Someone said: 2'.**

Someone said that children in our class have at least one pet.

Is this true?

Someone said that children in our class go to bed by 8 o'clock.

Is this true?

Someone said that most children in our class have at least one brother.

Is this true?

Someone said that most children in our class have cereal for breakfast.

Is this true?

Someone said that most children in our class come to school by car.

Is this true?

Someone said that most children in our class have fewer than 7 letters in their first name.

Is this true?

NOW TRY THIS!

- **Cut out your chosen question and stick it onto the 'Someone said: 2' activity sheet.**

Teachers' note This activity should be done in pairs. The children should choose a question from this sheet and stick it on to 'Someone said: 2'. They should then plan how they would go about answering the question. The focus should be on planning the investigation and time should be spent discussing all the children's work.

A Lesson for Every Day
Maths
6–7 Years
© A&C Black

Someone said: 2

- **Write your names.**

  _____

  _____

- **Show how you could find out if your statement is true.**

Stick your chosen question here

What information we need.

_____

_____

How we would collect it.

_____

_____

_____

_____

What we think we will find and why.

_____

_____

_____

How we would show the information.

_____

_____

_____

Teachers' note Use in conjunction with 'Someone said: 1'.

A Lesson for Every Day
Maths
6–7 Years
© A&C Black

Hold it!

• James is holding a |coin| in each hand. The coins are different and less than |£1|.

• What |coins| could he have?

• Show all the different ways below.

Ip and 2p

NOW TRY THIS!

James's two coins are |silver| coins.

• |Circle| the answers above that have only silver coins.

The total of the coins is between 20p and 40p.

• Write which coin you can be certain that

James is holding. _____

Teachers' note Encourage the children to discuss the possibilities and to work systematically, for example finding all the possibilities if one coin is a 1p, then a 2p etc. The extension activity could be changed before copying to provide variation and differentiation, for example saying that James's coins were bronze and silver and their total between 10p and 20p.

A Lesson for Every Day
Maths
6-7 Years
© A&C Black

- **Look at the picture on 'The vet: 2'.**
- **Which pets are waiting to see the vet?**
- **Make a list of the numbers of different pets.**

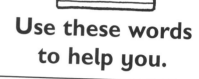

Use these words to help you.

cats

rabbits

dogs

hamsters

snake

parrots

tortoise

———————————

———————————

———————————

———————————

———————————

———————————

- **How many pets are waiting to see the vet?** ☐

NOW TRY THIS!

- **Think of some other pets to add to the list.**
- **Draw them in the picture.**

Teachers' note The children will need a copy of 'The vet: 2'. Let the children choose whether they write the words or draw pictures of the animals at the vets. During the plenary ask those that did the extension activity to share their work. As a further extension, ask the children questions that involve finding simple totals and differences.

A Lesson for Every Day
Maths
6–7 Years
© A&C Black

The vet: 2

Teachers' note Use this sheet in conjunction with 'The vet: 1'.

A Lesson for Every Day
Maths
6-7 Years
© A&C Black

111

Bird spotting

This table shows the birds Tim and his friends saw in the woods.

Robin	Sparrow	Blue-tit	Dove	Blackbird
Tim	Billy	Tim	Sally	Trixie
Billy	Pete	Pete	Tim	Tim
Sally	Tim	Sally	Pete	Susie
Trixie			Susie	

1 Who saw all the birds? _____

2 Who saw the fewest birds? _____

3 How many saw a dove? _____

4 Who saw a blue-tit? _____

5 Who saw a robin but not a sparrow? _____

6 Who saw a robin and a blackbird? _____

7 Who saw a robin and a dove but not a blackbird? _____

NOW TRY THIS!

- **Make up some more questions like these to ask a partner.**

112

Teachers' note Encourage the children to make marks on the data to help them answer the questions, for example by crossing out names or putting ticks. To simplify, edit this page to eliminate the last question and add a simpler one, such as 'How many saw a robin?' To extend the activity, edit the page so that there are more questions similar to the last one.

A Lesson for Every Day
Maths
6-7 Years
© A&C Black

In the fridge

What is in Danni's fridge?
- **Complete this** table .

Things in the fridge	How many

- **Make a** list **of the things you think you have in your fridge at home.**

Teachers' note The children should write the names of the food items in the table. They can illustrate with pictures if they wish. Once they have done this they count the number of each item and add that to the appropriate column.

A Lesson for Every Day
Maths
6–7 Years
© A&C Black

Longer or shorter?

You need your ruler.

- Find $\boxed{10}$ objects in your classroom.
- Make lists of the objects that are $\boxed{\text{shorter}}$ or $\boxed{\text{longer}}$ than your ruler.

Longer than my ruler

Shorter than my ruler

NOW TRY THIS!

- Find more objects so that you have the same number of objects in each list.

Teachers' note The children should find a variety of items and write the names of the objects, draw them or do both in the space provided. To extend the activity, ask them to find and list 10 items that are longer than their ruler. For the extension activity, encourage the children to be as accurate as they can, measuring to the nearest centimetre if possible.

A Lesson for Every Day
Maths
6-7 Years
© A&C Black

Dice

You need a dice.

- **Throw the dice 12 times.**
- **Make a list of the numbers you threw.**

Numbers I threw

Which number did you throw most often ?

Was there a number that you did not throw?

Write down the odd numbers in your list.

Write down the multiples of 2.

What is the highest total you can make when you add 2 of your numbers?

Which of your numbers make 10 when you add them?

NOW TRY THIS!

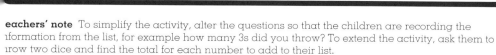

- **Think of 5 more questions to ask.**
- **Now answer them!**

eachers' note To simplify the activity, alter the questions so that the children are recording the information from the list, for example how many 3s did you throw? To extend the activity, ask them to irow two dice and find the total for each number to add to their list.

A Lesson for Every Day
Maths
6–7 Years
© A&C Black

The metre beater game

- ## Play this game with a partner.

> You need some counters.

☆ Cut out the cards and place them face down on the table.

☆ Each player picks a card. If the length on the card is longer than a metre the player collects a counter.

☆ Also, the player that has the longer length of the two collects a counter.

☆ Put the cards to one side and pick 2 new cards.

☆ Continue playing until all the cards have been used.

1 metre	20 centimetres	150 centimetres
1 metre and 10 centimetres	80 centimetres	99 centimetres
1 metre and 5 centimetres	60 centimetres	110 centimetres
1 metre and 30 centimetres	40 centimetres	120 centimetres
2 metres	6 centimetres	300 centimetres
1 metre and 99 centimetres	9 centimetres	87 centimetres
4 metres	50 centimetres	199 centimetres
2 metres and 50 centimetres	66 centimetres	180 centimetres

Teachers' note These cards can be used for a range of comparing activities, such as the following: individual children can pick two cards, say which is longer and record them using the < or > signs; pairs of children can pick a card and then use rulers and a metre stick to draw that length along the playground in chalk. Further ideas can be found on the notes on the activity on page 14.

A Lesson for Every Day
Maths
6-7 Years
© A&C Black

Doggy differences

• **Cut out these cards and work with a partner.**

Jack Russell	Chihuahua	Yorkshire Terrier	Corgi
5 kg	2 kg	3 kg	11 kg
St Bernard	**Dachshund**	**Border Collie**	**Great Dane**
80 kg	9 kg	18 kg	52 kg
Labrador Retriever	**Boxer**	**German Shepherd**	**Cocker Spaniel**
30 kg	32 kg	38 kg	12 kg
Scottish Terrier	**Miniature Poodle**	**Irish Wolfhound**	**Pug**
8 kg	7 kg	50 kg	6 kg

Teachers' note Children can play a simple game in pairs, where they place the cards face down and pick one each. The difference between the two weights can be found and the player with the larger weight wins the cards. Alternatively, the cards can be used in conjunction with the following sheet and some kilogram weights.

A Lesson for Every Day
Maths
6–7 Years
© A&C Black

Doggy dilemmas

- **You need the cards from the 'Doggy differences' sheet. This is a kilogram weight.**
- **Use the cards to help you work out which scales will balance. Tick or cross to show whether they balance.**

NOW TRY THIS!

- **Use the cards to find more sets that balance.**
- **Draw two of them on the back of this sheet.**

Teachers' note Encourage the children to use the cards to find the weights and to work out which balance. Provide kilogram weights so that the children can feel how heavy some of the smaller dogs are and find items in the classroom that are about the same weight as some of the dogs.

A Lesson for Every Day
Maths
6–7 Years
© A&C Black

Litre checker

• Tick whether each container in real life holds
$\boxed{\text{more}}$ **or** $\boxed{\text{less}}$ **than 1 litre.**

☑ more than 1 litre

☐ less than 1 litre

☐ more than 1 litre

☐ less than 1 litre

☐ more than 1 litre

☐ less than 1 litre

☐ more than 1 litre

☐ less than 1 litre

☐ more than 1 litre

☐ less than 1 litre

☐ more than 1 litre

☐ less than 1 litre

☐ more than 1 litre

☐ less than 1 litre

☐ more than 1 litre

☐ less than 1 litre

NOW TRY THIS!

• Draw pictures of other items that, in real life, hold: more than 1 kilogram

less than 1 kilogram

Teachers' note Ensure that children are introduced to 1-litre containers and that they begin to appreciate their size. Support this activity with practical measuring using sand or water containers.

A Lesson for Every Day
Maths
6-7 Years
© A&C Black

Scale trail

• **You need a counter for this activity.**

☆ Place your counter on the trail under A, B or C.

☆ Read the scale and move your counter on one place for each kilogram, for example for 3 kg move on 3 places.

☆ Read the new scale and keep moving in the same way.

☆ Which prize will you win for each starting position?

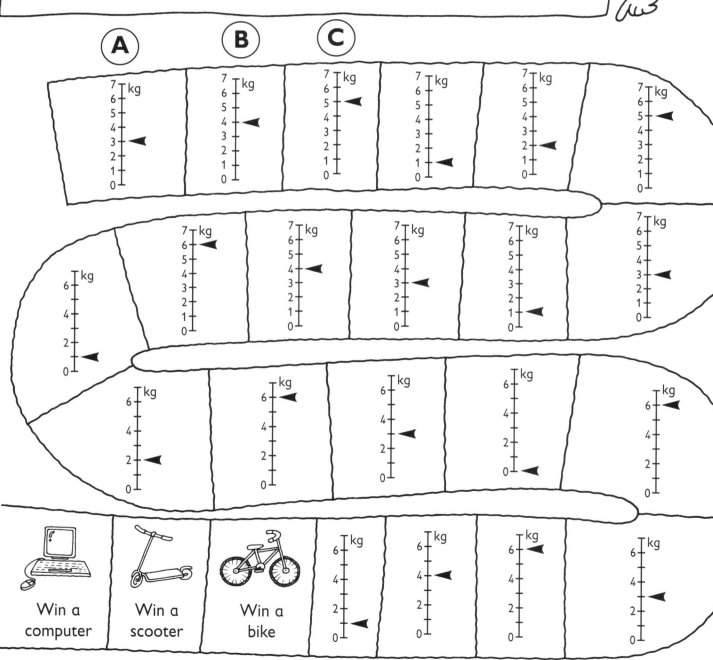

Teachers' note Note that the later scales are numbered in twos, with intermediate points unnumbered.

A Lesson for Every Day
Maths
6–7 Years
© A&C Black

T-shirt printer

There are 3 **types of T-shirts:**

round-necked	v-necked	straight-necked

There are 4 **pictures that can be printed onto the T-shirts.**

face	apple	bird	car

- **How many different T-shirts can be printed?**
- **Show your solutions here.**

NOW TRY THIS!

- **Draw a table to check that you have found all the solutions.**

Teachers' note Encourage the children to make their own decisions about how to list or draw the solutions. For the extension activity, demonstrate how a table could be drawn with three columns (one for each T-shirt type) and 4 rows (one for each picture). Encourage the children to notice how a table can be very useful in making sure that none are missed.

A Lesson for Every Day
Maths
6–7 Years
© A&C Black

Unusual pets

The people in the Animal Club have some unusual pets.

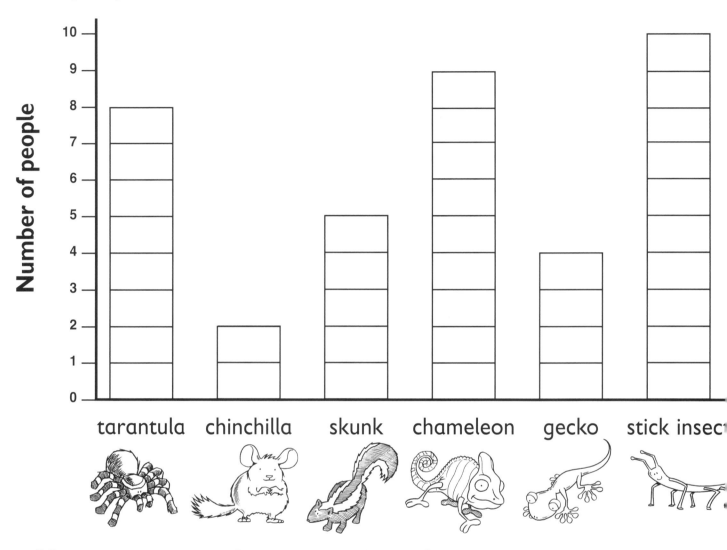

- **How many people own each pet?**

  tarantula _____ chinchilla _____ skunk _____

  chameleon _____ gecko _____ stick insect _____

- **How many people are in the Animal Club?** _____

NOW TRY THIS!

- **Make up some more questions to ask your partner.**

Teachers' note To simplify, encourage the children to put a ruler on top of each block to line up with the vertical axis. For the extension activity, ask them to make up questions that include finding totals and differences. During the plenary invite children to ask their questions for the class to answer.

A Lesson for Every Day
Maths
6–7 Years
© A&C Black

Chocolate bars

Mr Sweetiman can only stock 4 types of chocolate bar. This block graph shows which bars his friends like best.

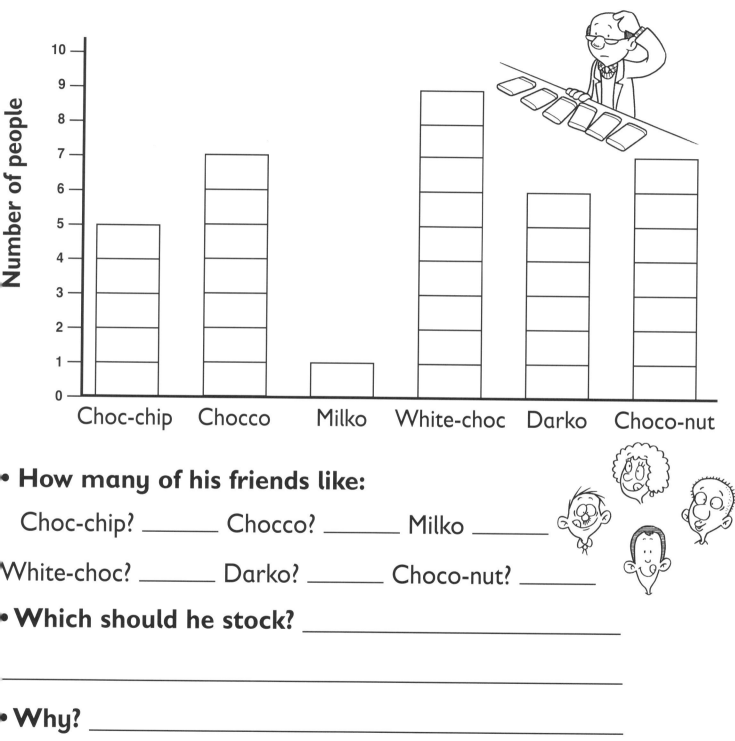

- **How many of his friends like:**

  Choc-chip? _____ Chocco? _____ Milko _____

  White-choc? _____ Darko? _____ Choco-nut? _____

- **Which should he stock?** _____

  _____

- **Why?** _____

  _____

Teachers' note Set the scene by telling the children that Mr Sweetiman owns a newsagents and needs to order some stock. As an extension activity, children could do a group or class survey to find out which chocolate their friends like best and then make a block graph to show the information. During the plenary share the children's graphs and ask questions from them.

A Lesson for Every Day
Maths
6–7 Years
© A&C Black

Celebrations

The tally chart shows
the cards Lily has to buy.

• Use the tally chart to draw
  a block graph .

Birthday ⦀⦀ ////

Wedding ////

Birth of baby //

Passing driving test ////

0

| Birthday | | | |

Teachers' note Ensure the children know how much the tallies are worth. You could demonstrate tallying by going round the class and asking the children to say what month their birthday is in. Ensure that children write the numbers beside the lines on the vertical axis and not between them. To simplify the activity, add the labels and numbers to the graph before copying.

A Lesson for Every Day
Maths
6-7 Years
© A&C Black

Favourite circus acts

The ⬚table⬚ shows the clowns' favourite acts.

• **Show the information in a** ⬚block graph⬚.

Circus acts	Number of clowns
High wire	10
Juggling	5
Trapeze	8
Tumbling	7
Unicycle	6
Acrobats	4

High wire

NOW TRY THIS!

• **Ask your friends what circus acts they would most like to see.**
• **Make a block graph to show what they say.**

Teachers' note To simplify, add the labels and numbers with the children. To extend, encourage the children to label alternate intervals. As a further extension, encourage the children to make a list of their own circus acts and ask the whole class for one favourite or a few children for two or three choices.

A Lesson for Every Day
Maths
6–7 Years
© A&C Black

Clothes: 1

- **Cut the cards from 'Clothes: 2'.**
- **Sort the clothes into two piles.**
- **Write a label for each set.**

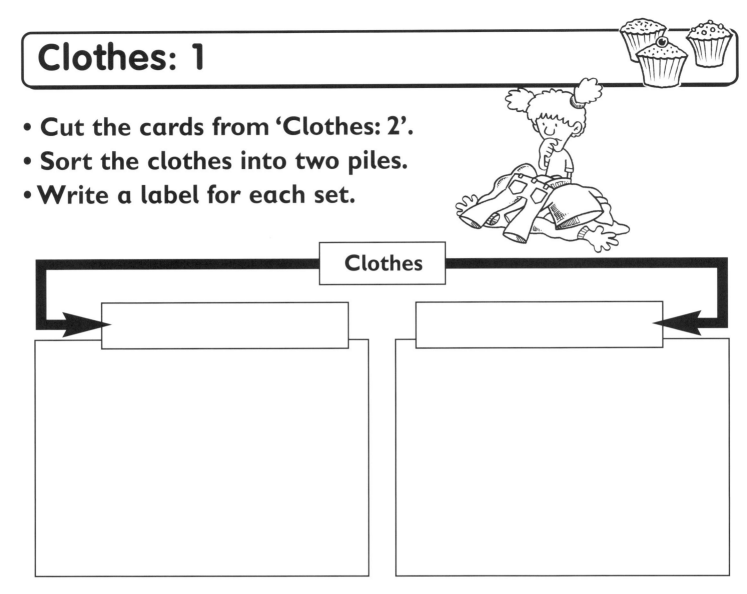

Clothes

- **Think of another way to sort the clothes.**

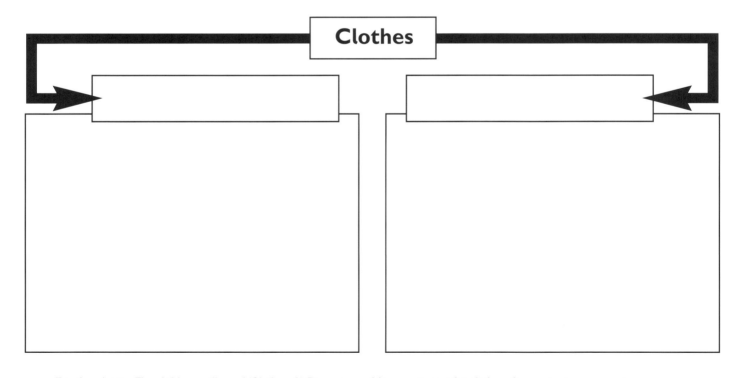

Clothes

Teachers' note The children will need 'Clothes: 2'. Discuss possible ways to sort the clothes; the most obvious would be those to wear in cold weather and those to wear in hot. As an extension activity, ask the children to think about ways of sorting each of the two sets into two further sets, for example footwear and body wear.

A Lesson for Every Day
Maths
6–7 Years
© **A&C Black**

Clothes: 2

• ## Cut out the cards.

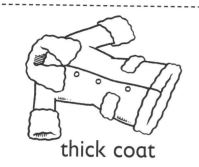

thick coat

thick jumper

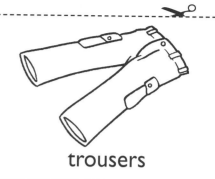

trousers

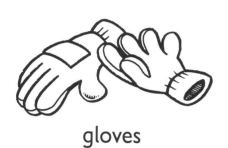

gloves

scarf

wellington boots

shorts

summer dress

sandals

flip-flops

swimsuit

T-shirt

sun hat

woolly hat

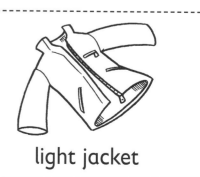

light jacket

eachers' note Use this sheet in conjunction with 'Clothes: 1'. You may wish to colour and laminate
1ese cards to make a more permanent resource.

A Lesson for Every Day
Maths
6-7 Years
© A&C Black

Crunchy carrots

- ## **Play this game with a partner.**

☆ Take turns to choose a carrot.

☆ Estimate its length in centimetres. Your partner checks your estimate by measuring the carrot with a ruler.

☆ Score 2 points if you are exactly right and 1 point if your estimate was only 1 centimetre away.

☆ The winner is the player with the highest score at the end.

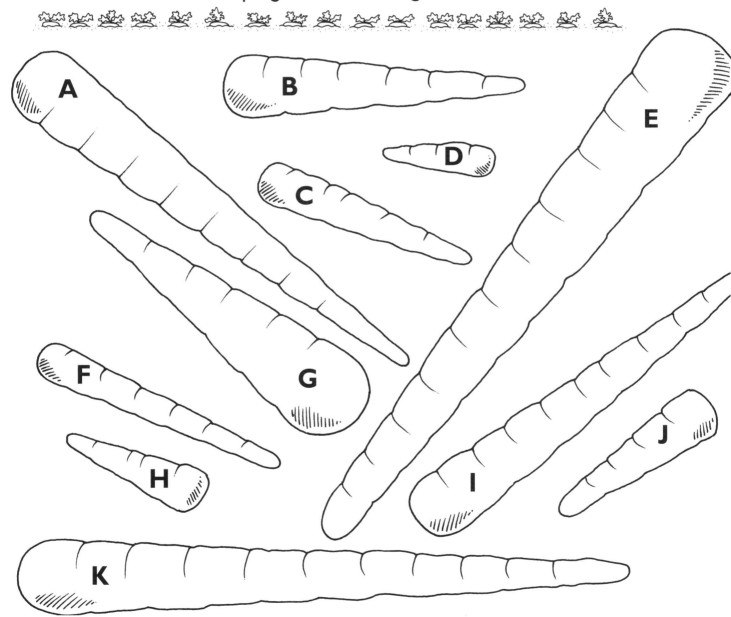

Teachers' note Ask the children to record the letter of the carrot, the estimate and the actual length. This could be drawn as a table on the board at the start of the lesson for them to copy and complete. As an extension activity, the children could be asked to list the carrots in order of size, starting with the smallest.

A Lesson for Every Day
Maths
6–7 Years
© A&C Black

Marble mania

A small marble weighs 5 g

A large marble weighs 50 g

A glass jar weighs 500 g

Write the total weight of the items on each card.

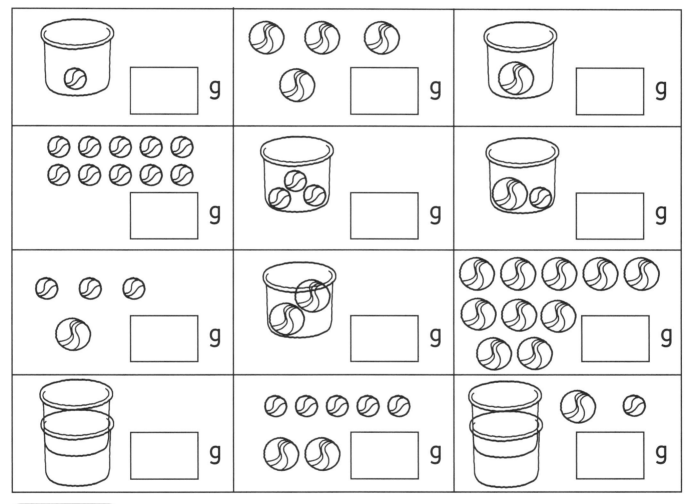

NOW TRY THIS!

- Cut out the cards and put them in order of weight, starting with the lightest.
- Which are lighter than half a kilogram?
- Which are heavier than half a kilogram?

eachers' note Invite the children to say which picture shows a weight greater than one kilogram nd ask them to write the amount in different ways, such as in kilograms and grams or just in grams. ncourage the children to weigh objects such as marbles practically to reinforce this activity.

A Lesson for Every Day
Maths
6–7 Years
© A&C Black

Monster weights

• **Read the scales to find the weight of each monster.**

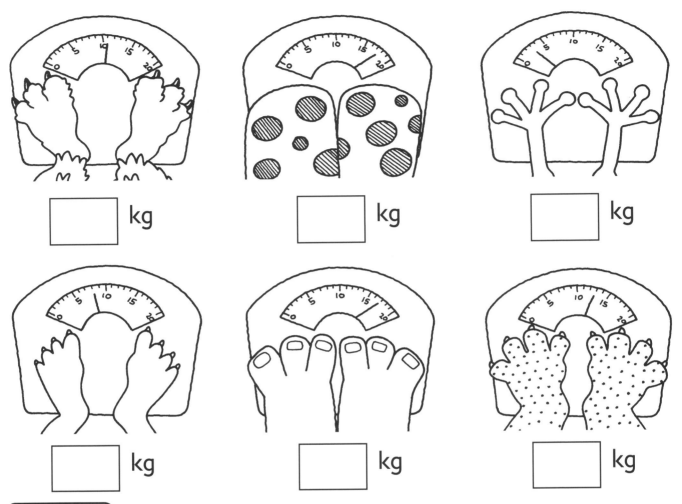

☐ kg   ☐ kg   ☐ kg

☐ kg   ☐ kg   ☐ kg

NOW TRY THIS!

• **Draw arrows on these scales to show the weight of each monster.**

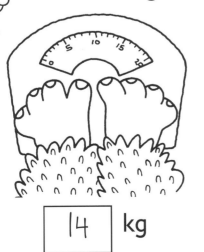 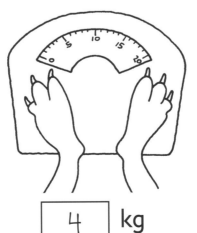 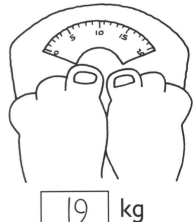

14 kg   4 kg   19 kg

Teachers' note Ask the children to say which monster is the heaviest and which is the lightest. Encourage them to describe how they worked out how heavy each monster was using the scale. The arrows on the scales could be changed to create variety.

A Lesson for Every Day
Maths
6-7 Years
© A&C Black

Spaghetti spikes

- **Use a ruler to measure the lengths of uncooked spaghetti in centimetres.**

Spaghetti

◻ cm

◻ cm

◻ cm

◻ cm

◻ cm

◻ cm

NOW TRY THIS!

- **Use some string to measure the lengths of these pieces of cooked spaghetti.**

◻ cm

◻ cm

◻ cm

eachers' note For the extension activity demonstrate how to place string along the line and then ark the string at the end before placing along a ruler, pulled tight. Children can then work in pairs hen measuring with string. Discuss the children's answers to see who was most accurate.

A Lesson for Every Day
Maths
6–7 Years
© A&C Black

Let's measure: 1

- **Work with a partner.**
- **Read through the questions and choose one of them to work with.**
- **You need a copy of 'Let's measure: 2'.**

Someone said that children in our class are over 130 cm tall.

Is this true?

Someone said that children in our class have feet that are less than 20 cm long.

Is this true?

Someone said that each shoe owned by children in our class weighs less than 1 kg.

Is this true?

Someone said that our teacher's mug holds less than 500 ml.

Is this true?

Someone said that the length of our classroom is about 4 metres.

Is this true?

Someone said that, in our class, the distance around each child's head is more than 35 cm.

Is this true?

NOW TRY THIS!

- **Cut out your chosen question and stick it onto the 'Let's measure: 2' sheet.**

Teachers' note This activity should be done in pairs. The children should choose a question from this sheet and stick it onto 'Let's measure: 2'. They should then plan how they would go about answering the question. The focus should be on planning the measuring and deciding what equipment to use and time should be spent discussing all the children's work.

A Lesson for Every Day
Maths
6–7 Years
© A&C Black

Let's measure: 2

• **Write your names.**

_____

_____

• **Show how you could find out if your statement is true.**

Stick your chosen question here.

What information we need.

_____

_____

What equipment we need.

_____

_____

How we would measure.

_____

_____

What we think we will find and why.

_____

_____

_____

How we would show the information.

_____

_____

A Lesson for Every Day
Maths
6–7 Years
© A&C Black

133

Wheels

Mr Carr recorded the vehicles he saw on Monday morning. He wants his village to win an award for the least amount of traffic.

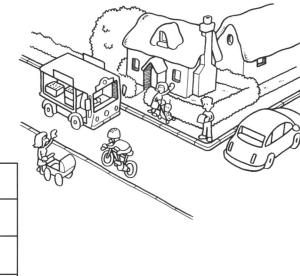

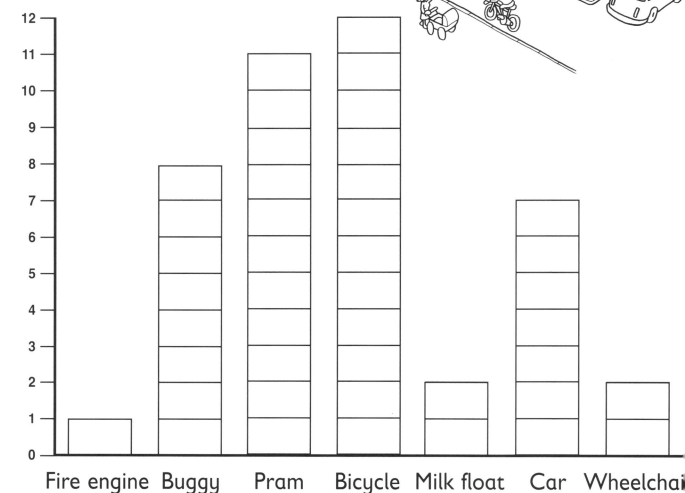

- **How many vehicles did he see?**

Fire engine _____ Milk float _____ Pram _____

Car _____ Bicycle _____ Wheelchair _____ Buggy _____

- **Do you think his village might win the award?** _____

- **Why or why not?** _____

134

A Lesson for Every Day
Maths
6-7 Years
© A&C Black

Macy and her kittens

Ben wants to know how many tins of cat food
to buy for his cat Macy and her four kittens.
• Use the ⎡pictogram⎤ to find out.

 = 1 tin

	Number of tins
Sunday	🥫 🥫 🥫 🥫 🥫 🥫 🥫 🥫
Monday	🥫 🥫 🥫 🥫 🥫 🥫 🥫
Tuesday	🥫 🥫 🥫 🥫 🥫 🥫 🥫 🥫
Wednesday	🥫 🥫 🥫 🥫 🥫 🥫 🥫
Thursday	🥫 🥫 🥫 🥫 🥫 🥫
Friday	🥫 🥫 🥫 🥫 🥫
Saturday	🥫 🥫 🥫 🥫 🥫 🥫 🥫

Number of tins

• **How many tins of cat food did the cats eat on:**

Sunday _____   Monday _____   Tuesday _____   Wednesday _____

Thursday _____   Friday _____   Saturday _____

• **How many tins should Ben buy this week?** _____

Teachers' note Tell the children that this is a pictogram which shows how many tins of cat food
Macy and her kittens ate last week. As an extension activity, ask the children how many tins of cat
food Ben would need to buy each week if he had to buy 1 more tin each day.

A Lesson for Every Day
Maths
6–7 Years
© A&C Black

In the garden

Adam has been planting flowers in the garden.

His mum wants to know how many of each he has planted.

- Make a ⬚pictogram⬚ to show her.

Tulip 10 Daffodil 19 Crocus 12 Snowdrop 16 Bluebell 8 Pansy 14

❀ = 1 flower

Tulip	Daffodil	Crocus	Snowdrop	Bluebell	Pansy

NOW TRY THIS!

- **Write 5 things that the pictogram shows you.**

_____

_____

Teachers' note To simplify, reduce the number of plants to a maximum of 10. To extend, increase the number of plants to 30 and encourage the children to use a bee symbol to represent two plants. For the extension activity, ask the children to make statements that involve more than simply reading the numbers of flowers. They could do this orally to an adult to scribe, or in writing.

A Lesson for Every Day
Maths
6–7 Years
© A&C Black

Goal!

The list shows goals scored so far in The Planet league.

• Draw a pictogram of the information.

| Mars: 8 |
| Jupiter: 12 |
| Saturn: 18 |
| Pluto: 3 |
| Mecury: 8 |
| Venus: 15 |

 = 1 goal

Mars	
Jupiter	
Saturn	
Pluto	
Mercury	
Venus	⚽⚽⚽⚽⚽⚽⚽⚽⚽⚽⚽⚽⚽⚽⚽

Goals scored

The team who scores the most wins the cup.

• Who will win the cup?_____

• Who needs to practise more?_____

NOW TRY THIS! Craig scored half of Saturn's goals.

• How many did he score? _____

Teachers' note To simplify, reduce the number of goals scored to a maximum of 10. To extend, increase the number of goals to 30.

A Lesson for Every Day
Maths
6-7 Years
© A&C Black

Multiples

- **Look at these numbers.**
- **List the numbers that are** $\boxed{\text{multiples of 5}}$ **and those that are** $\boxed{\text{not}}$ **a multiple of 5.**

| 12 | 3 | 15 | 10 | 45 | 6 | 44 | 5 |
| 25 | 18 | 30 | 32 | 40 | 21 | 20 | 50 |

Is a multiple of 5

Is not a multiple of 5

- **Think of another way to sort these numbers and make a new list.**

Teachers' note Encourage the children to cross out the numbers as they add them to their list. To simplify the activity, delete some of the numbers. To extend, add extra numbers to 100.

A Lesson for Every Day
Maths
6-7 Years
© A&C Black

Numbers

Katie sorted some numbers into 2 hula hoops.

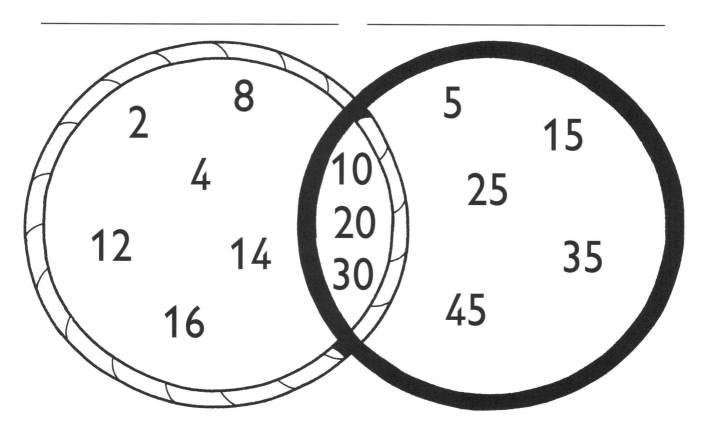

2   8   4   12   14   16

10   20   30

5   15   25   35   45

1 What types of number are inside the stripy hoop?

_____

2 What types of number are inside the black hoop?

_____

3 What types of number are in the overlap of the hoops?

4 Write a label for each hoop. _____

NOW TRY THIS!

• Add 2 more numbers to each part of the diagram.

Teachers' note To simplify the activity, reduce the numbers to: 2, 4, 6 and 8 in the left-hand part of the stripy hoop; 10 and 20 in the intersection; 15, 25 and 35 in the right-hand part of the black hoop. For the extension activity, encourage the children to go through the multiples of 2, 5 and 10 to help work out which numbers go where.

A Lesson for Every Day
Maths
6-7 Years
© A&C Black

Pets: 1

You need the worksheet 'Pets: 2'.
- Look at the pictures of the children.
- Write their names in the correct places on the diagram.

Has a pet	Has not got a pet
_____ _____	_____ _____
_____ _____	_____ _____
_____ _____	_____ _____
_____ _____	_____ _____
_____ _____	_____ _____
_____ _____	_____ _____
_____ _____	_____ _____
_____ _____	_____ _____

1 How many children have a pet? _____

2 How many children do not have a pet? _____

NOW TRY THIS!
- **Who has a pet in your class?**
- **Draw a diagram to show what you find out.**

Teachers' note The children will need 'Pets: 2'. As a further extension activity, different groups of children could ask different classes and then display their diagrams for the school to see.

A Lesson for Every Day
Maths
6–7 Years
© A&C Black

Pets: 2

A Lesson for Every Day
Maths
6–7 Years
© A&C Black

Teachers' note Use this sheet in conjunction with 'Pets: 1'.

Toys

Sally and Steve were sorting their toys.
This is how they did it.

	Has blue eyes	Does not have blue eyes
Has blonde hair		
Does not have blonde hair		

1 How many toys do Sally and Steve have?_____

2 How many toys have:

(a) Blue eyes and blonde hair?_____

(b) Not blue eyes and not blonde hair?_____

(c) Blonde hair but not blue eyes? _____

(d) Blue eyes but not blonde hair? _____

NOW TRY THIS!

• **Draw a different diagram about Sally and Steve's toys.**

Teachers' note For the extension activity, the children should draw their own diagram on plain paper and sort the toys out again according to their own criteria. Encourage them to cross out the pictures in this diagram as they work.

A Lesson for Every Day
Maths
6-7 Years
© A&C Black

Right angles: 1

- **You need the cards from 'Right angles: 2'.**
- **Arrange the cards in the diagram.**

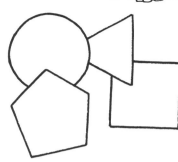

	Has one right angle or more	Has no right angle
Has one curved side or more		
Has no curved side		

1 How many shapes have right angles? _____

2 How many of your shapes have only straight sides? _____

NOW TRY THIS!

- **Use the shapes to make up another diagram with different headings.**

eachers' note Enlarge the sheet to A3. Children need the shape cards from 'Right angles: 2'.
Children arrange the cards in the diagram and then stick them in place. For the extension activity,
he children use the cards to make up another Carroll diagram with different criteria.

A Lesson for Every Day
Maths
6-7 Years
© A&C Black

• **Cut out the cards.**

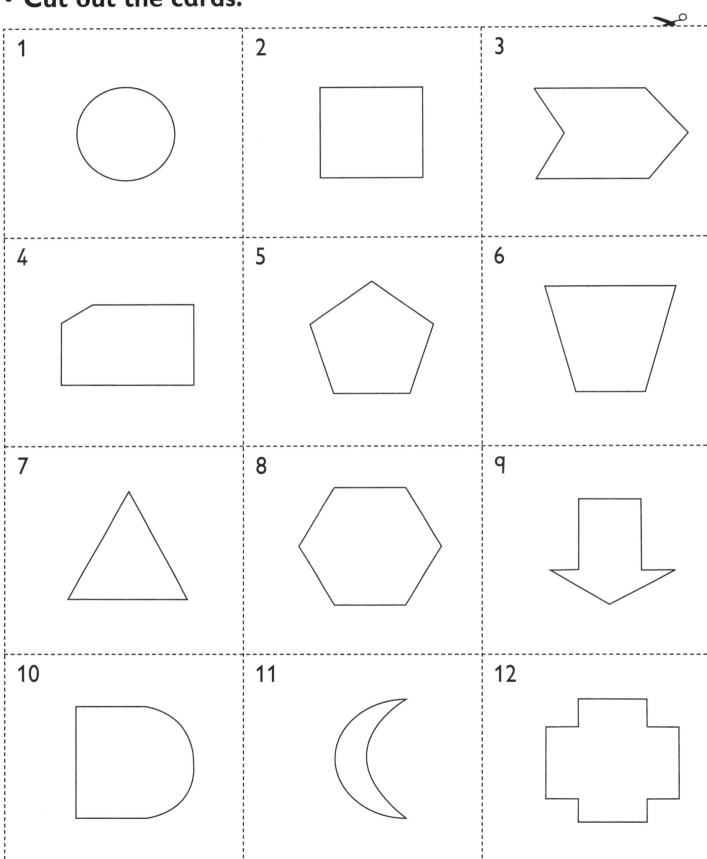

Teachers' note Use this sheet in conjunction with 'Right angles: 1'. You could laminate the cards to make a more durable resource.

A Lesson for Every Day
Maths
6–7 Years
© A&C Black

Going to great lengths

- You can use centimetres or metres to measure these things. Write which is best.

1. length of a lorry

metres
_____

2. width of a butterfly
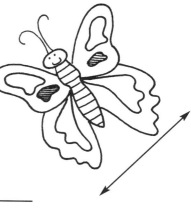
_____

3. length of a rabbit

_____

4. height of a house

_____

5. width of a laptop

_____

6. depth of a bucket
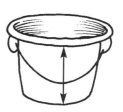
_____

7. length of the school hall

_____

8. height of a lamp post
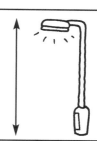
_____

9. thickness of a book

_____

10. distance from our playground to the school hall

_____

NOW TRY THIS!

- **Draw 4 other things you would measure in metres or centimetres.**

Teachers' note Encourage the children to realise that the words 'length', 'width', 'height', 'depth', 'thickness' and 'distance' all refer to types of length that can be measured in centimetres or metres.

A Lesson for Every Day
Maths
6-7 Years
© A&C Black

145

Deep water

- **Colour to show the correct amount of water in each bucket.**

A

just over 1 litre

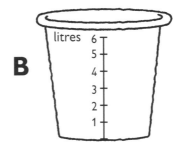

B

about 3 litres

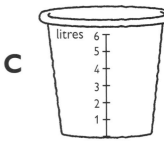

C

nearly 5 litres

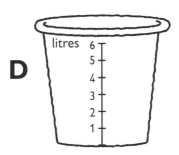

D

just less than 6 litres

E

just under 4 litres

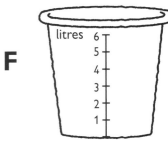

F

about half a litre

G

2 and a bit litres

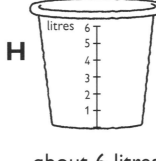

H

about 6 litres

I

just over 3 litres

NOW TRY THIS!

- **Which bucket is holding the most water?** _____
- **Which bucket is holding the least water?** _____

Teachers' note Ensure that the children are introduced to 1-litre containers and that they begin to appreciate their size. Support this activity with practical measuring using sand or water containers.

A Lesson for Every Day
Maths
6-7 Years
© A&C Black

Rick's restaurant

Rick is preparing tables in his restaurant.
What calculations are needed?
- Write the calculation and the answer.

1 There are 12 tables in Rick's restaurant. Tonight 7 tables are booked. How many are not booked?

$$12 - 7 = 5$$

2 Tonight, 8 couples are booked to come to the restaurant. How many people is this?

3 There are 4 places on Table 1. Rick puts 2 forks at every place. How many forks does he need?

4 There are 2 places on Table 2. He puts 6 bread rolls on the table. How many rolls per person?

5 On Table 3, Rick puts 2 knives at every place. He puts out 8 knives. How many places is this?

6 On Table 4, Rick puts 20 flowers. There are 5 flowers for each person. How many places are there?

NOW TRY THIS!

In the restaurant, 6 tables have 2 places and 6 have 4 places. How many places altogether?

On Sunday 33 people came. This was 5 more than on Saturday. How many came over both nights in total?

achers' note The focus of this activity is to write the number sentence rather than just to find the nswer. Ensure that children understand this. Look out for children who involve the table number their answer. Such children are not correctly interpreting the questions but merely picking out mbers and performing an operation on them.

A Lesson for Every Day
Maths
6-7 Years
© A&C Black

London Eye

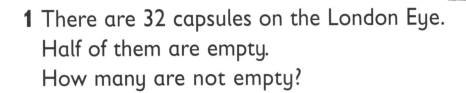

- **Solve these problems.**
- **What calculations are needed?**
- **How did you decide?**

1 There are 32 capsules on the London Eye.
Half of them are empty.
How many are not empty?

2 There were 18 people in a capsule.
9 people got out. How many people in now?

3 There were 7 people in a capsule.
16 people got in. How many people in now?

4 Capsules 1, 2, 3 and 4 each have 20 people inside.
How many people is this?

5 There were 12 people in a capsule.
9 people got out and then 15 got in.
How many people in the capsule now?

6 If it costs £8 per child, how much for 3 children?

7 Each capsule holds 25 people.
How many are needed for 75 people?

8 If it costs £16 per adult, how much for 2 adults?

NOW TRY THIS!

- **Write a** $\boxed{\text{number fact}}$ **for each question above to show what you did.**

Teachers' note Encourage the children to describe their strategies for working the answer out. Encourage them to demonstrate this in different ways, for example using practical material, number lines, a 100-square, place value cards. The numbers can be altered before copying to provide differentiation.

A Lesson for Every Day
Maths
6–7 Years
© A&C Black

Beaver away

• **Answer the questions on each pile of logs.**

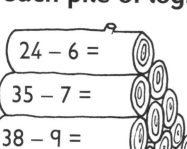

24 – 6 =	31 – 5 =	28 – 9 =
35 – 7 =	21 – 8 =	23 – 6 =
38 – 9 =	26 – 7 =	32 – 4 =
41 – 3 =	33 – 6 =	25 – 8 =
31 – 8 =	32 – 9 =	26 – 8 =
34 – 7 =	22 – 9 =	35 – 9 =

62 – 4 =	81 – 5 =	92 – 6 =
53 – 7 =	52 – 4 =	73 – 4 =
82 – 8 =	63 – 9 =	95 – 6 =
72 – 9 =	52 – 8 =	66 – 7 =
82 – 4 =	95 – 7 =	84 – 5 =
97 – 9 =	67 – 9 =	93 – 8 =

NOW TRY THIS!

• **Write five more subtraction questions with the answer** 57 .

61 – 4 = 57 _____

_____   _____

_____   _____

eachers' note These questions all involve crossing a tens boundary. Discuss strategies for solving
ie questions, such as counting back to the next multiple of 10 and then counting back the remaining
umber of places, for example 52 – 8 is the same as 52 – 2 – 6. Ensure that children know their
umber pairs with a total of 10, for example 6 and 4 to help them find 50 – 6 = 44.

A Lesson for Every Day
Maths
6-7 Years
© A&C Black

I 'eight' a cucumber

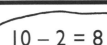

$10 - 2 = 8$	$12 - 4 = 8$	$14 - 6 = 8$	$16 - 8 = 8$
$11 - 3 = 8$	$13 - 5 = 8$	$15 - 7 = 8$	$17 - 9 = 8$

- **Colour** green **the cucumber questions that have an answer with the units (ones) digit** 8 .

$53 - 5 =$

$46 - 7 =$

$44 - 6 =$

$32 - 8 =$

$26 - 8 =$

$73 - 6 =$

$51 - 3 =$

$92 - 4 =$

$47 - 9 =$

$65 - 9 =$

$36 - 7 =$

$53 - 7 =$

$60 - 2 =$

$85 - 7 =$

$91 - 3 =$

$94 - 5 =$

$93 - 5 =$

$58 - 9 =$

$74 - 6 =$

$57 - 9 =$

$42 - 7 =$

$35 - 7 =$

NOW TRY THIS!

- **Write four more subtraction questions that have an answer with the units digit** 8 .

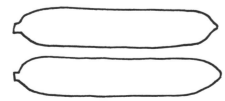

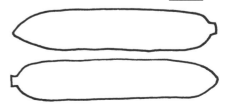

Teachers' note Encourage the children to use the number facts at the top of the page to help them spot units/ones digits that will produce a units/ones digit of 8, for example if 14 – 6 = 8, then 54 – 6 will also have the units/ones digit 8.

A Lesson for Every Day
Maths
6-7 Years
© A&C Black

Flea party

Draw lines with a ruler to join pairs of fleas together.
Measure each line to the nearest centimetre and complete the sentences.

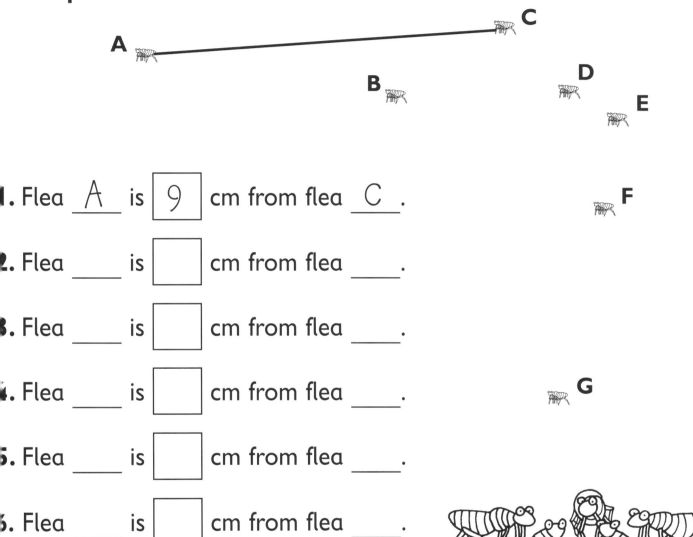

1. Flea __A__ is ⎡9⎤ cm from flea __C__ .

2. Flea ____ is ⎡ ⎤ cm from flea ____ .

3. Flea ____ is ⎡ ⎤ cm from flea ____ .

4. Flea ____ is ⎡ ⎤ cm from flea ____ .

5. Flea ____ is ⎡ ⎤ cm from flea ____ .

6. Flea ____ is ⎡ ⎤ cm from flea ____ .

7. Flea ____ is ⎡ ⎤ cm from flea ____ .

NOW TRY THIS!

• **Which 2 fleas are closest together?** _____
• **Which 2 are furthest apart?** _____

Teachers' note Ensure that children understand that they can join any two fleas and measure the distance between them with a ruler. Demonstrate how to hold the ruler and to place it so that the cm or zero mark is at the first flea. They should then read where the second flea is. Encourage them to turn the paper as appropriate.

A Lesson for Every Day
Maths
6-7 Years
© A&C Black

Frog tongues!

These frogs have long tongues for catching flies.
The length of each tongue is given in centimetres.

- Use a ruler to draw each tongue to see if the frog will reach the fly.

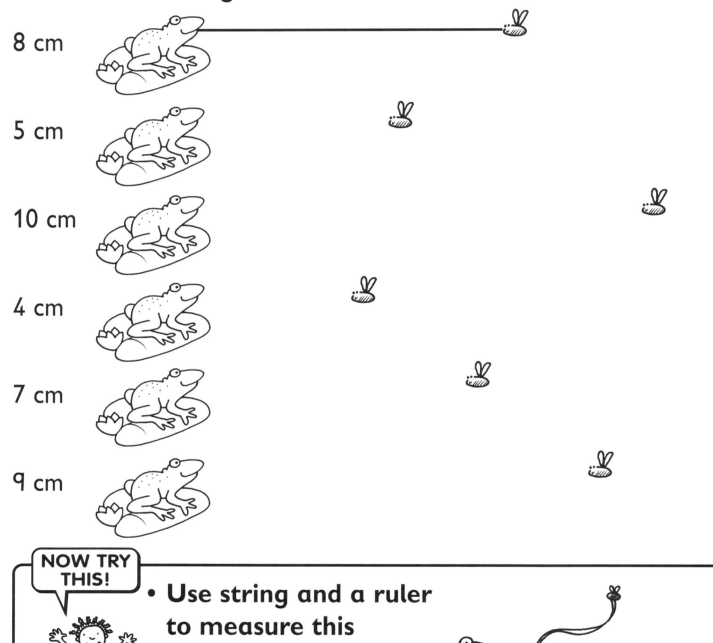

8 cm

5 cm

10 cm

4 cm

7 cm

9 cm

NOW TRY THIS!

- Use string and a ruler to measure this frog's tongue.

Teachers' note Ensure that children are not given rules (where the end of the rule is zero) but are given rulers (where the zero position is a little way along the ruler). Remind them to position the cm or zero mark on the ruler at each frog's mouth and to make a mark at the number of centimetres given, before joining the two.

A Lesson for Every Day
Maths
6-7 Years
© A&C Black

Fun time

Alfie was taken to the theme park.
Fill in the missing unit of time in each box.
Choose from: | seconds | | minutes | | hours |

1. We took the train to the theme park. It took about 1 [hour].

2. We had to queue for tickets. That took about 5 [   ].

3. I went on the Big Wheel. I was on there for about 10 [   ].

4. I fed a carrot to a horse. It ate it in about 20 [   ].

5. We had fish and chips for lunch. That took about 15 [   ].

6. We went on a boat trip for about 20 [   ].

7. Then I ate an ice cream. That took about 8 [   ].

8. We were at the theme park for about 5 [   ] altogether.

NOW TRY THIS!

• **Write some things you do that take:**

10 minutes _____

5 seconds _____

8 hours _____

eachers' note At the start of the lesson describe a visit to a theme park such as Alfie's day and iscuss how we can describe how long things take. Ask the children to say which takes longer, a ninute, an hour or a second, and invite them to say how long they think activities usually take, for xample eating breakfast, doing the register, sitting in assembly.

A Lesson for Every Day
Maths
6-7 Years
© A&C Black

Charlie and Chester

The chimps, **Charlie** and **Chester**, take different lengths of time to do the same thing.

- **Tick who takes** longer **each time.**

		Charlie	**Chester**
1. swinging in the trees		☐ 20 seconds	✔ 1 minute
2. hunting for food		☐ 1 hour	☐ 40 minutes
3. playing		☐ 30 minutes	☐ 1 hour
4. sleeping		☐ 1 hour	☐ 65 minutes
5. making a nest		☐ 6 minutes	☐ 5 minutes
6. eating a banana		☐ 1 minute	☐ 50 seconds
7. sheltering from the rain		☐ 1 day	☐ 25 hours

NOW TRY THIS!

- **Who takes longer?**

	Charlie	**Chester**
Peeling fruit	☐ 2 minutes	☐ 100 seconds

Teachers' note At the start of the lesson, discuss the relationships between the units of time: seconds, minutes, hours and days and write the relationships on the board, for example 60 seconds is the same as 1 minute. As a further extension activity, the children could work in pairs to time each other doing a simple activity to see who takes the longest.

A Lesson for Every Day
Maths
6–7 Years
© A&C Black

Pirate map

- **Cut out the pictures at the bottom of the sheet.**

- **Arrange the pictures onto the grid so that all these statements are true.**

The chest is to the left of the volcano.

The bridge is to the right of the volcano.

The flag is above the chest.

The cave is above the volcano.

The cannon is between the cave and the ship.

The skull is below the ship.

The tree is above the ship.

The parrot is next to the tree.

The hut is between the anchor and the parrot.

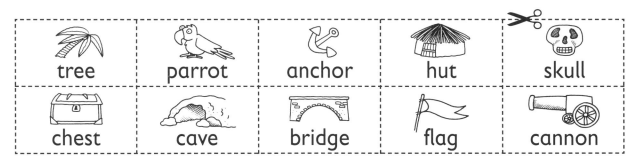

Teachers' note As an extension activity, ask the children to write five different statements of their own about the position of the items, after the pieces have been correctly stuck onto the grid. These statements could be displayed on the wall alongside an enlarged pirate map.

A Lesson for Every Day
Maths
6-7 Years
© A&C Black

155

Let's swim again

Work with a friend to solve these problems.
- **What calculations are needed?**
- **How did you decide?**

Cut out the cards.

1 James swam 12 widths and then 7 more. How many did he swim in total?

2 Suzi went to the pool 7 times in one week and 5 times in the next week. How many times did she go?

3 Sam swam 9 lengths which was 4 more than he had swum before. How many had he swum before?

4 It costs £2.20 for each child to swim. How much does it cost for 3 children?

Child | £2.20

5 There were 17 children in the pool. 12 more arrive. How many are there now?

6 There were 16 children in the pool. 12 more arrive and 7 get out. How many are there now?

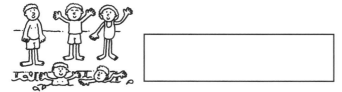

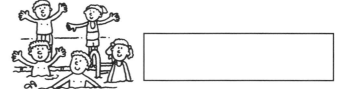

7 Jack swam 45 metres. This was 5 metres fewer than Kylie swam. How far did Kylie swim?

8 Chloe swam 35 metres. This was 10 metres further than Raz swam. How far did Raz swim?

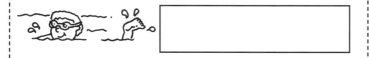

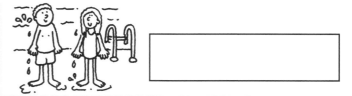

Teachers' note Some of these problems contain distracting words such as 'times' (as in the second question) or 'more' when multiplication or addition respectively is not the operation required. It is important that children interpret questions correctly rather than looking for trigger words to tell them what to do.

A Lesson for Every Day
Maths
6–7 Years
© A&C Black

Hopping frog

- **Use the number lines to answer these questions.**

Use the next multiple of 10 to help you.

$27 + 15 = \boxed{42}$

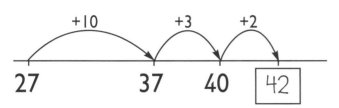

```
   +10        +3      +2
27         37      40    42
```

27   37   40 $\boxed{42}$

$35 + 24 = \boxed{}$

```
      +20            +4
35                        
```

35                          $\boxed{}$

$36 + 28 = \boxed{}$

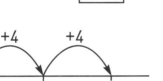

```
   +20      +4      +4
36
```

36

$44 + 17 = \boxed{}$

44

$39 + 26 = \boxed{}$

_____

$58 + 37 = \boxed{}$

_____

NOW TRY THIS!

- **Pick pairs of numbers, one from each lily pad, and find their totals.**

78   86   95
  67   59

26   47   38
  49   35

Teachers' note This activity can help to introduce children to the idea of using number lines to cross a tens boundary. The children should develop these ideas by drawing their own number lines.

A Lesson for Every Day
Maths
6–7 Years
© A&C Black

Calendar puzzle

- **Draw a square of 4 small squares on this calendar.**
- **Add the numbers in each column.**

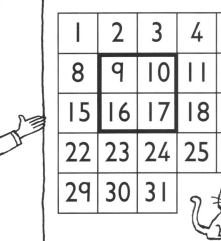

1	2	3	4	5	6	7
8	9	10	11	12	13	14
15	16	17	18	19	20	21
22	23	24	25	26	27	28
29	30	31				

One has been started for you.

9	10
16	17

9 + 16 = _____

10 + 17 = _____

_____
_____

_____
_____

_____
_____

_____
_____

- **Talk to a partner about any patterns you notice.**

NOW TRY THIS!

- **Draw six squares on this grid and add the numbers in each column.**

41	42	43	44	45	46	47
48	49	50	51	52	53	54
55	56	57	58	59	60	61
62	63	64	65	66	67	68

Is the pattern the same?

Teachers' note Discuss appropriate strategies for adding pairs of two-digit numbers, such as using an empty number line, partitioning and recombining, or using an expanded method in columns. In the extension activity, when the children draw their own six squares, make sure that they draw three columns of two.

A Lesson for Every Day
Maths
6–7 Years
© A&C Black

Dizzy the baker: 1

Dizzy baked some cakes. Each cake needed a different length of time in the oven.
- Join each cake with the timer set to the correct length of time.

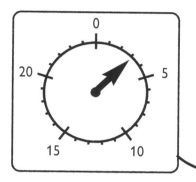

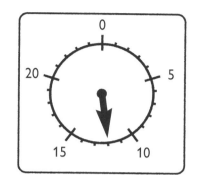

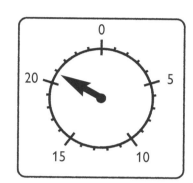

8 minutes

19 minutes

12 minutes

3 minutes

23 minutes

21 minutes

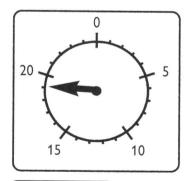

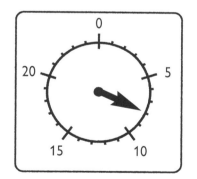

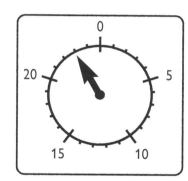

NOW TRY THIS!

- Draw an arrow on each dial to show these times.

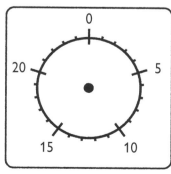

13 minutes

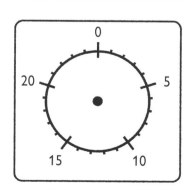

24 minutes

Teachers' note Draw children's attention to the fact that the timer shows up to 25 minutes only. The following sheet can be used as an extension activity as the timer shows up to one hour.

A Lesson for Every Day
Maths
6–7 Years
© A&C Black

Dizzy baked some cakes. Each cake needed
a different length of time in the oven.

- Join each cake with the timer set to
  the correct length of time.

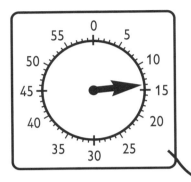

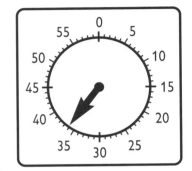

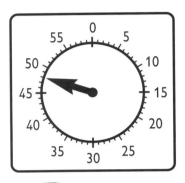

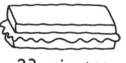

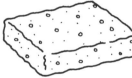

29 minutes

23 minutes

14 minutes

48 minutes

36 minutes

59 minutes

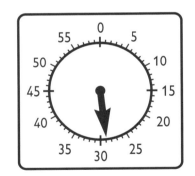

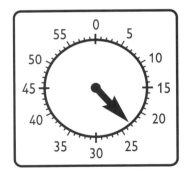

NOW TRY THIS!

- **Draw an
  arrow on
  each dial
  to show
  these times.**

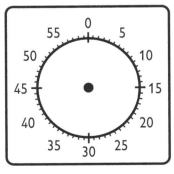

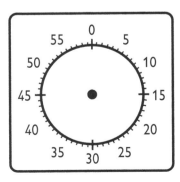

44 minutes

58 minutes

Teachers' note Watch out for children who make errors such as thinking that the position to the
right of 30 is 31 rather than 29. Draw attention to the multiples of 5 and ask which two of them 29 lies
between.

A Lesson for Every Day
Maths
6-7 Years
© A&C Black

Wally's wonder watch: 1

Draw hands on Wally's watch to match the times.

It's half past three.

It's six o'clock.

It's quarter past nine.

It's quarter to two.

It's ten thirty.

It's 15 minutes past eight.

It's six forty-five.

It's twelve fifteen.

NOW TRY THIS!

- **Which of these times is closest to lunch time?**

eachers' note This activity can be used as an assessment to see which forms of describing times
hildren are comfortable with, for example many will know quarter and half past but may be less
amiliar with six fifteen and seven forty-five. Draw attention to the fact that the hour hand points
rectly to the hour only at 'o'clock'.

A Lesson for Every Day
Maths
6–7 Years
© A&C Black

- **Write the times shown on Wally's watch in words.**

It's five o'clock.

It's

It's

It's

It's

It's

It's

It's

NOW TRY THIS!

- **Write the times on the last 4 watches in a different way.**

Teachers' note This activity can be used as an assessment to see how confident the children are in describing time in words. Note that there are several ways of describing time, for example six fifteen, quarter past six, 15 minutes past six, or half nine, half past nine, nine thirty, 30 minutes past nine.

A Lesson for Every Day
Maths
6–7 Years
© A&C Black

Carol's classy clock: 1

Write the digital time on Carol's clock to match the times.

It's eight o'clock.

It's ten thirty.

It's two fifteen.

It's nine forty-five.

It's half past eleven.

It's 15 minutes past one.

It's quarter past three.

It's quarter to twelve.

NOW TRY THIS!

• **Write the time you usually get up in the morning on this clock.**

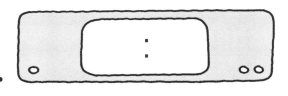

eachers' note This activity can be used as an assessment to see which forms of describing digital
nes children are comfortable with, for example many will find writing times such as six fifteen and
ven forty-five in digital form much easier than writing half past seven or quarter to nine.

A Lesson for Every Day
Maths
6-7 Years
© A&C Black

Carol's classy clock: 2

- **Write the times on Carol's clock in words. Use words from this list:**

o'clock   quarter past   half past   quarter to

5:30

It's half past five.

11:00

It's

7:15

It's

8:45

It's

9:00

It's

6:15

It's

12:30

It's

4:45

It's

 **NOW TRY THIS!**

- **Which of the times above is closest to 5 o'clock?** _____

Teachers' note This activity can be used as an assessment to see whether the children are confident in relating the times shown on digital clock with half past, quarter past, quarter to, etc. Remind children that the hour comes first when shown on a digital clock and draw attention to the fact that for times with :45, it is the next hour that is written, for example 2:45 is quarter to three.

A Lesson for Every Day
Maths
6-7 Years
© A&C Black

Rotating pictures

This picture has been turned | clockwise | **through** | a quarter turn | **4 times.**

• **Draw what these pictures will look like if you do the same.**

    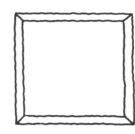

 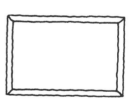  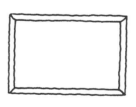 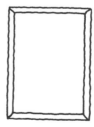

NOW TRY THIS!

• **On the back of the sheet draw a picture of your own and show** | anticlockwise | **quarter turns.**

eachers' note Tracing paper could be used for this activity or the children could cut out the original cture and rotate it. Encourage them to appreciate that four quarter turns return the picture back to s original position. Children can be shown this function on a computer, for example using drawing ols in word-processing software.

A Lesson for Every Day
Maths
6-7 Years
© A&C Black

In a spin

Beth is playing a turning game.
She makes turns to face different letters.

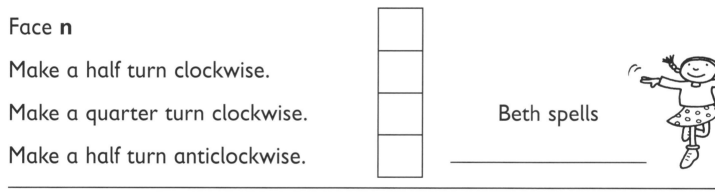

• **Write the words that she spells out.**

Face **m**

Make a half turn clockwise.

Make a quarter turn clockwise.

Make a half turn anticlockwise.

m

Beth spells

_____

Face **n**

Make a half turn clockwise.

Make a quarter turn clockwise.

Make a half turn anticlockwise.

Beth spells

_____

Face **m**

Make a quarter turn anticlockwise.

Make a half turn clockwise.

Make a quarter turn clockwise.

Beth spells

_____

NOW TRY THIS!

• **Write instructions for how to spell:**

man, men.

Teachers' note Draw attention to the fact that turning clockwise or anticlockwise through half a turn produces the same result.

A Lesson for Every Day
Maths
6–7 Years
© A&C Black

School play

- Follow the instructions. Start at the arrow each time.
- Colour to show who sits where.

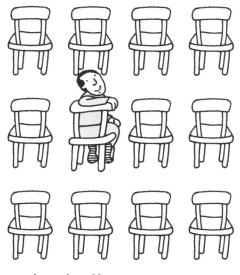

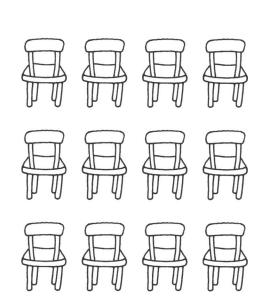

Enter the hall.

Mr Green   Go straight until you reach the **third row** of chairs.
Turn [left] and sit in the **second** chair.

Mrs Black   Go straight until you reach the **second row** of chairs.
Turn [right] and sit in the **fourth** chair.

Ms Yellow   Turn [left] when you reach the **first row** of chairs.
Sit in the **third** chair.

Mr Blue   Go straight until you reach the **third row** of chairs.
Turn [right] and sit in the **first** chair.

Mrs Red   Go straight until you reach the **second row** of chairs.
Turn [left] and sit in the **fourth** chair.

NOW TRY THIS!

Mr Grey is already seated.
- **Write directions for how he reached his seat.**

Teachers' note This activity encourages the children to follow directions and begin to use the words 'left' and 'right' correctly. If necessary the words 'left' and 'right' can be written on the sheet with arrows for those children who are finding it difficult.

A Lesson for Every Day
Maths
6-7 Years
© A&C Black

Avoid the zombies

• **Work with a partner.**

☆ Take it in turns to place a counter at the start.

☆ Move to the finish avoiding all the zombies.

☆ Describe the route to your partner.

Use these words.

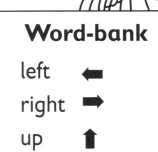

							finish
					zombie		zombie
person			zombie				
						zombie	
start		zombie					zombie

Word-bank

left ←

right →

up ↑

down ↓

• **With your partner, write a list of instructions to show 3 different routes.**

'Right 1' means 'move right 1 square'.

Route 1	Route 2	Route 3
right 1		
up 3		

NOW TRY THIS!

• **Draw Route 3 on the grid.**

• **Write the instructions going back from the** finish **to the** start **.**

Teachers' note An additional activity can be played with this maze. Give each pair a set of cards marked Left, Right, Up and Down and a counter each. The children should take it in turns to pick a card and, where possible, move in that direction until a zombie is reached. A target square can be agreed in advance and the winner is the first to reach it.

A Lesson for Every Day
Maths
6–7 Years
© A&C Black

The hamster run

- **Work with a partner.**
- **Tell the story of where the hamster went.**
- **Use these words in your story.**

Word-bank

left	right	under	over	between	up	down
round	through	along	beside	turn	straight	

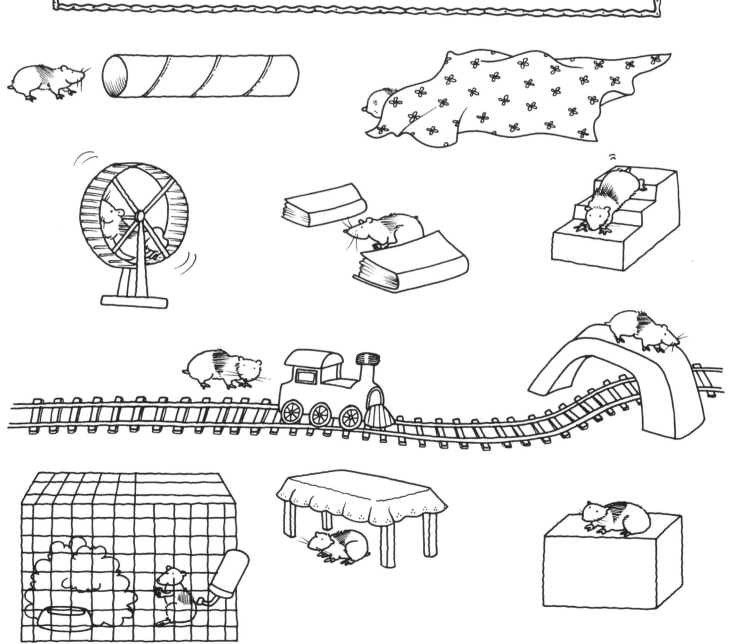

Teachers' note Before the children begin the activity, discuss what is happening in the illustration. The children can describe the journey to a partner or could record it on paper. Ensure the children understand that they can use more words than just those given in the word-bank.

A Lesson for Every Day
Maths
6–7 Years
© A&C Black

169

Cubs and Brownies

Here is some information about Cub scouts and Brownies.

There are ⬚12⬚ Cubs.

There are ⬚7 more⬚ Brownies than Cubs.

Each Cub has ⬚2⬚ badges.

Each Brownie has ⬚3⬚ badges.

• Write ⬚4⬚ questions about the information for a friend to answer. Start your questions with

How many….?   How many more….?   How many

 **NOW TRY THIS!** • Swap sheets with a friend and answer their questions.

Teachers' note This activity encourages the children to make up their own questions using appropriate vocabulary. When children exchange sheets for the extension activity, ask them to describe how they decided what to do and encourage them to use number sentences to show the operation used. The numbers could be adjusted to make them appropriate for the children's abilities.

A Lesson for Every Day
Maths
6-7 Years
© A&C Black

Hop, skip and jump

- **Use the number lines to answer these questions.**
- **Count up** **from the smaller number.**

74 – 27 = 47

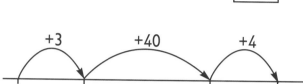

+3   +40   +4

27   30   70   74

82 – 36 = ☐

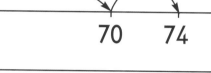

36   40   80   82

53 – 25 = ☐

_____

25

61 – 48 = ☐

_____

48

93 – 37 = ☐

_____

62 – 26 = ☐

_____

NOW TRY THIS!

- **Pick pairs of numbers, one from each set, and find their** **differences** **.**

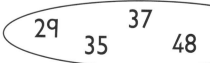

52   75   83   91   64

29   37   35   48   16

eachers' note For more information on this recommended calculation approach, see the Guidance aper on Calculations at: www.standards.dfes.gov.uk/primaryframeworks/mathematics/Papers/

A Lesson for Every Day
Maths
6–7 Years
© A&C Black

Ant trail

An ant is walking all the way around the sides of each shape.

- Use a ruler to measure how far it walks for each shape.

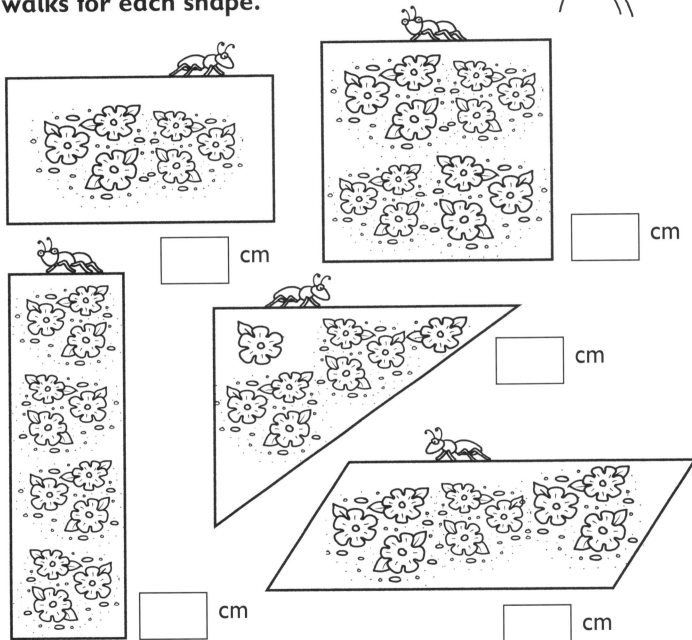

$\boxed{}$ cm

$\boxed{}$ cm

$\boxed{}$ cm

$\boxed{}$ cm

$\boxed{}$ cm

NOW TRY THIS!

- **On the back of the sheet draw a rectangle that has an ant trail of 30 cm.**

172 Teachers' note Encourage the children to write the length of each side on the shape and then to find the total of the four lengths at the end. This can help them to further appreciate that opposite sides of rectangles are the same length and that only two sides of rectangles need to be measured.

A Lesson for Every Day
Maths
6-7 Years
© A&C Black

TV times: 1

The time now is	Cartoons are at	The time now is	The Y factor is at

The time now is	The news is at	The time now is	Football is at

The time now is	Art-magic is at	The time now is	Em street is at

The time now is	Nowastory is at	The time now is	Dinoworld is at

The time now is	Dina Warrior is at	The time now is	Westenders is at

eachers' note This sheet should be used in conjunction with 'TV times: 2'. It could also be used lone by asking the children to write down how long they would have to wait for each programme.

A Lesson for Every Day
Maths
6-7 Years
© A&C Black

Teachers' note Ask the children to cut out the cards from TV times: 1 and 2 and sort them into pairs. The sheet could also be used alone. Children could be given a time and told to find what time each programme would start. Both sets of cards could also be used by children working in pairs, such as by turning over a card of each type and seeing whether they match.

A Lesson for Every Day
Maths
6–7 Years
© A&C Black

Time quiz

- **Help the team answer the questions.**
- **Circle the correct answer.**

1. It is 8:00. What time will it be in half an hour?

a	7:30	**b**	8:00
c	8:30	**d**	8:15

2. It is 5:30. What time was it 30 minutes ago?

a	6:30	**b**	6:00
c	5:15	**d**	5:00

3. It is 3:00. What time will it be in 15 minutes?

a	3:30	**b**	2:45
c	3:15	**d**	2:30

4. It is 1:15. What time was it 45 minutes ago?

a	12:45	**b**	12:15
c	12:30	**d**	1:30

5. It is 10:00. What time was it half an hour ago?

a	10:30	**b**	9:00
c	9:30	**d**	11:15

6. It is 6:45. What time was it 15 minutes ago?

a	7:00	**b**	6:15
c	7:30	**d**	6:30

7. It is 4:45. What time will it be in three quarters of an hour?

a	6:30	**b**	4:30
c	5:30	**d**	6:00

8. It is 7:30. What time will it be in quarter of an hour?

a	7:15	**b**	7:45
c	8:00	**d**	8:15

NOW TRY THIS!

- **Make up four more questions for a partner to solve.**

eachers' note The times can be altered before copying to provide more challenging questions, ch as involving time to the nearest 5-minute intervals rather than to quarters of an hour. Point out at some questions involve moving forwards and others moving backwards in time.

A Lesson for Every Day
Maths
6-7 Years
© A&C Black

Feeding time

• **Play this game with a partner.**

☆ Cut out the cards and place them face down.

☆ Take turns to pick a card and say what the angle is.

☆ If your partner agrees, score the points shown on the scoreboard above.

Score

right angle	5 points
smaller than a right angle	1 point
larger than a right angle	3 points

Teachers' note See notes on the activity on page 20 for an introductory activity to help the children to recognise right angles.

A Lesson for Every Day
Maths
6–7 Years
© A&C Black

Hexagon handiwork

**A hexagon has been drawn on the first grid.
Draw a different hexagon on each grid.**

**NOW TRY
THIS!**

• **Write how many right angles each
hexagon has.**

achers' note Remind the children that a closed shape with six sides is called a hexagon, so the
ape on the sheet is a hexagon. For the extension activity ensure that children recognise right
gles in different orientations, for example noticing that the first hexagon has two right angles.

A Lesson for Every Day
Maths
6-7 Years
© A&C Black

Power-robots!

Here are drawings of 2 power-robots.

- Carefully cut out the right-angle gobbler from the bottom of the page.
- Use it to find which power-robot has more right angles.
- Mark each right angle like this.

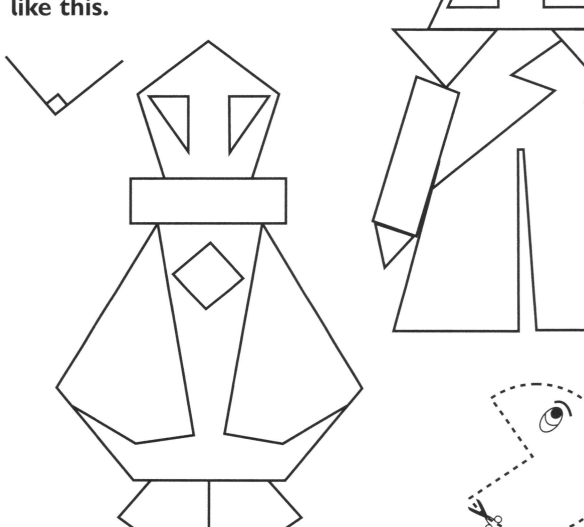

NOW TRY THIS!

- Write how many right angles each hexagon has.

Teachers' note At the start of the lesson, demonstrate how to use the right-angle gobbler to test angles. Ensure the children realise that they need to line up one edge of its 'mouth' with a line or edge and make sure that where the two lines or edges join is at the corner of its 'mouth'.

A Lesson for Every Day
Maths
6–7 Years
© A&C Black

What a match: 1

Work with a partner.
Match each question with a | number sentence |.

Some number sentences can be used more than once.

1 There are | 18 | daisies. Beth takes away | 3 | of them. How many daisies are there now?

2 There are | 18 | counters in a pile. Fred puts | 3 | more in the pile. How many now?

3 There are | 18 | people on a bus. | 3 | people get off. How many are there now?

4 | 18 | sweets were shared between | 3 | friends. How many sweets do they each get?

5 Ben had | 18p |. He buys a cake costing | 3p |. How much money does he have now?

6 A plant was | 18 cm | tall. It grew | 3 | times as tall. How tall is it now?

7 | 18 | grapes were shared equally between Lee and 2 friends. How many grapes did Lee get?

$$18 - 3 = 15$$

$$18 \times 3 = 54$$

$$18 + 3 = 21$$

$$18 \div 3 = 6$$

NOW TRY THIS!

- **Make up a new story to match each number sentence.**

achers' note The questions are one-step calculations and the children should work together in irs to discuss them. Some children may find it easier to work out the answer to help them recognise nich number sentence is the correct one. The following sheet can be given to more confident ildren to help them tackle two-step problems.

A Lesson for Every Day
Maths
6-7 Years
© A&C Black

What a match: 2

- **Work with a partner.**
- **Match each question with a** number sentence .
- **Some number sentences can be used more than once.**

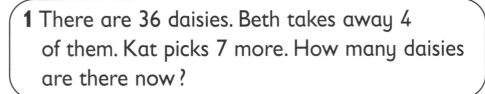

1 There are 36 daisies. Beth takes away 4 of them. Kat picks 7 more. How many daisies are there now?

2 There are 36 counters. Fred takes 4 and Sean takes 7. How many are left?

3 There are 36 people on a bus. 4 people get off and 7 get on. How many are left?

4 36 sweets were shared between Josh and 3 friends. Josh ate 7 of his sweets. How many does he have left?

5 Ben had 36p. He buys a cake costing 4p and a drink costing 7p. How much money does he have now?

6 A plant was 36 cm tall. It grew 4 cm and then a further 7 cm. How tall is it now?

7 36 grapes were shared between Lee and 3 friends. Then Lee was given 7 more grapes as well. How many has he now?

8 Harry was given 36p each day for 4 days. He spent 7p of this money. How much does he have now?

$36 - 4 + 7 = 39$

$(36 \times 4) - 7 = 137$

$36 - 4 - 7 = 25$

$36 + 4 - 7 = 33$

$(36 \div 4) + 7 = 16$

$(36 \times 4) + 7 = 151$

$(36 \div 4) - 7 = 2$

$36 + 4 + 7 = 47$

Teachers' note The questions are two-step calculations and the children should work together in pairs to discuss them. Explain that the brackets show which part of the number sentence is worked out first. Some children may find it easier to work out the answer to help them recognise which number sentence is the correct one.

A Lesson for Every Day
Maths
6–7 Years
© A&C Black

Make 26

- Cut out each piece of the jigsaw.
- Fit all the pieces together to make a rectangle .
  The numbers of faces in each column must be 26.

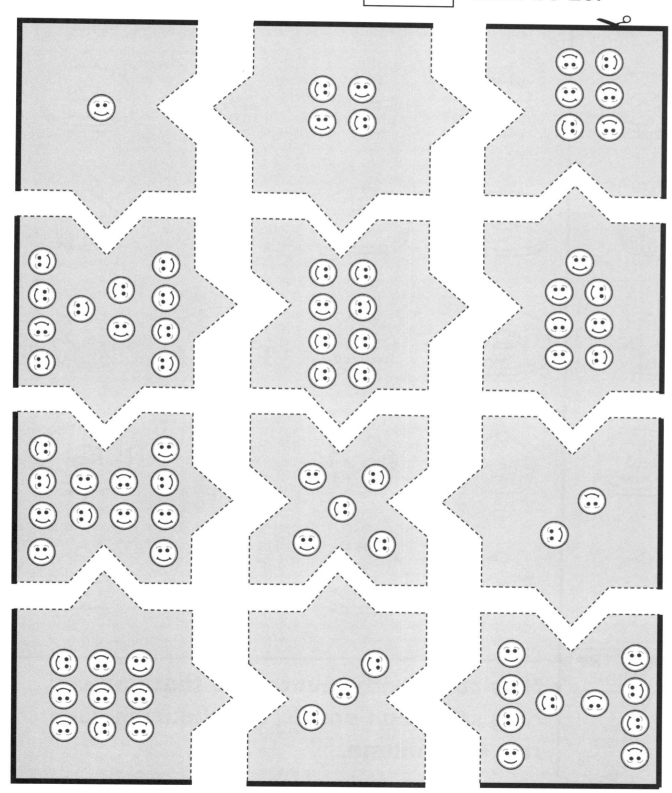

eachers' note Children will need to cut out these pieces and, as such, may benefit from the sheet ing copied onto thin card or enlarged onto to A3 paper. A large class set of these could be copied d laminated for a more permanent resource. As an extension activity ask the children to find the tal number of faces in the rows.

A Lesson for Every Day
Maths
6-7 Years
© A&C Black

Hide the cakes

- **Put counters on the cakes to hide them, so that you can only see 2 buns and a doughnut in each row and column.**

NOW TRY THIS!

- **Now cover with counters so that you can only see a bun and 2 doughnuts in each row and column.**

 Teachers' note It is vital that children understand what is meant by row and column for this problem-solving activity. Provide them with counters and explain that they can cover any of the cakes, but you must be able to still see 2 buns and a doughnut in each row, going across, and 2 buns and a doughnut in each column, going down

A Lesson for Every Day
Maths
6–7 Years
© A&C Black

Building bricks

The bumps on these bricks show an array .

• **Write two multiplication facts for each brick.**

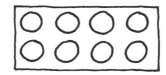

$2 \times 4 = 8$

$4 \times 2 = 8$

_____

_____

_____

_____

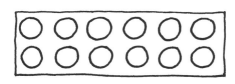

_____

_____

_____

_____

_____

_____

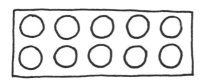

_____

_____

_____

_____

_____

_____

• **Write one multiplication fact for each brick.**

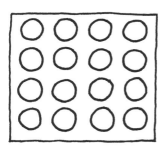

_____

_____

_____

eachers' note Use Lego bricks (or similar) to introduce the activity. Encourage the children to xplain why the last three shapes will only have one multiplication fact. As an extension, the children ould draw their own bricks and write the corresponding multiplication facts.

A Lesson for Every Day
Maths
6–7 Years
© A&C Black

Market stall

- **Write a number sentence for each number story.**
- **Use** $\boxed{+}$, $\boxed{-}$, $\boxed{\times}$, $\boxed{\div}$ **and** $\boxed{=}$.

5 boxes of 4 cabbages is 20 cabbages altogether.

$5 \times 4 = 20$

There are 20 potatoes. 7 are bought. There are 13 left.

There are 24 shoppers. 32 more arrive, making 56 altogether.

45 apples are shared between 5 people. Each gets 9 apples.

14 mangoes are grouped into 2s. There are 7 groups.

6 bags of 5 oranges is 30 oranges altogether.

There are 31 pears. 12 are rotten. 19 are ok.

There are 6 leeks and 4 times as many plums. There are 24 plums.

 **NOW TRY THIS!**

- **Write two number stories for a partner to solve.**

Teachers' note Some situations could be described in more than one way, for example 31 – 12 = 19 or 12 + 19 = 31. Ensure the children are aware that it is correct for an answer to be written 31 = 12 + 19, where the equals sign comes nearer the beginning of the number sentence.

A Lesson for Every Day
Maths
6–7 Years
© A&C Black

Fraction webs

• **Write** $\frac{1}{2}$, $\frac{1}{4}$ **or** $\frac{3}{4}$ **to show what fraction of each web is shaded.**

 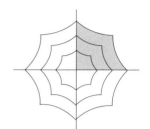 $\frac{1}{4}$   $\frac{}{}$

  $\frac{}{}$  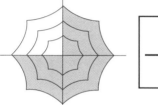 $\frac{}{}$

 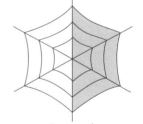 $\frac{}{}$   $\frac{}{}$

 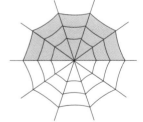 $\frac{}{}$  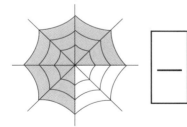 $\frac{}{}$

NOW TRY THIS!

• **Shade each web to match the fraction shown.**

$\frac{1}{2}$  $\frac{3}{4}$  $\frac{1}{4}$

eachers' note The extension activity can also be used to help children begin to understand ideas of equivalence, such as realising that $\frac{1}{2}$ is equivalent to $\frac{2}{4}$, and that $\frac{1}{4}$ is equivalent to $\frac{2}{8}$.

A Lesson for Every Day
Maths
6-7 Years
© A&C Black

Quarter shapes

Emily has been folding, cutting and colouring paper shapes.

• **Cut out the cards. Sort them into groups to show what fraction of each shape is shaded.**

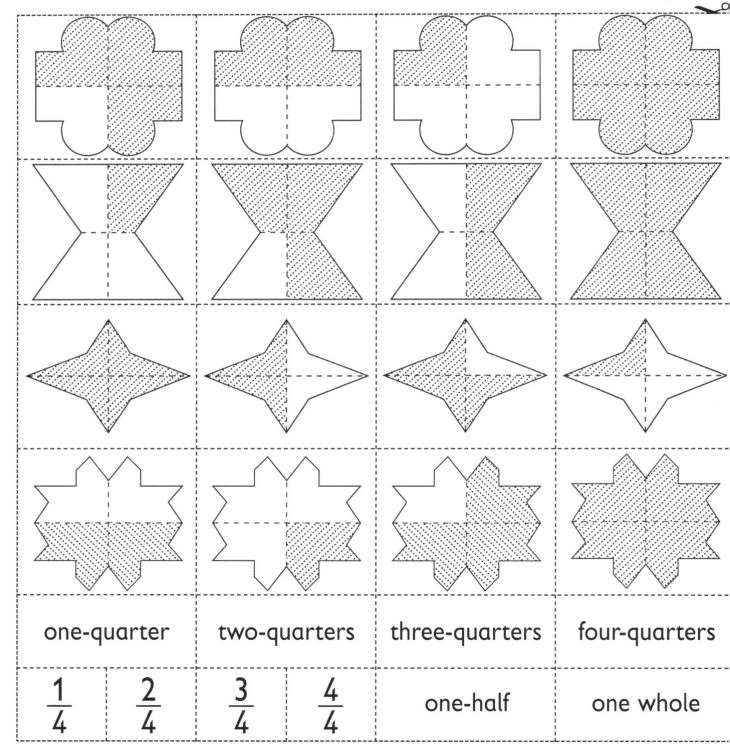

| one-quarter | two-quarters | three-quarters | four-quarters |

| $\frac{1}{4}$ | $\frac{2}{4}$ | $\frac{3}{4}$ | $\frac{4}{4}$ | one-half | one whole |

Teachers' note This sheet can also be used as a pairs game, where the children spread the cards face down on the table and take it in turns to turn over two. If the cards match, they can keep the cards. The winner is the player with the most cards.

A Lesson for Every Day
Maths
6-7 Years
© A&C Black

Crazy custard machine

- **Say whether the arrow on the dial has turned through** `one-half` , `one-quarter` **or** `three-quarters` **of a full turn.**

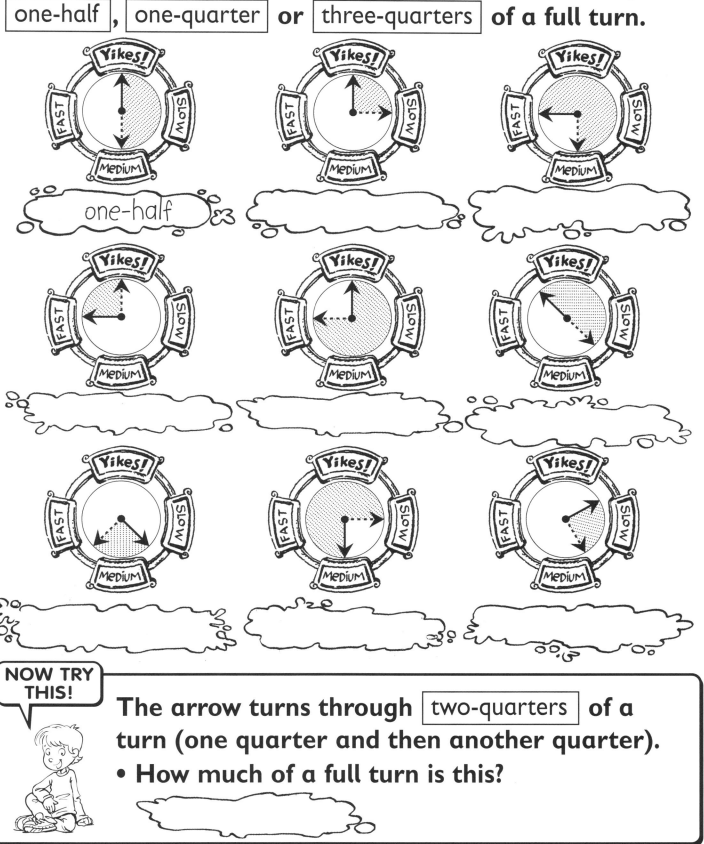

one-half

NOW TRY THIS!

The arrow turns through `two-quarters` of a turn (one quarter and then another quarter).
- **How much of a full turn is this?**

Teachers' note Begin the lesson by asking the children to stand pointing forwards to the board. Call out 'Half turn' and ask the children to turn to face the opposite direction, so that they are pointing away from the board. Repeat for one-quarter and three-quarters of a turn.

A Lesson for Every Day
Maths
6-7 Years
© A&C Black

Wheels away

• **Use the information in this box to solve each puzzle.**

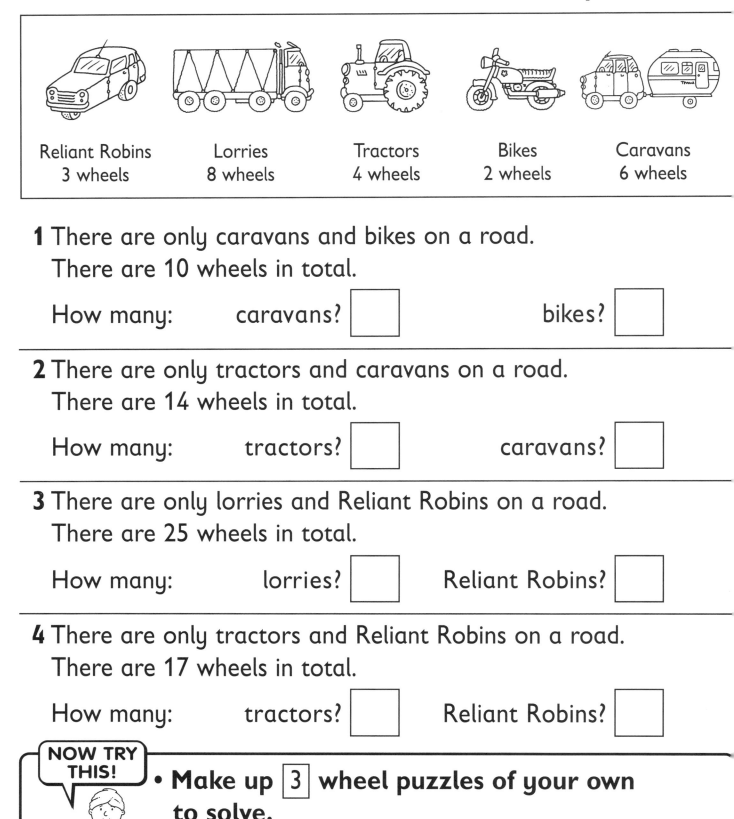

| Reliant Robins | Lorries | Tractors | Bikes | Caravans |
| 3 wheels | 8 wheels | 4 wheels | 2 wheels | 6 wheels |

1 There are only caravans and bikes on a road.
There are 10 wheels in total.

How many: caravans? ☐   bikes? ☐

2 There are only tractors and caravans on a road.
There are 14 wheels in total.

How many: tractors? ☐   caravans? ☐

3 There are only lorries and Reliant Robins on a road.
There are 25 wheels in total.

How many: lorries? ☐   Reliant Robins? ☐

4 There are only tractors and Reliant Robins on a road.
There are 17 wheels in total.

How many: tractors? ☐   Reliant Robins? ☐

NOW TRY THIS!

• **Make up ③ wheel puzzles of your own to solve.**

Teachers' note Each of the questions above has only one possible solution, but the children's own puzzles are likely to have several. Discuss all possible answers to their questions. It could be useful to have multiple pictures of the vehicles for some children to manipulate practically.

A Lesson for Every Day
Maths
6–7 Years
© A&C Black

Triangle tricks: 1

- **Shade** each of the pieces in the colours shown and cut them out.
- **Arrange them to make a large triangle.**
- **Find as many different ways as you can.**
- **Record your answers on 'Triangle tricks: 2'.**

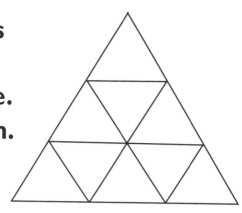

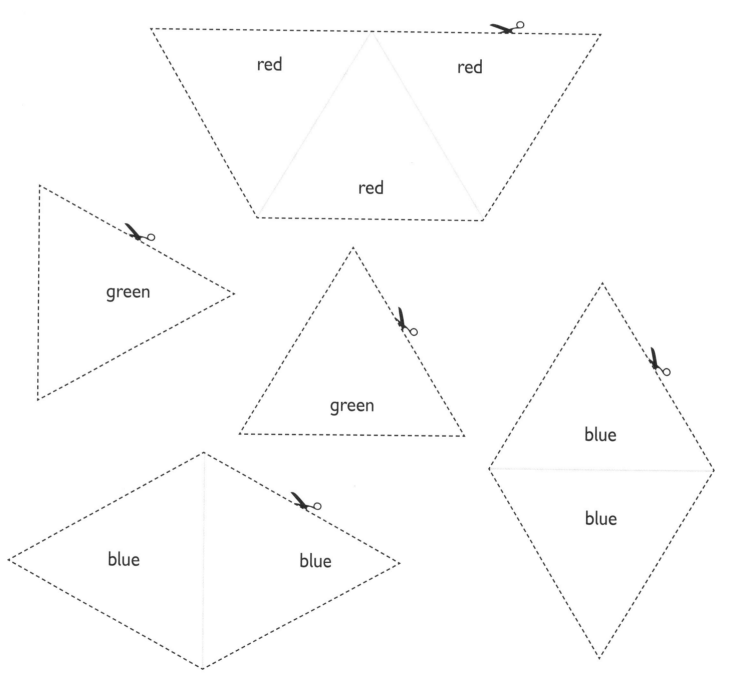

red red

red

green

green

blue

blue

blue

blue blue

eachers' note Provide children with the following recording sheet and coloured pencils. Encourage hem to cut out their solutions and rotate them in order to compare which are the same. Provide irrors for children to test whether any are reflections of each other. Compile an exhaustive class list f the solutions.

A Lesson for Every Day
Maths
6-7 Years
© A&C Black

- ## Use the 'Triangle tricks: 1' pieces.
- ## Record your answers here.

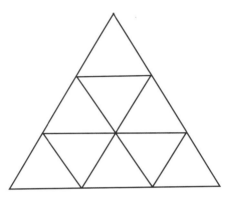
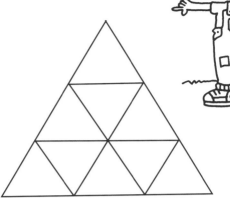
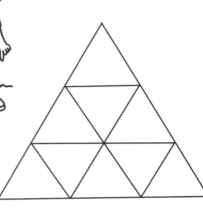

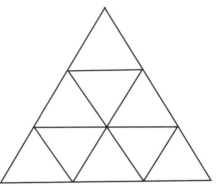
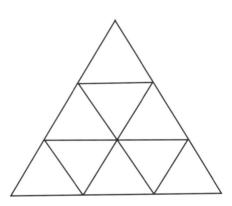
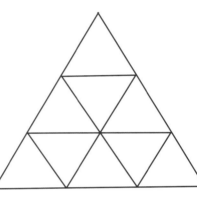

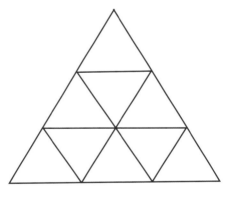
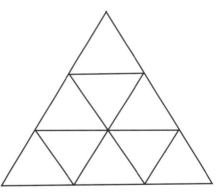
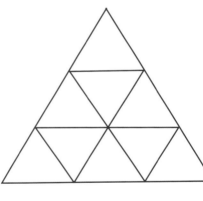

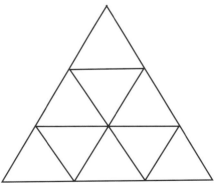
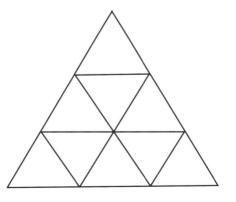
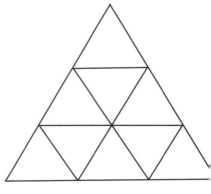

• Are any of your solutions the same?

Teachers' note Use this sheet in conjunction with 'Triangle tricks: 1'.

A Lesson for Every Day
Maths
6–7 Years
© A&C Black

Wendy's window box

Wendy divided her window box into ☐10☐ parts. She planted 3 seeds in each part.

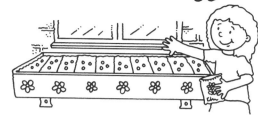

1 How many seeds did she plant in total?

$$10 \times 3 = 30$$

2 She had 35 seeds altogether.
How many didn't she plant?

3 The 35 seeds cost 70p altogether.
How much did each seed cost?

4 15 of the seeds were flower seeds.
The rest were vegetable seeds.
How many was this?

5 Only 6 of the 15 flower seeds grew.
How many did not grow?

6 Wendy picked 5 tomatoes from each
of her 3 tomato plants.
How many tomatoes did she pick?

7 Wendy dug up 12 small potatoes.
She shared them equally with her friend.
How many did they each have?

NOW TRY THIS!

• Make up ☐2☐ of your own window box questions for a partner to solve.

Teachers' note Encourage the children to use number sentences to show what they have decided to do for each calculation and ask them to describe their methods for answering each question.

A Lesson for Every Day
Maths
6-7 Years
© A&C Black

Traffic jam

There are ⬚15⬚ vehicles in a traffic jam.

1 The postman is ⬚5th⬚ in line.
How many vehicles are behind him?

2 The window cleaner is ⬚9th⬚ in line.
How many vehicles are behind him?

3 Each vehicle has ⬚2⬚ headlights.
How many altogether?

4 Each vehicle has ⬚4⬚ wheels.
How many wheels in total?

NOW TRY THIS!

• **Show your working.**
There are ⬚8⬚ people in the bus, ⬚1⬚ person in the postman's van and ⬚3⬚ people in each of the other vehicles.
• **How many people are in the traffic jam?**

192

Teachers' note The numbers can be altered before copying to provide differentiation. For the extension activity, the children should be encouraged to describe how they worked out the solution and the strategies they used.

A Lesson for Every Day
Maths
6-7 Years
© A&C Black

Marching Mummies

- **Work with a partner to solve these problems.**
- **What calculations are needed?**
- **How did you decide?**

1 The mummy takes 7 steps and then 9 steps more. How many steps so far?

2 The mummy walks 20 steps altogether. How many more steps to go?

After $\boxed{4}$ **steps the mummy had walked** $\boxed{2 \text{ metres}}$.
Each step the mummy takes is the same length.

---

3 How far had the mummy walked after:

a) 8 steps?    **b)** 12 steps?

c) 2 steps?    **d)** 1 step?

e) 10 steps?    **f)** 20 steps?

NOW TRY THIS!

- **If the mummy walked a distance of** $\boxed{30 \text{ metres}}$, **how many steps was this altogether?** _____
- **Show your working.**

Teachers' note The numbers can be altered before copying to provide differentiation. For the extension activity, the children should be encouraged to describe how they worked out the solution and the strategies they used.

A Lesson for Every Day
Maths
6-7 Years
© A&C Black

Farmer Palmer's diary: 1

• **Read the diary and answer the questions.**

Monday:
*Bought **9** more chickens to go with the **22** that I already had.*
***6** of my chickens are cockerels. The rest are hens.*

Wednesday:
*Every hen I have laid **2** eggs today!*

Friday:
*Every hen I have laid **3** eggs today!*

Sunday:
*This week my hens laid **250** eggs altogether!*

1 After buying more chickens, how many
did Farmer Palmer have altogether? _____

2 How many are hens? _____

3 On Wednesday, how many eggs
were laid in total? _____

4 On Friday, how many eggs were laid? _____

5 If each hen laid the same number of eggs
during the week, how many was this? _____

NOW TRY THIS!

• **If Farmer Palmer sold** half
**of his cockerels, how many
chickens will he have now?**

Teachers' note Read through the diary entries together. Encourage the children to describe their decision-making when choosing which operation to use and their strategies for working out the answer. Encourage them to work out answers in different ways, such as using practical material, number lines, place value cards etc. See the notes on the activity for more details.

A Lesson for Every Day
Maths
6–7 Years
© A&C Black

Read the diary and answer the questions.

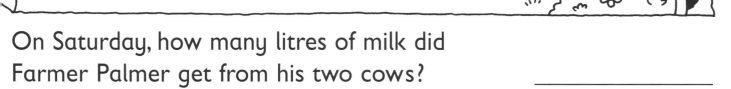

Saturday:
*Maisie and Daisy, my milking cows, both made **25** litres of milk today.*

Sunday:
*Maisie made **18** litres of milk and Daisy made **23** litres today!*

Monday:
*Maisie made **9** litres more than Daisy. Daisy made **17** litres.*

Tuesday:
*Maisie made **8** litres more than Daisy. Maisie made **26** litres.*

On Saturday, how many litres of milk did Farmer Palmer get from his two cows? _____

How many litres did he get on Sunday? _____

On Monday, how many litres of milk did Maisie make? _____

On Tuesday, how many litres of milk did Daisy make? _____

From Saturday to Tuesday, which cow made the most milk? _____

NOW TRY THIS!

On Wednesday, Maisie made twice as much milk as Daisy. Daisy made 16 litres.
• How much milk did Farmer Palmer get? _____

eachers' note Read through the diary entries together. Encourage the children to describe their ecision-making when choosing which operation to use and their strategies for working out the nswer. Encourage them to work out answers in different ways, such as using practical material, umber lines, place value cards etc. See the notes on the activity for more details.

A Lesson for Every Day
Maths
6-7 Years
© A&C Black

Sponsored spell

Class A are doing a sponsored spell for charity.

- **Work out how much each person raised.**

1 Urvi raised 5p per word. She got these words correct.

| red | because | night | blue | children | weigh | cried |

Urvi raised _____

2 Sean raised 7p per word. He got these words correct.

| red | blue | children | cried |

Sean raised _____

3 Ben raised 4p per word. He got these words correct.

| red | because | special | night | blue | children | cried | through |

Ben raised _____

4 Josie raised 6p per word. She got these words correct.

| red | because | night | blue | children | cried |

Josie raised _____

NOW TRY THIS!

Jason raised 24p in total.
He got these words correct.

| red | because | special | night | blue | children | cried | through |

- **How much did he raise per word?** _____

Teachers' note Encourage the children to describe their strategies for working out the answers. Encourage them to demonstrate this in different ways, for example using practical material, number lines, a 100 square, place value cards. The numbers can be altered before copying to provide differentiation.

A Lesson for Every Day
Maths
6-7 Years
© A&C Black

Hungry as a horse

- ## Share the carrots equally.
- ## Use a cube to be each carrot.

You need some cubes.

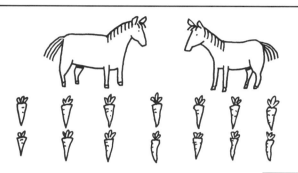

14 shared between 2 is $\boxed{7}$

12 shared between 4 is $\boxed{}$

18 shared between 3 is $\boxed{}$

16 shared between 4 is $\boxed{}$

20 shared between 4 is $\boxed{}$

21 shared between 3 is $\boxed{}$

NOW TRY THIS!

- ## Write each question as a division sentence:

$$14 \div 2 = 7$$

Teachers' note The children need to understand the difference between types of division, for example sharing between two and dividing into equal groups of two. This activity looks at sharing.

A Lesson for Every Day
Maths
6–7 Years
© A&C Black

Monkey tricks

- **Share the bananas equally.**
- **Use a cube to be each banana.**

You need some cubes.

$12 \div 2 = \boxed{6}$

$12 \div 3 = \boxed{}$

$16 \div 4 = \boxed{}$

$18 \div 3 = \boxed{}$

$21 \div 3 = \boxed{}$

$20 \div 4 = \boxed{}$

NOW TRY THIS!

- **Use 24 cubes to help you answer these.**

$24 \div 2 = \boxed{}$ $24 \div 3 = \boxed{}$ $24 \div 4 = \boxed{}$

Teachers' note The children need to understand the difference between types of division, for example sharing between two and dividing into equal groups of two. This activity looks at sharing.

A Lesson for Every Day
Maths
6-7 Years
© A&C Black

Playful kittens

• **Write each question as a division and answer it.**

How many groups of 5 are in 30? 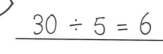 $30 \div 5 = 6$

How many groups of 10 are in 50?    _____

How many groups of 2 are in 14?    _____

How many groups of 5 are in 15? 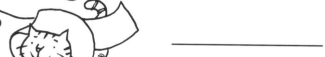   _____

How many groups of 10 are in 90?    _____

How many groups of 2 are in 18?    _____

How many groups of 5 are in 35?    _____

How many groups of 10 are in 60?    _____

How many groups of 2 are in 16? 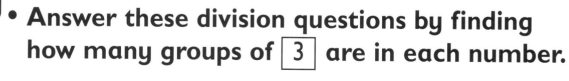   _____

NOW TRY THIS!

• **Answer these division questions by finding how many groups of** $\boxed{3}$ **are in each number.**

$18 \div 3 = \boxed{}$ $15 \div 3 = \boxed{}$ $21 \div 3 = \boxed{}$

Teachers' note For the extension activity, provide the children with cubes or counters. Ask them to count out the correct number and then to see how many groups of three they can make. This activity looks at grouping.

A Lesson for Every Day
Maths
6-7 Years
© A&C Black

Pirate gold

Each pirate gets the same number
of gold coins.

- **How many pirates are on each ship?**

Use cubes
to help you.

Our ship has **18** gold coins. Each pirate will get **2** gold coins.

On this ship are 9 pirates.

Our ship has **35** gold coins. Each pirate will get **5** gold coins.

On this ship are ☐ pirates.

Our ship has **80** gold coins. Each pirate will get **10** gold coins.

On this ship are ☐ pirates.

Our ship has **15** gold coins. Each pirate will get **3** gold coins.

On this ship are ☐ pirates.

Our ship has **24** gold coins. Each pirate will get **4** gold coins.

On this ship are ☐ pirates.

Our ship has **24** gold coins. Each pirate will get **3** gold coins.

On this ship are ☐ pirates.

Our ship has **16** gold coins. Each pirate will get **4** gold coins.

On this ship are ☐ pirates.

Our ship has **28** gold coins. Each pirate will get **4** gold coins.

On this ship are ☐ pirates.

NOW TRY THIS!

- **Write each question as a division sentence.**

$$18 \div 2 = 9$$

Teachers' note The children need to understand the difference between types of division, for example sharing between two and dividing into equal groups of two. This activity looks at dividing into equal groups.

A Lesson for Every Day
Maths
6-7 Years
© A&C Black

Counter covering

A counter is covering one number in each
multiplication or division sentence.
Write the number on the counter.

$2 \times \boxed{5} = 10$ 　　　 $5 \times \bigcirc = 15$ 　　　 $10 \times \bigcirc = 40$

$25 \div \bigcirc = 5$ 　　　 $12 \div \bigcirc = 6$ 　　　 $50 \div \bigcirc = 5$

$10 \times \bigcirc = 50$ 　　　 $2 \times \bigcirc = 8$ 　　　 $5 \times \bigcirc = 25$

$70 \div \bigcirc = 7$ 　　　 $20 \div \bigcirc = 10$ 　　　 $45 \div \bigcirc = 9$

$5 \times \bigcirc = 40$ 　　　 $10 \times \bigcirc = 80$ 　　　 $2 \times \bigcirc = 16$

NOW TRY THIS!

• **Try these in the same way.**

$\bigcirc \times 2 = 14$ 　　　 $\bigcirc \times 5 = 35$ 　　　 $\bigcirc \times 10 = 60$

$\bigcirc \div 2 = 7$ 　　　 $\bigcirc \div 10 = 4$ 　　　 $\bigcirc \div 5 = 4$

$\bigcirc \times 10 = 90$ 　　　 $\bigcirc \times 2 = 18$ 　　　 $\bigcirc \times 5 = 45$

$\bigcirc \div 5 = 10$ 　　　 $\bigcirc \div 10 = 10$ 　　　 $\bigcirc \div 2 = 9$

Teachers' note Demonstrate to the children how the inverse operation can sometimes be used to find a missing number, for example □ ÷ 5 = 9 can be solved by multiplying 9 and 5.

A Lesson for Every Day
Maths
6-7 Years
© A&C Black

Cake calculations

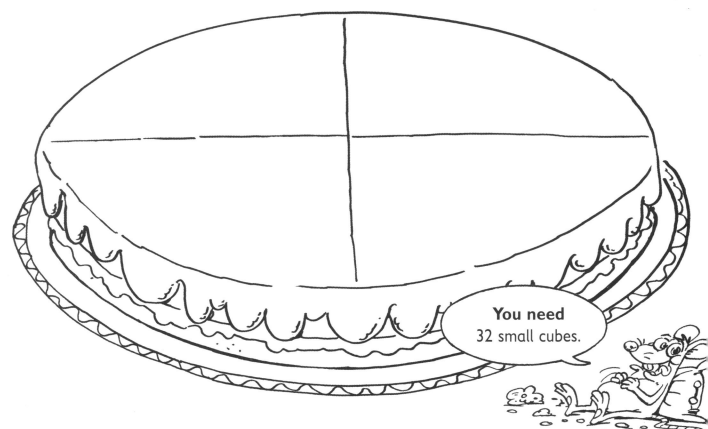

You need
32 small cubes.

This cake is cut into four pieces.

- **Put an equal number of cubes on each piece of cake.**

- **Count how many cubes on three pieces to find $\frac{3}{4}$.**

Use 12 cubes	Use 16 cubes	Use 28 cubes
$\frac{3}{4}$ of 12 is ☐	$\frac{3}{4}$ of 16 is ☐	$\frac{3}{4}$ of 28 is ☐
Use 20 cubes	Use 24 cubes	Use 32 cubes
$\frac{3}{4}$ of 20 is ☐	$\frac{3}{4}$ of 24 is ☐	$\frac{3}{4}$ of 32 is ☐

NOW TRY THIS!

- **Find $\frac{3}{4}$ of 100, <u>without</u> using your cubes.**

Teachers' note This activity can help the children to appreciate a fraction as not only an area of a shape, but also as part of a set of objects. Encourage them to arrange the 'cubes' into four equal sets and then to find the total number of cubes in three of those sets.

A Lesson for Every Day
Maths
6-7 Years
© A&C Black

Cross out

Cross out one number from each [row]
and [column] so that the total of
each row and column is 30.

10	2	6	12	~~9~~	= 30
5	7	7	3	15	= 30
12	5	8	8	2	= 30
3	15	4	12	8	= 30
5	6	12	7	5	= 30
= 30	= 30	= 30	= 30	= 30	

NOW TRY THIS!

• **This is even harder!**

6	7	5	~~6~~	9	= 30
8	8	8	4	10	= 30
7	10	7	6	7	= 30
9	8	10	6	6	= 30
9	5	5	14	2	= 30
= 30	= 30	= 30	= 30	= 30	

achers' note Discuss suitable strategies for finding which number to cross out, for example by
ding up all the numbers in a row and subtracting 30 to see the number of the one to be crossed
. If there are several of that number in a row the same should be done for a column.

A Lesson for Every Day
Maths
6-7 Years
© A&C Black

Soldiers on parade

8 soldiers are standing in a straight line.
4 wearing red and then 4 wearing blue.

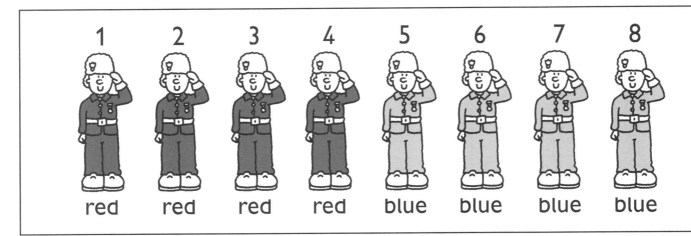

1	2	3	4	5	6	7	8
red	red	red	red	blue	blue	blue	blue

The soldiers can only move 2 together at a time.
The soldiers have to be next to each other.

• How many moves will it take until they are in the order:
red, blue, red, blue, red, blue, red, blue?

• Show your working here.

Teachers' note Ensure that children understand the puzzle and that the soldiers can shuffle along the line once two have been moved. Encourage them to use pictures/diagrams to present solutions. Some children may choose to use equipment such as red and blue pencils to physically move the soldiers. The focus should be on presenting solutions clearly so that someone else could follow it.

A Lesson for Every Day
Maths
6-7 Years
© A&C Black

Jumping Jack

Jack has used a number line to do some sums.
For each number line, tick ✓ the sum that
Jack did.

0 1 2 3 4 5 6 7 8 9 10 11 12 13 14

| 0 + 7 + 3 = 10 | 2 + 5 + 3 = 10 | 2 + 7 + 1 = 10 |

0 1 2 3 4 5 6 7 8 9 10 11 12 13 14

| 4 + 2 + 6 = 12 | 4 + 10 + 2 = 16 | 4 + 6 + 2 = 12 |

0 1 2 3 4 5 6 7 8 9 10 11 12 13 14

| 3 + 7 + 2 = 12 | 3 + 4 + 5 = 12 | 3 + 7 + 5 = 15 |

0 1 2 3 4 5 6 7 8 9 10 11 12 13 14

| 5 + 3 + 5 = 13 | 0 + 5 + 9 = 14 | 5 + 4 + 4 = 13 |

NOW TRY THIS!

• **Mark arrows to show how Jack works out
3 + 7 + 4.**

0 1 2 3 4 5 6 7 8 9 10 11 12 13 14

Teachers' note Ask the children to describe their strategies for working out the answer. Encourage
them to demonstrate this in different ways, for example, using practical material, number lines,
100-square, place value cards. The numbers can be altered before copying to provide differentiation.

A Lesson for Every Day
Maths
6-7 Years
© A&C Black

- **Show how each person could have worked out the answer**

Mattie worked out the correct answer to 9 × 5. Her answer was 45.

Will worked out the correct answer to 4 + 4 + 4 + 4 + 4 + 4. His answer was 24.

Deepa worked out the correct answer to 100 – 19. Her answer was 81.

Josh worked out the correct answer to 20 ÷ 5. His answer was 4.

NOW TRY THIS!

- **Talk to a friend about which question you found hardest.**

Teachers' note It is important that children are given the opportunity to consider the different ways that answers to calculations could be found, such as drawing, using practical material, number lines, 100-square, place value cards etc. Compare the children's completed sheets and encourage them to say which methods they think are most useful or easy to work with.

A Lesson for Every Day
Maths
6–7 Years
© A&C Black

These lines of mine

- **Show how Sam could have worked out the answer to each question on the number line.**

13 + 9

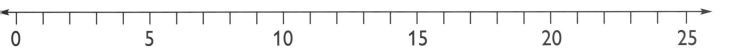

21 – 17

7 × 3

18 ÷ 3

 **NOW TRY THIS!**

- **Talk to a friend about which question you found hardest.**

Teachers' note It is important that children are given the opportunity to consider different ways that answers to calculations could be found, including different ways such as drawing, using practical material, number lines, 100-square, place value cards etc. Compare children's completed sheets and encourage them to say which methods they think are most useful or easy to work with.

A Lesson for Every Day
Maths
6-7 Years
© A&C Black

Going crackers!

- **For each cracker write the multiplication question and answer.**

$2 + 2 + 2 + 2 + 2 + 2 + 2 =$ $7 \times 2 = 14$

$5 + 5 + 5 + 5 + 5 + 5 =$

$10 + 10 + 10 + 10 + 10 + 10 + 10 =$

$3 + 3 + 3 + 3 + 3 =$

$2 + 2 + 2 + 2 + 2 + 2 + 2 + 2 + 2 =$

$4 + 4 + 4 + 4 + 4 =$

$5 + 5 + 5 + 5 + 5 + 5 + 5 + 5 =$

$10 + 10 + 10 + 10 + 10 + 10 =$

NOW TRY THIS!

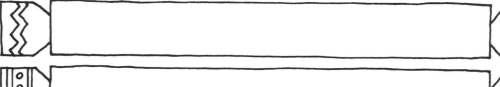

- **Fill in the crackers for these multiplication questions.**
- **Write the answers.**

$6 \times 4 =$ ☐

$7 \times 3 =$ ☐

Teachers' note For this activity, encourage the children to interpret the multiplication sign as meaning 'lots of', such as 7 lots of 2, 6 lots of 5, and so on.

A Lesson for Every Day
Maths
6–7 Years
© A&C Black

Cross-number puzzles

- **Solve these puzzles.**
- **Write missing clues for the numbers in the grid.**

Use these **multiples** to help you.

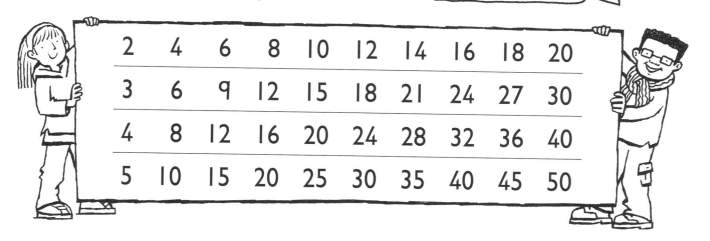

2	4	6	8	10	12	14	16	18	20
3	6	9	12	15	18	21	24	27	30
4	8	12	16	20	24	28	32	36	40
5	10	15	20	25	30	35	40	45	50

Across
1. 3×5
2. 5×5
3. double 7
4. 8×5
6. _____
7. double 13
8. 10×5

Down
1. 6×3
2. 8×3
3. _____
4. 9×5
5. double 8
6. 6×5
7. 4×5

Across
1. 4×4
2. 7×3
3. 6×3
4. 7×5
6. _____
7. _____
8. 8×3

Down
1. 3×4
2. 7×4
3. _____
4. 6×5
5. double 17
6. 9×5
7. double 12

Teachers' note Encourage the children to interpret the multiplication sign as meaning 'lots of' for this activity. Demonstrate how the lists of multiples can help them find the answers, for example 4×5 means '4 lots of 5' and can be found by looking at the fourth multiple of 5 in the list. As an extension, the children could make up their own cross-number puzzle.

A Lesson for Every Day
Maths
6–7 Years
© A&C Black

209

Special sheep

- **You need a large L shape of card or paper for this activity.**

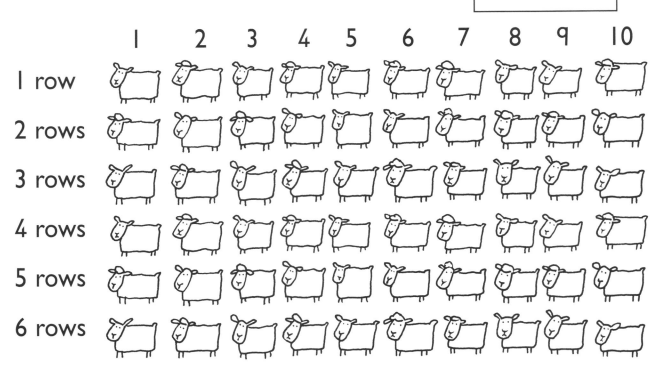

| | 1 | 2 | 3 | 4 | 5 | 6 | 7 | 8 | 9 | 10 |

1 row

2 rows

3 rows

4 rows

5 rows

6 rows

- **Cover some of the sheep to help you answer these.**

3 rows of 4 sheep = | 12 | 2 rows of 5 sheep = [ ]

2 rows of 8 sheep = [ ]   4 rows of 7 sheep = [ ]

3 rows of 6 sheep = [ ]   3 rows of 8 sheep = [ ]

4 rows of 4 sheep = [ ]   5 rows of 6 sheep = [ ]

3 rows of 9 sheep = [ ]   4 rows of 6 sheep = [ ]

4 rows of 8 sheep = [ ]   3 rows of 7 sheep = [ ]

NOW TRY THIS!

- **Write each question as a multiplication sentence:** $3 \times 4 = 12$

Teachers' note See the notes on the activity for the approximate size of the L shape. Demonstrate carefully how the L shape can be used to cover some of the sheep to leave the correct number of rows with the given number of sheep in each row. When answering the questions, the children should say what they think the number of sheep will be and then count them.

A Lesson for Every Day
Maths
6–7 Years
© A&C Black

Grape remainders

• Play this game with a partner.

> **You need** cubes for grapes.

☆ Spread the cards face down on the table.

☆ Take turns to pick a card and answer the question.

☆ Score 1 point if the remainder is 1.
  Score 2 points if the remainder is 2.

☆ The player with the most points wins the game.

---

15 grapes shared between 2 is

grapes ☐   remainder ☐

---

19 grapes shared between 3 is

grapes ☐   remainder ☐

---

13 grapes shared between 2 is

grapes ☐   remainder ☐

---

13 grapes shared between 3 is

grapes ☐   remainder ☐

---

14 grapes shared between 4 is

grapes ☐   remainder ☐

---

17 grapes shared between 5 is

grapes ☐   remainder ☐

---

26 grapes shared between 5 is

grapes ☐   remainder ☐

---

22 grapes shared between 3 is

grapes ☐   remainder ☐

---

21 grapes shared between 5 is

grapes ☐   remainder ☐

---

21 grapes shared between 4 is

grapes ☐   remainder ☐

---

13 grapes shared between 4 is

grapes ☐   remainder ☐

---

9 grapes shared between 2 is

grapes ☐   remainder ☐

---

12 grapes shared between 5 is

grapes ☐   remainder ☐

---

10 grapes shared between 3 is

grapes ☐   remainder ☐

Teachers' note Ensure that the children have had plenty of practice sharing sets of objects equally.
t the start of the lesson, discuss how remainders are written when there are some left over after
haring. When playing the game, a third child could act as adjudicator.

A Lesson for Every Day
Maths
6–7 Years
© A&C Black

Ghostly grids

- ## Fill in the missing numbers to make <u>true</u> division and multiplication facts.

50	÷	50	=	I
÷	■	÷	■	×
10	×	5	=	
=	■	=	■	=
	×		=	

20	÷	20	=	I
÷	■	÷	■	×
5	×	4	=	
=	■	=	■	=
	×		=	

12	÷	12	=	I
÷	■	÷	■	×
2	×	6	=	
=	■	=	■	=
	×		=	

45	÷	45	=	I
÷	■	÷	■	×
5	×	9	=	
=	■	=	■	=
	×		=	

70	÷	70	=	I
÷	■	÷	■	×
10	×	7	=	
=	■	=	■	=
	×		=	

16	÷	16	=	I
÷	■	÷	■	×
2	×	8	=	
=	■	=	■	=
	×		=	

NOW TRY THIS!

- ## Use the numbers ⬚40⬚, ⬚5⬚ and ⬚8⬚ to make some multiplication and division facts.

Teachers' note Remind the children that multiplication is the inverse of division and so if they know a tables fact it can be made into a related division fact. Here, all four facts are required to complete each grid. When completing the grid, remind the children that each row and column must show a true number fact.

A Lesson for Every Day
Maths
6–7 Years
© A&C Black

Group survey

- Work in a group of four.
- ✔ or ✗ whether each statement is true or false for each of you.

Names _____ _____ _____ _____

I am aged 7	☐	☐	☐	☐
I am a boy	☐	☐	☐	☐
I like the colour pink	☐	☐	☐	☐
I have two sisters	☐	☐	☐	☐
I have no brothers	☐	☐	☐	☐
I like football	☐	☐	☐	☐

- **Now write $\frac{1}{4}$, $\frac{1}{2}$, $\frac{3}{4}$ or $\frac{4}{4}$ to make each statement true.**

In our group:

☐ are aged 7

☐ are boys

☐ like pink

☐ have two sisters

☐ have no brothers

☐ like football

Teachers' note This activity can help the children to appreciate a quarter as not only an area of a shape, but also as a proportion of a whole, such as a whole group of children. The children must work in groups of four for this activity, although for more confident children, a group of eight could be introduced, and the fractions $\frac{1}{8}$, $\frac{1}{4}$, $\frac{3}{8}$, $\frac{1}{2}$, $\frac{5}{8}$, $\frac{3}{4}$, and $\frac{7}{8}$ included.

A Lesson for Every Day
Maths
6-7 Years
© A&C Black

Wilma and Thelma

Two sisters split some money.

Wilma gets one-quarter .

Thelma gets three-quarters .

• Write how much money each sister will get.

NOW TRY THIS!

• Check your answers to each question by adding together the sisters' amounts.

Teachers' note At the start of the lesson, introduce Wilma and Thelma as imaginary people or by using puppets. Ask the children to first find one-half, and then to halve that to get one quarter (Wilma's amount). They could either find Thelma's amount by seeing what is left or they could be shown that Thelma will always have three times as much as Wilma.

A Lesson for Every Day
Maths
6-7 Years
© A&C Black

2 sheep, sheep, sheep, cow, cow
FIELD 3 cow, cow, cow, cow
FIELD 1 horse, horse, horse, cow
FIELD 2 sheep, horse, horse,
cow, cow, cow, sheep
FIELD 1 horse, cow, cow, sheep
FIELD 2 sheep, cow, cow, horse, horse,
FIELD 3 cow, cow, cow, horse
FIELD 1 cow, cow, cow, sheep
FIELD 2 cow, cow, horse, horse,
FIELD 2 sheep, horse, horse, horse,
FIELD 3 sheep, sheep, sheep, cow
FIELD 2 cow, cow, cow, cow
FIELD 3 sheep, sheep, sheep, sheep
FIELD 2 horse, horse, horse, horse
FIELD 1 horse, cow, cow, cow
FIELD 2 horse, sheep, horse, horse,
FIELD 3 sheep, horse, horse, horse,
FIELD 1 cow, cow, cow,
FIELD 2 cow, cow, horse, horse,
FIELD 3 sheep, sheep, sheep, sheep,
SUGGESTED QUESTION:
• How could you record these solutions?

Triplet trouble: 1 and 2 – page 26–7
EXAMPLE SOLUTION:
VARIATIONS ON:
ABC   ABC
CAB   CAB
BCA   ABC

13, 14, 15, 16, 17, 19
18 is missing

NTT
1, 2, 4, 6, 7, 8, 9, 10, 12, 20, 30, 60

At the sweetshop – page 30
SOLUTIONS:
30, 26, 24
32, 64
66

The pirates' library – page 31
SOLUTIONS:
35   42
48   29
37   43

Pasta party – page 34
SOLUTIONS:
35   41   38
48   24   32
44   22   36

---

2 sheep, sheep, sheep, sheep
FIELD 3 cow, cow, cow
FIELD 1 horse, horse, horse,
FIELD 2 sheep, horse,
FIELD 3 cow, cow, cow, sheep
FIELD 1 horse, cow, cow, sheep
FIELD 3 cow, cow, cow, horse,

Animal magic – page 38
SOLUTIONS:
7 – 4 = 3   8 – 4 = 4
9 – 3 = 6   10 – 7 = 3
6 – 3 = 3   8 – 5 = 3
6 – 1 = 5   10 – 6 = 4

Domino decisions: 1 and 2 – page 39–40
SOLUTIONS:

2	4	5
6	0	0
3	2	6

5	3	1
0	5	3
4	2	3

2nd page

5	3	1	6	2	6	1
0	5	3	2	4	6	4
4	2	3	1	5	4	3	5

Find Bo-Peep's sheep! – page 41
SOLUTIONS:

0	8	1	0	5	6	3	9	5
1	5	0	7	1	9	8	7	2
7	5	4	6	9	2	3	8	9
6	4	0	9	3	1	6	4
1	9	6	3	4	0	1	3	4

Storytime – page 47
SOLUTIONS:
16 × 4 28 + 5 36 – 3 4 27 ÷ 3

Whose pet? – page 50
SOLUTIONS:

Hide and seek – page 28
SOLUTIONS:

Missing digits – page 61
POSSIBLE SOLUTIONS:
Q1
12 + 10 = 22   11 + 11 = 22   10 + 12 = 22
9 + 13 = 22   8 + 14 = 22   7 + 15 = 22
6 + 16 = 22   5 + 17 = 22   4 + 18 = 22
3 + 19 = 22

Dinner time – page 52
SOLUTIONS:
10   24   33
14   20   4
32   2   28
30   48   1
40   18   52   6
20   38   50   8
10   73   82   1
40   43   13   70
81   22   30   3

Q3
5 + 38 = 43   15 + 28 = 43   25 + 18 = 43
35 + 8 = 43
NTT
21 + 10   20 + 11   19 + 12   18 + 13
17 + 14   16 + 15   15 + 16   14 + 13
13 + 18   12 + 19

Check it out – page 62
SOLUTIONS:
1 true   2 false
3 true   4 false
5 true   6 false

Cherry time – page 63
SOLUTIONS:
14 + 15 + 16 = 45   (smallest)
14 + 15 + 17 = 46
14 + 15 + 18 = 47
14 + 16 + 17 = 47
15 + 16 + 17 = 48
14 + 16 + 18 = 48
14 + 17 + 18 = 49
15 + 16 + 18 = 49
15 + 17 + 18 = 50
16 + 17 + 18 = 51   (largest)

Loop the loop – page 64
SOLUTION
The phrase from start to finish is ONE FINE DAY

Hoopla – page 65
SOLUTIONS:
6   8
6   11
12
9   11   15
11   13   14
13   16   18
11   13   16
NTT
5 + 9   9 + 5   9 + 5   6 + 8   8 + 6   7 + 7

Cross out – page 66
SOLUTIONS:

Weaving – page 72
SOLUTIONS:

Round to check – page 73
SOLUTIONS:
37   46   68
61   87   49
88   83   64
NTT
58   94

£3.00   £4.30   £4.30
£4.50   £3.80   £5.20
£3.90   £3.90   £4.50
£3.90   £3.00   £4.80

True or false? – page 76
SOLUTIONS:
true   false
true   true
true   false
true   false
true   false

Shape shifting: 1 and 2 – page 78–9
SOLUTIONS:

NTT

All change! – page 80
SOLUTIONS
1 1p £1 £1 £1   2 2p £1   3 5p £1 4 1p
10p
NTT
£5.00 – £1.99 = £3.01   £5.00 – £3.98 = £1.02
£5.00 – £2.95 = £2.05   £5.00 – £4.88 = £0.11 or 11p

Bikers! – page 81
SOLUTIONS:
seat
bell
pedal
tyres
brakes
wheels
helmet

Guess the shape – page 89
SOLUTIONS:
sphere
cube
square-based pyramid
cylinder
tetrahedron (or octahedron)
cone
cuboid (or cube)

Billy's door – page 95
SOLUTIONS:
open
shut
shut
open

Amy's seat – page 96
SOLUTIONS:
blue
blue
blue
white

Car boot sale – page 98
SOLUTIONS
1 5 + 7 = 12   5 25 – 17 = 8
2 11 * 3 = 30   6 9 * 2 – 6 = 12
3 12 + 5 = 17   7 4 + 8 = 12
4 16 ÷ 2 = 8

---

8 slices of bread, 8 pieces of bacon, 12 leaves
of lettuce.

Animal races – page 103
SOLUTIONS:
9
55
51
15
12

Hold it! – page 109
SOLUTIONS:
1p 2p   2p 5p   5p 10p *   10p 20p **
1p 5p   2p 10p   5p 20p **   10p 50p *
1p 10p   2p 20p   5p 50p   20p 50p *
1p 50p   2p 50p
NTT * silver coins only
** silver coins with total between 20p and 40p
The coin must be a 20p

The vet: 1 and 2 – page 110–1
SOLUTIONS:
9 cats
2 rabbits
4 dogs
3 hamsters
1 snake
2 parrots
1 tortoise
22 animals in total

Bird spotting – page 112
SOLUTIONS:
1 Tim
2 Trixie, Billy and Susie
3 4
4 Tim, Pete, Sally
5 Sally and Trixie
6 Tim, Trixie
7 Sally

In the fridge – page 113
SOLUTIONS:
butter: 2
milk: 3
yoghurts: 6
sausages: 8
roast chicken: 1
tomatoes: 7
lettuce: 1
apples: 5

Litre checker – page 119
SOLUTIONS:
More than one litre   Less than one litre
Less than one litre   Less than one litre
More than one litre   More than one litre
Less than one litre   More than one litre

Scale trail – page 120
SOLUTIONS:
Starting point A: computer
Starting point B: scooter
Starting point C: bike

T-shirt printer – page 121
SOLUTION:
There are 12 different T-shirts possible.

Unusual pets – page 122
SOLUTIONS:
tarantula 8   chinchilla 2   skunk 5
chameleon 9   gecko 4   stick insect 10
6 people

215

Chocolate bars – page 123
Solutions:
Choc-chip 5   Chocco 7
Milko 1   White-choc 9
Darko 6   Choco-nut 7
He should stock White-choc, Chocco, Choco-nut, Chocco and Darko. They are the ones most people like.

Celebrations – page 124
Solutions:
Birthday 9, Birth of baby 2, Passing driving test 4, Wedding 4

Favourite circus acts – page 125
Solutions:
Block graph with labels, intervals, and blocks to the height of the information on the table.

Monster weights – page 130
Solutions:
11 kg 18 kg 3 kg 8 kg 17 kg 13 kg

Spaghetti spikes – page 131
Solutions:
10 cm   12 cm   15 cm   9 cm   5 cm
Now try this!
14 cm   13 cm   24 cm

Wheels – page 134
Solutions:
1 16   2 9   3 23   4 80
5 18   6 £24   7 3   8 £32

Macy and her kittens – page 135

In the garden – page 136
Solutions:
Fire engine 1 Milk float 2 Pram 11
Car 7 Bicycle 12 Wheelchair 2 Buggy 8

Goal! – page 137
Solutions:
Pictogram answers as shown in table
More practice: Saturn
Winner: Pluto
Now try this!
9 goals

Multiples – page 138
Solutions:
Multiples of 5: 5, 10, 15, 20, 25, 30, 40, 45, 50
Other numbers: 3, 6, 12, 18, 21, 32, 44

Numbers – page 139
Solutions:
1 Multiples of 2
2 Multiples of 5
3 In the overlap: multiples of 10 (i.e. multiples of 2 and 5)
4 Label hoops: Multiples of 2, Multiples of 5

Pets: 1 and 2 – page 140–1
Solutions:
Has a pet: 11, Susie, Emma, Ann, Eli, Kate, Liz, Liah, Tom, Beth, Liam, Alex
Has not got a pet 17, Luke, Lucy, Ben, Josh, Isabel, Sam, Harry, Holly, Ian, Dave, Daisy, Jake, Sadie, Ruby, Suki, Brett, Rosie

Toys – page 142
1 22 toys   2(a) 6 (b) 7 (c) 5 (d) 4

Right angles: 1 and 2 – page 143–4
Solutions:
Right angles/curved: 10
Not right angles/curved: 1, 11
Right angles/not curved: 2, 3, 4, 9, 12
Not right angles/not curved: 5, 6, 7, 8
1 6
2 10

Going to great lengths – page 145
Solutions:
1. metres   2. centimetres
3. centimetres   4. metres
5. centimetres   6. centimetres
7. metres   8. metres
9. centimetres   10. metres

Rick's restaurant – page 147
Solutions
1 12 – 7 = 5   2 8 * 2 = 16
3 2 * 4 = 8   4 6 ÷ 2 = 3
5 8 ÷ 2 = 4   6 20 ÷ 5 = 4
NTT
(6 * 2) + (6 * 4) = 36
33 + (33 – 5) or 33 + 28 = 61

London Eye – page 148
Solutions:
1 16   2 9   3 23   4 80
5 18   6 £24   7 3   8 £32
NTT
1 32 – 16 = 16   2 18 – 9 = 9
3 7 + 16 = 23   4 4 * 20 = 80
5 12 – 9 + 15 = 18   6 8 * 3 = 24
7 75 ÷ 25 = 3   8 16 * 2 = 32

Beaver away – page 149
Solutions:
18 26 19
28 13 17
29 19 28
38 27 17
23 23 18
27 13 26
58 76 86
46 48 69
74 54 89
63 44 59
78 88 79
88 58 85

I 'eight' a cucumber – page 150
Solutions:
Green cucumber questions:
53 – 5   44 – 6   26 – 8   51 – 3   92 – 4
47 – 9   40 – 2   85 – 7   91 – 3   93 – 5
74 – 6   57 – 9   35 – 7

Fun time – page 153
Solutions:
hour, minutes, minutes, seconds, minutes, minutes, minutes, hours

Charlie and Chester – page 154
Solutions:
Charlie, Charlie, Chester, Chester, Charlie, Charlie, Chester
Now try this!
Charlie

Pirate map – page 155
Solutions:
anchor   hut   parrot   tree
flag   cave   cannon   ship
chest   volcano bridge   skull

Let's swim again – page 156
Solutions:
1 12 + 7 = 19   2 7 + 5 = 12
3 9 – 4 = 5   4 £2.20 * 3 = £6.60
5 17 + 12 = 29   6 16 + 12 – 7 = 21
7 45 + 50 = 95   8 35 – 10 = 25

Calendar puzzle – page 158
Solutions:
The sum of the numbers in the first column is always two less than the sum of those in the second column.

Ant trail – page 172
22cm   24cm   24cm   26cm   26cm

Time quiz – page 175
c 8:30   d 5:00
c 3:15   c 12:30
c 9:30   d 6:30
c 5:30   b 7:45

Power-robots! – page 178
Solutions:
The left-hand robot has 18 right angles.
The right-hand robot has 15 right angles.

What a match: 1 and 2 – page 179–80

Sheet 1	Sheet 2
1 18 – 3 = 15	1 6 – 4 – 7 = 25
2 18 + 3 = 21	2 36 – 4 – 7 = 25
3 18 ÷ 3 = 15	3 36 – 4 – 7 = 39
4 18 ÷ 3 = 6	4 36 ÷ 4 – 7 = 2
5 18 × 3 = 54	5 36 – 4 – 7 = 25
6 18 × 3 = 54	6 36 + 4 + 7 = 47
7 18 ÷ 3 = 6	7 36 + 4 + 7 = 16
	8 36 × 4 – 7 = 137

Make 26 – page 181
Solution:
For example:
1   12   5   3
7   8   6   2   10
4

Building bricks – page 183
Solutions:
2 × 4 = 8   2 × 3 = 6   1 × 6 = 6
4 × 2 = 8   3 × 2 = 6   6 × 1 = 6
1 × 3 = 3   2 × 6 = 12   1 × 2 = 2
3 × 1 = 3   6 × 2 = 12   2 × 1 = 2
3 × 5 = 15   2 × 5 = 10   3 × 4 = 12
5 × 3 = 15   5 × 2 = 10   4 × 3 = 12
NTT
2 × 2 = 4   3 × 3 = 9   4 × 4 = 16

Market stall! – page 184
Solutions:
Possible answers include:
5 × 4 = 20   20 – 7 = 13
24 + 32 = 56   45 ÷ 5 = 9
14 ÷ 2 = 7   6 × 5 = 30
31 – 12 = 19   6 × 4 = 24

Wheels away – page 188
Solutions:
1 1 caravan   2 bikes
2 2 tractors   1 caravan
3 2 lorries   3 Reliant Robins
4 2 tractors   3 Reliant Robins

Triangle tricks: 1 and 2 – page 189–90
Solutions to original questions on the sheet:

reflections of 5 above

Wendy's window box – page 191
Solutions:
1 10 * 3 = 30   2 35 – 30 = 5
3 70p ÷ 35 = 2p   4 35 – 15 = 20
5 15 – 6 = 9   6 5 * 3 = 15
7 12 ÷ 2 = 6

Traffic jam – page 192
Solutions:
1 10   2 6   3 30   4 60
NTT
48 people (8 + 1 + (3 * 13)

Marching mummies – page 193
Solutions:
1 16   2 4   3 a) 4 m b) 6 m c) 1 m
d) 7 m or 50 cm e) 5 m f) 10 m
NTT
60 steps

Farmer Palmer's diary: 1 and 2 – page 194–5
Solutions:
Page 20
1 31   2 25   3 50   4 75   5 10
NTT 28 (25 hens and 3 cockerels)
Page 21
1 50 litres   2 41 litres   3 26 litres   4 18 litres
5 Maisie made 95 litres and Daisy made 83 litres. Maisie made the most.
NTT 48 litres

Sponsored spell – page 196
Solutions:
1 35p   2 28p   3 32p   4 36p
NTT
3p per word

Playful kittens – page 199
Solutions:
30 ÷ 5 = 6   50 ÷ 10 = 5   14 ÷ 2 = 7
15 ÷ 5 = 3   90 ÷ 10 = 9   18 ÷ 2 = 9
35 ÷ 5 = 7   60 ÷ 10 = 6   16 ÷ 2 = 8
NTT
18 ÷ 3 = 6   15 ÷ 3 = 5   21 ÷ 3 = 7

Cake calculations – page 202
Solutions:
9   12   21
15   18   24
NTT
75

Cross out – page 203
Solutions:

10	2	X	6	12	X
5	7	X	3	8	4
12	X	8	1	7	6
3	15	X	8	X	4
X	6	12	7	5	X

(rows summing to 30)

6	7	5	X	9
8	X	3	8	4	10
7	10	7	6	X
X	8	10	6	6
X	14	2	7

Soldiers on parade – page 204
Possible solution:

R	R	B	B	B	B	R	B	B	B
R	R	B	R	B	B	B	B	R	B
R	B	B	B	B	B	B	R	R	B
R	B	R	B	B	B	B	R	R	B
R	B	R	B	B	B	B	B	R	B

Jumping Jack – page 205
Solutions:
2 + 5 + 3 = 10
4 + 6 + 2 = 12
3 + 4 + 5 = 12
5 + 4 + 4 = 13

Going crackers! – page 208
Solutions:
7 × 2 = 14
6 × 5 = 30
7 × 10 = 70
5 × 3 = 15
9 × 2 = 18
5 × 4 = 20
8 × 5 = 40
6 × 10 = 60
NTT
If the 'x' sign has been interpreted as meaning 'lots of', these will be the solutions:
4 + 4 + 4 + 4 + 4 + 4
3 + 3 + 3 + 3 + 3 + 3 + 3

Cross-number puzzles – page 209
Solutions:

1	2		8		1		2
			2	1	8		8
8	4				3	5	
	4	0				2	4
3	5	0		4	0		
				5		0	

Wilma and Thelma – page 214
Solutions:
£1   £3   £9
£10   £30   £6
£15   £45   £4
£20   £60   £18